THE
LONG
HOT
WALK

A TRUE STORY

DEB McCARROLL

The Long Hot Walk
Copyright © 2014 by Deborah McCarroll

The names and identifying details of some characters in this book have been changed.

ISBN: 978-0-692-33269-6

Design by Deborah McCarroll

Studio Pacific Works, LLC
studiopacific.com

debmccarroll.com

For Shayba, my hero.

Acknowledgements

Thank you to my sisters for their care and example and thank you to my brother for his strength and kindness. Thanks, too, to my Seattle family. To all the friends and supporters who cheer through the thickest thick and thinnest thin. A big, fat, HUGE thank you to Gladys. For everything. Most of all thanks to my mother for all that I am. Ma, I miss you every day.

Foreward

All within these pages is as true as I can recall. A lot of people populate a lifetime, so some individuals have been substituted to keep things tidy and a good number of names have been changed to protect the guilty. Also, some events have been combined to show ongoing occurrences or themes but the major stuff, it's all as it happened. Cross my heart.

"We're all mad here."

- Lewis Carroll,
Alice in Wonderland

One

WHEN I WAS AIR

My mother was a soft-spoken woman, with short hair cascading over her head in soft, dark waves and even in the brutal heat of the desert afternoon, her lips were dressed up with a pretty shade of coral lipstick. I squinted up at her profile and then out at the endless blacktop, the distant road melting into a shivering, silver ribbon. I wiped sweat from my lip with the back of my hand and tasted salt.

She'd arrived up at my classroom door, a brown vinyl satchel, pressed to look like leather, dangling from one pale hand. Mrs. Sanchez had been writing on the streaked board and she'd whispered off to the side with my mother before searching the desks. "Debbie? Your mother is here."

The heel of my shoe skittered on a loose bit of gravel and it rolled off the side of the rough blacktop and into the dirt, carving a soft rut behind it. I wondered how long it would take the wind to scour the ground smooth again. "I'm thirsty," I said.

My mother's hand was warm and dry as it pulled me along. "Ma, I'm thirsty." I tugged at her.

She looked down, as if surprised to see me attached to the end of her arm. She blinked. "What?"

"I need a drink."

She stopped and looked at the long stretches of nothing here and nothing there, as if noticing for the first time that we were standing on an cracked, empty highway in the middle of nowhere under the baking sun. "Well, let's see what's over the next rise," she said, shading her eyes.

Further down the road, the sound of tinkling laughter blended with the wind as we crossed the broken yellow line to scan the valley below. A travel trailer squatted down the bluff, looking like a fat white beetle burrowed in the sand. A striped awning jutted from the side, shading a trio of empty plastic folding chairs straight out of the grassy, lush pages of the SEARS & ROEBUCK catalog. I couldn't think why anyone would choose this empty place to set up housekeeping. I followed the whole of it with my eyes, trying to see just what they saw. What made this place better than anywhere else? All I could see was somewhere to be blurred outside the car window until you got to where you were going.

My mother dropped the satchel and adjusted the waistband of her skirt. "Wait here," she said, and she started down the bluff through the sagebrush and the hot, shifting sand. I watched her get smaller and smaller, until she was swallowed by the awning's black square of shade. She swept the hair from her forehead and straightened the strand of pearls around her neck before knocking. A shadow surfaced in the film of the small screen door, like a trout lunging for a fly. A man in white shorts, with a smooth red scalp, leaned out.

My mother moved her hands through the warm air as she talked. A woman in a straw hat came to the door and peeked around the man. My mother gestured up the bluff and they turned their pink faces to me. They stood for a long moment, looking up the rise, before the man disappeared inside. The woman crossed her arms. My mother shooed a fly. When the man came back, he handed my mother a white Styrofoam cup. She said something to him, took the cup, and turned to make her way back to me.

She carried the cup carefully, only taking her eyes off it to glance at a bit of sagebrush or to check the sand where she put her hand to steady herself up the rise. When she reached me, she was breathing hard, her face red and damp with sweat. "Here," she panted, as she held the cup out to me. The hem of her black skirt was rimmed with red dust.

I stared at the blinding white spot of water. It seemed to be lit from inside. "Go on, take it."

I took the cool water into my mouth and held it there for a while, trying to make it last. I downed half the cup and then held it out to her.

"No, Q.T. That's for you."

I thought about saving it, carrying the cup along the strip of road with me, carefully changing hands and keeping it safe, like a baby bird, until my elbows would begin to quiver. I tipped the cup back and swallowed the last drop before crushing the cup in my fist like the tough guys crush beer cans in the movies.

My mother picked up the satchel. "Better?" She pulled a tissue from her sleeve and wiped my face. The tissue came away smudged with dirt. She kissed my cheek and gave my ear a soft tug. "Well...shall we?"

I flattened the cup between my palms and shoved it into my pocket. My finger touched the cat eye marble nestled deep in the linty corner. I made a game of rolling the smooth glass up the flattened cup and letting it fall back into the deep well of my pocket in time with my steps. It was the only thing I'd taken with me. The only thing I ever took.

I'd plucked it from the smooth rut carved into the desk, a place to neatly lay your pencil so it wouldn't roll to the floor and spoil the lead point. I'd left the schoolwork and the Big Chief writing pad. I'd been working on my letters. Carefully, r r r r then s s s s. So far away. It was like I'd dreamed it all now.

The marble in my pocket rolled through my fingers down a crack in the cup to land solidly in the corner with every turn. I imagined the soft taffy stripes in the marble turning against the white. As I walked, I studied the side of my mother's face. Her mouth was open slightly, her dark eyes fixed on the road ahead. I tried to imagine her behind the wheel of a car, how she'd hold her hands, at ten and two, checking the rearview mirror regularly, or casually maybe, with manicured fingers dangling from the wheel, one arm thrown over the passenger seat, all cool and sophisticated. She never had learned to drive, or if she did, she didn't think she was good enough at it. I'd heard a story once about somebody trying to teach her. One

3

of the husbands, or her father maybe, but it didn't take. So we walk, or if we have a little money, we climb onto one of the belching buses that crawl the streets of Albuquerque day and night.

About a million years ago, my mother was a registered nurse. She'd kiss me goodbye in the kitchen and close the door behind her, usually leaving me with my sister, Judith, something neither of us particularly enjoyed. Judith was a teenager, restless and anxious to be riding in cars or sneaking cigarettes with her friends instead of babysitting. But my brother, Ben, worked and my sister, Isabelle, had cheerleading practice, so it was up to Judith. She'd sigh in a heavy way, roll her eyes, and say, "Well, come on, scrounge." Then we'd cross the street in front of our house and head to the football field to meet her friend Lila, me trailing behind like a new puppy. To me, Judith always seemed wild and beautiful and dangerous. At home, she was like a cat in a cage, pacing and bright eyed, just waiting for her escape. Eventually, she met a boy and that's just what she did.

My mother had her own way of talking and her own words for things. Sometimes you understood, sometimes you didn't. She had her own name for each of us that was not our name. Words that had nothing to do with us on the surface, but to her, each name described who we were and summed up the whole of us. Molly Kay, Deuce, Pokey Dale. These funny little words made each child whole in her mind, as if she'd been rushed into the naming at our births, and only after much hard thought and trial and error had she come upon just the perfect word, with the perfect number of syllables and right feel in her mouth, to fit us like a set of tailored clothes. She hardly ever called me by my given name, except to introduce me to the ladies in the grocery or if she was angry. Almost always, she'd touch my cheek or smooth my hair and say, "How's my Q.T.?"

I'm starting to forget my siblings. They're all gone now, like so much dandelion fluff on the breeze. Isabelle went to college in Texas, where she lives with my flashy aunt Charlene.

Judith dropped out of school to marry a boy just as young and full of fire as her own self. And my brother Benjamin went off to carry a gun in Vietnam.

I don't remember that much about my brother. He was tall, I remember that. Like one of the strong, cool trees that grow on the banks of the muddy Rio Grande. I'd have to bend way back just to look up at him.

He would put his hand down and I'd hang onto it, fingers wrapped tight, and he'd lift me clean over his head. I'd get a tickle in my stomach, same as flying down those steep hills in his Chevy, not entirely pleasant but not scary enough to stop. Other than that, I don't remember much about him. I was a real little kid when he left and he wasn't around much to begin with. I have this memory of him lying on the couch, pretending to be asleep. I'd poke him on the shoulder and he'd start singing a song rhyming pickles with motorcickles. He'd have his eyes shut tight and he'd thrash around like he was lost in a dream. I'd laugh and then we'd do the whole thing all over again.

Then one day, he was just gone. My big, strong brother, off to be a Marine and fight in a war a world away. I wouldn't have thought someone who could fill up a room like that could just one day be gone.

After everyone left, Ma lost her job. She was a registered nurse at St. Jude's Hospital, usually working the night shift, and by that time she'd whisper and shout to herself all the time. I can just picture the faces of those poor startled patients as Ma screamed at the empty white walls to leave her alone. It was understood that everyone at the hospital liked my mother. They would smile and nod and say how sweet she was, but really, what could they do?

First, we lost power to the house because the bills sat in the basket by the door for months. Then the water got cut off. After that, I'd sneak under the chain-link fence that circled the water tower next door and I'd fill that red bucket as far as I could with water for drinking and washing. By the time I'd get back home, arms wrapped tight around the middle of it, most of the water would have sloshed out and my shirt would be soaked. Ma cooked beans and tortillas on a heavy iron skillet, and sopapillas–which are a kind of fried bread–in a can of melted shortening over a little fire dug into a hole in the back yard. I'd sit there in the glow, happy and full, staring up at the stars and the black outline of that fat-bellied water tower next door. Every town in New Mexico has one. There isn't much rain in the summer, so you gotta have a good water supply to keep the town going when the ditches dry to mud and the sidewalks get too hot to walk in bare feet.

Our cat, Kalina, (pronounced kal-eye-nah) got caught up there once. Kalina was a big orange tabby. Mom named him, of course. He sure didn't look much like a Kalina to me, with all those scars and chewed up ears on that big wide head of his, but she said that he was pretty and that he needed a pretty name.

I have no idea what got into that cat's head, making him decide to climb up to the top of that tower. Maybe a bird taunted him. Maybe once he started up he couldn't back down, or maybe he did it on a dare. Who knows? All I know is that one fine day, he decided to climb higher than any cat should, and then he was too afraid to climb back down. If it was me, I wouldn't have gone near that tower, but you can't tell a cat anything.

He howled and cried and did his best to put one timid paw after another on the rungs, only to give up and climb back to the top again. I craned my neck way up, up, up and shaded my eyes so I could make out the orange dot that was my cat. Mother stood on the sidewalk, calling after Kalina and shifting her weight from foot to foot.

The fire department was called and eventually, a fireman in a clean white shirt and a shiny badge started up the tower ladder. I guess that old cat didn't care much for that fireman, because he looked like he'd murder the guy if he got the chance. He even took a swipe at him, clawing and yowling with his fur all puffed up.

Down on the ground, the other firemen stretched a blanket out tight between them and eventually Kalina got yanked off and came flying down in a striped and twisting fury. He hit the blanket, took one big bounce, and raced off like an orange bullet. He never did come back.

I'd see him in town once in awhile at the gas station, where he took up residence. He always seemed to give me the dirtiest look, like it was my fault that he got trapped up there. What could I do about it? I didn't tell him to get himself stuck on top of a water tower, and I sure didn't tell that fireman to fling him off of it. I still felt pretty sorry for him, though.

That was before school. Before we started walking and before Judith saved my life on that gray, wet day. It seemed like it had rained for weeks, though really, it had probably just drizzled through the afternoon.

I was bored and tired of coloring books and the three channels on the T.V. When it finally let up enough to go out, I grabbed my coat, put on my rubber boots, and ran outside–free at last.

Our house sat right across from the high school, a constant embarrassment to my sisters. The grounds had a military cannon, a relic from some war or other. I dearly loved that hunk of machinery. It had a flat bit on the top that you could sit on as you pedaled a set of wheels around and round, like a bicycle. Those wheels were smooth as silk, metal gears meshing perfectly, the force of my legs and feet driving the steel mechanism. It felt like the whole thing could leave the ground at any moment and I'd soar and glide above our house, waving at Ma as I swooped by.

On that day, the beast was wet and shiny from barrel to base. I put my hands to the steel and begin to climb. Near the top, panting and straining above the dripping world below, I swung one booted leg over the top of my perch, just as the foot supporting my full weight slipped, sending me bumping downward to the concrete below.

On her walk back from the drug store, in the fading afternoon light, Judith found me lying on the cement slab under the cannon, out cold. Maybe she first saw my boot jutting from the corner of the base. Or maybe it wasn't until she saw my face—still and pale in the gloom—that she realized I wasn't faking. However it happened, it must have scared the stuffing out of her, because she gave me a very hard time about it later, which I thought was awfully unfair since I was the one with the goose egg.

When I woke up, it was dark outside and I was lying on the bed beside Ma. The lamp on the side table burned gauzy shadows around the room and she was reading a paperback. When I stirred, she'd laid her book on her chest and said, "Well, if it isn't Sleeping Beauty." Then she'd made me a cheese sandwich, which I remember was very good.

After walking all day, we had dinner in a run-down diner and found a trailer park that had a makeshift launderette in a drab little cinder block room. It consisted of three washers and dryers and a couple of molded plastic chairs that were scuffed and ready for the landfill.

I sat on the stairs out in the growing darkness, smelling detergent and residue from the dryers as it mingled with the frying of various trailer park dinners.

A chill crept up across the desert as stars winked on. It gets cold in the desert at night. You wouldn't think so in the baking oven heat of the day.

My feet were sore and I was so tired that I imagined myself to be an overcooked noodle as I slumped my ribs over my knees. I took a look at my shoes, black numbers, open on the top with buckles on the sides. Mary Jane's. They were shoes made of dirt now. I couldn't even see my socks through the top strappy part, just dust. I attempted to wipe some of it off and clean them with my thumb and a bit of spit, but it just seemed to rearrange the dirt, so I gave it up.

No one came to do their laundry that night, which was good because we looked pretty suspicious, hanging around with no clothes to wash and no money with which to wash them.

After awhile, sleep got the best of me and I curled up on the washing machines. I'd wake throughout the night, fluorescent lights painting everything with a green tinge, including Ma. She was always awake, sitting up straight in that hard chair, lips working, as if reading an invisible book or magazine. Now and then she'd laugh, her eyes glassy and unfocused. I'd turn over and go back to sleep.

I woke up in the morning, stiff and cold. She was still in the chair. She looked up at me and said, "Well, good morning."

I washed my face and hands in the utility sink, drying them on the rough brown paper from the dispenser. Ma did the same and applied lipstick, combed her hair, and performed a virtual scalping on me, yanking a wet Goodies comb through my tangles.

"Youch, Ma-a-a!"

"Oh, don't be such a baby," she said, checking her face in the warped paper towel dispenser. "We're ladies, you know. And any lady knows that it hurts to be beautiful."

"I'm not a baby, and I think that's enough. My hair is good." I rubbed the sore spots on my head and smoothed my damp hair.

She smiled, gave me a kiss on my cheek, and rubbed the red smudge with a thumb. She held my chin in one hand. "Your bangs are so long. Doesn't that bother you, your hair in your way like that?" She brushed the strands from my eyes with soft fingers and stared down at me with an almost amazed look on her face. Finally, she smiled at just one corner of her mouth. "Now, when did you get so big, huh? When?" she said. "My little girl. You're growing up too fast." She looked a little sad, for just an instant, and then she sighed and dropped the lipstick into the satchel pocket. "All right, Q.T. Let's get going."

We walked to a McDonald's and she ordered an Egg McMuffin and a water. We sat at a table that smelled like pine cleaner. We bowed heads and she whispered a prayer. Then she cut the sandwich in half with a plastic serrated knife and slid the half on the paper wrapper over to me.

"I like that top on you," she said, wiping her mouth with a paper napkin.

"You think so? I was thinking it was getting a little too, you know, baby for me."

"Oh no. Girls are wearing them like that now."

I got up and crossed the table to her side. "Your pearls are turned around," I said, working the clasp to the back of her neck.

"Oh thank you, Q.T. I just hate that." She tied a knot in the base of the strand and patted at them. "There, that ought to fix it. Aw, would you look at that? Now I've got a run." She ran a finger over the silvery nick, scarring the fabric of her stocking just above the ankle. "I'm just a mess," she muttered.

"Why are we going to Gallup, Ma?"

"Hmm? Gallup? I have a cousin who lives there and I'll be able to find work." She dabbed a bit of clear nail polish on the run and removed her shoe to work the line around to the inside, where it wouldn't be as noticeable.

Talking to my mother was like reading the newspaper. She only gave you the who, what, when, and where of it. Straight out. Just the facts, ma'am. Other people said things like "maybe" and "perhaps" or "I don't know." But Ma? Never, and so how could a person not believe in her? How could they not believe that everything was just fine and dandy when she'd put out that hand and say, "It's time to go."

But eventually, someone always finds us and these footsore miles evaporate like steam on a breeze. This last time, it was my sister Judith, coaxing us out of that shabby little motel. She'd convinced Ma that we should come live with her and her brand new husband, Bob.

We took the satchel and moved into the spare bedroom at the end of that long, narrow hallway in my sister's rented house. Ma was pretty sick, all right, talking to herself and laughing and screaming into the night. And then came the day that my sister told Mother she had to go downtown to sign some papers for her Social Security. We all piled into the car and we ended up in front of a boxy brown building that turned out to be the Saint Joseph Psychiatric Hospital. Judith got out of the passenger side and Bob sprinted around the back of the car to help Mother out of the back seat.

Boy, was she mad. He was able to get her to go as far as the front steps peaceably and then she started clocking him with this heavy tortoiseshell makeup case she'd sometimes use as a purse. I sat wincing in the back seat while he ducked and clung to the sleeve of her coat.

I guess she thought she'd be able to make a run for it once they got outside the car, but Bob was on to her. He clearly had no idea what he was up against, however, because he looked completely stunned when that hunk of luggage came flying at his head. Poor guy. Can you imagine marrying into this family? Surprise!

Ma was in the lockup a couple of months that time. I stayed with Judith and her hero hubby, which was not even a little bit like living with my mother.

They had a lot of hippy friends and they smoked a lot of pot. They even had a room especially for that purpose. It had black lights and posters in loud, glowing colors. There were long strings of beads in the doorway and a big velvet pillow in the middle of the floor that said *Zig Zag*.

A lot of people with long hair and colorful clothes would shuffle in and lie around that pillow while sucking on a bubbling water bottle, smoke curling lazily from the top.

I tried it once. It tasted spicy and dark. It hurt my lungs and made me gag and cough. Everyone around the pillow laughed and patted me on the back, mussing my hair and making noises about what a big girl I was.

It was in those electric days, under the care of my wild sister, that I experienced what it is to be free. I mean, really free. Bob had a green hulk of a station wagon I called the Green Machine and during one warm summer night, we went driving down Central Avenue in Albuquerque, with all the windows thrown open and me in the very back, with the seats folded down. There was more room in the back of that car than some of the motel rooms for which Ma had plunked down good money.

Warm wind whooshed through the wide window over the tailgate, whipping at my hair and face, the radio blasting while Bob and my sister sat miles away under the bright lights of the city street. I was lifted as joy washed over me and I was flying with the breeze and the music and the lights and I became the air itself, free to fly high above treetops and chimneys, with no work or chore to hold me to the earth. I was one with the same wind that blew through the wide, dry desert, where I would soon walk with my mother under a constant sun. The same draft that would whip at my ankles and eventually find its way into my thirsty mouth.

It's funny how life is, isn't it? It seems to me that most people live every day hoping to grasp something that will give them that feeling, that sweetness. You can see it in their eyes, the waiting. In between the boredom and the average, every once in awhile, they find something magical. And there's no telling where it's going to come from. Day in and day out, people are carefully stitching moments together. Throwing parties, getting married, having babies–just trying to grab a little corner of that something special. And usually, all of that is pretty good, but there's no guarantee that it's going to be the lighter-than-air, can't-wipe-the-smile-off-your-face good.

Then one day, you hear a song, say. And the stars are out and you're having just the right conversation with just the right person and, boom. Absolute bliss. It's fleeting, of course. Throughout the years, we all walk around collecting bits of it, squirreling them away in photo albums and old love letters, living across the in-between, and finally, we look back and we say, "All right, that was good. I did good." Or we look back and all we remember is the in-between.

I occasionally got to visit my mother while she was in that lonely hospital. They don't let little kids onto the ward, so I had to wait outside the double doors, which had wire crisscrossing the skinny windows, while they told her she had visitors. They bent the rules and let her come out to see me. She'd sit, her folding chair next to mine, her arm draped over me, and she'd talk about the place.

"Mr. Garcia lost his wife and now he doesn't know where he is half the time, poor thing..." or, "Oh, that Margaret makes so much noise at night, I can't hardly get any sleep!" or, "He thinks he's one of the apostles and he's always trying to heal everyone–you know, a laying on of hands type thing? Just here, on your head. I tell him only Jesus could do that." And always she would say, "I was so confused. I can't believe the things I thought were happening."

The pills they gave her made her hands shake so bad. She'd sit, talking with her fingers working in the air, as if turning radio knobs over and over. They'd be still for a few seconds if she'd work at it, but they'd just start right back to shaking as soon as she forgot about them.

Eventually, they let her out and she came back to live with us at Judith's house, saying it was only until she could find work. She didn't want to impose. My sister and Bob didn't use the room with the *Zig Zag* pillow again–at least not that I saw–and everything was good and relatively normal for awhile. Ma and I would go for walks, breathing in the sweet grasses and listening for Starlings and Cactus Wrens. She'd make up songs and sometimes we'd dance. On Sunday mornings, I'd crawl up on her lap so we could see what Beetle Bailey and Hi and Lois were up to.

Then one day, she didn't hear me the first time I spoke. Her eyes had gone all glassy, her lips moving to secret conversations. She spent more time off on her own, staring down the dirt roads with a hand shading her eyes, a faraway look just at the edges. And I knew. I knew it wouldn't be long before she'd grab that old brown satchel again and we'd leave my sister and her whitewashed house and the lush green chili fields of that dusty farm town for the open road and the wild desert air.

Two

THE CATHOLIC FREAKIN' INDIAN CENTER

On our way out of Albuquerque, we visited Annie and Pete. Annie and Pete were old friends of my mother. I don't know how they met or how long they'd known each other. I only know that though they rarely saw each other, they had a relaxed ease and familiarity that only comes with time. Some relationships are like that. They're solid and worn in all the right places, like a favorite chair.

Both Annie and Pete liked good food in healthy portions and it showed on their short, stocky frames. Pete cut a dashing figure. His lean upper lip supported a perfect pencil-thin mustache. He had leather brown skin and thin glossy hair, pasted in place with Vitalis so it gleamed as it swept back from his face. His clothes always seemed a little too tight for him and his breathing was labored beneath his stuffed rayon shirts. He had a rumbling, sandpaper voice with a thick Mexican accent. He liked to slip me quarters and he'd explode into booming laughter at his own jokes. He had dark, lazy eyes and an eagle tattooed on the inside of his forearm. He always smelled of clean aftershave and I never saw him without a cigar.

Annie had light, smooth skin. Her hair was short and brunette, wavy soft, and her clothes could have stood to go up a size or two as well. She liked silk blouses that tended to ride up on her generous hips. Her voice was deep, earthy. A little too breathy, maybe, with a slight accent on certain words, but nothing close to Pete's. She wore polyester slacks in bright colors and I never saw her lips without a coat of fire engine red lipstick.

When all the hugging and cheek kissing was done, Annie, Pete, and my mother sat around the Formica kitchen table, talking over strong coffee and a haze of smoke. My mother laid it out for them. The conspiracies, the hospitals, all of the usual stuff she said to people that made them get that nervous look in their eyes and move quickly away.

But Annie and Pete just listened. They nodded and made an occasional joke. They commiserated with my mother, putting a hand over hers now and then. They loved her and they quietly let her know that she could trust them. I don't know that I had ever seen my mother trust anyone. Maybe I only thought I could recognize it.

"Hey, how about that one, huh? She driving yet?" Pete said, nodding at me.

"I wouldn't be surprised. I'll tell you right now, that little girl is eight going on forty. And she is smart as a whip. Aren't you? Sometimes too smart, right?" My mother shifted in her chair and dangled one hand over the back.

"I remember when she was born. You could plainly see she was something special." Annie wheezed, as she freshened up my mother's coffee cup. I sat on the living room sofa and chewed my thumbnail.

"Well, maybe this whiz kid would like to go get some ice cream, huh? Or are you too old for that?"

Pete walked me right down to the Woolworth's store and bought me a vanilla cone. We took our time getting back to their small house, chatting easily and sauntering past weed-choked fields and sagging adobe houses. He told me stories about when he was a little boy, about when he was in the Army, and when he first married Annie.

His stories painted a picture of a man that had gone through life like a sponge, soaking in everything that came along. "How you doing, you doing all right?" he said, looking way down at me.

I nodded between licks on my ice cream.

"Your mama, she's special, you know that? She talks to angels. Hell, she may be one, for all I know. You take care of her, you hear?"

When we closed the squeaking screen behind us and stepped back onto the avocado carpet in the dim living room, I could hear my mother and Annie laughing in the kitchen. Pete dropped his cold cigar stub into a large, blue glass ashtray and pulled another one from his shirt pocket.

He bit off the end and discarded it. He rolled the cigar between his fingers and then lit the tip with a paper match from a plain white book. He gingerly picked a bit of tobacco from his tongue.

"Hey, what the heck's all the racket in here, huh? You gonna have the neighbors calling the cops on us," he called, stepping into the kitchen.

This sent the two women into peals of laughter all over again. He rocked on his heels, grinning behind his stogie. My mother's face had gone red and shiny from laughing. It had been awhile since I'd seen her so relaxed and at ease, the usual weight of the world far away. Occasionally she'd drift off, her attention on conversations we couldn't share. Annie and Pete fussed over what to have for dinner and whether there was enough beer.

The meal turned out to be left over tamales, with beans and rice, and homemade bread—crispy and chewy all at the same time. I ate until I couldn't breathe. They talked about friends here and gone. Photo albums were dusted off and spread open on the kitchen table. Mother told them how my sisters were doing and about my brother in Vietnam. Annie made the sign of the cross. Pete said their son Johnny was in the Navy. A letter had come from him just last week. They worried, of course, but God would protect him.

The next thing I knew, it was morning. I woke up in clean sheets on the textured, turquoise sofa. I rubbed my eyes and sat up. Ma was rummaging around in her purse. She pulled out a compact and applied lipstick, smacking at the end of it.

"Go wash your face and brush your teeth so that we can get going," she said, handing me a change of underwear. The yellow ones, with the white flowers. My favorites. I jumped up and grabbed them before Annie and Pete could catch sight of my personal property.

I washed up in the pink pedestal sink with a sliver of pink bar soap. The tub was a matching pink too, small in length and short in height.

While brushing, I thought that a bath in there would be a pretty tight squeeze for Annie and Pete. It probably took hardly any water at all to fill it up around them.

I glanced around the bathroom. Green aftershave, a mangled toothpaste tube, Vitalis, a washrag wrung out and folded on a hook. All the things that were so familiar, so personal to these two people, that the very sight of them made me blush and lower my eyes.

I dried my face on the fluffy towel hanging near the sink and changed my underwear. I stuffed the used underpants down the waistband of my trousers.

Mother was in the kitchen with Annie and Pete, so I removed the undies and jammed them into the side pocket of the travel bag, securely zipping the pocket shut.

A fter leaving Annie and Pete's, we walked the streets of Albuquerque, thick with people and belching buses, out into the sparse regions of the city's edge. We walked past lush chili farms and through desolate towns with only a few houses and one gas station. That night, we stayed at the Zuni Motor Lodge and we ate in the little attached diner. I watched the big neon sign outside the window blink as I ate my chicken dinner. After a bubble bath and a Coca-Cola from the ice bucket, I fell asleep to the cheerful on-again, off-again glow beyond the motel curtains. Then, when the morning sun replaced the splash of neon, we let the desert swallow us up again.

We spent one night on a cot in a Salvation Army shelter, where rows and rows of small beds held tired looking women with toothless smiles and wild hair. Another night passed on the couch of my mother's second cousins. She was not close with them, having even to explain who we were. They looked somewhat baffled at our dusty shoes and sunburnt faces, but they opened their doors and offered us bedding and a share in their supper.

In the morning, we wolfed down eggs and tortillas and gratefully took the water they offered in a plastic juice bottle.

"Take care of your mother," they said, and then we were back on the road.

Again, civilization faded away and all that was left were the billboards cautioning that this was the last chance for gas or souvenirs. Then there was only sagebrush and barbed wire.

Several cars slowed along the highway where we walked to offer us a ride. My mother would keep her steady pace, eyes ahead, and offer them a firm "No, thank you," and each time, my heart sank watching those cars pull away and eventually fall into the watery horizon. She said it wasn't safe to take rides from strangers.

As the sun dropped down the horizon, the temperature started to fall, and there wasn't a soul as far as the eye could see. She continued to plod ahead at that maddening, sure and relentless pace.

The sky turned inky black and the stars peeked on one by one. So many stars, clear and bright, with no selfish moon to steal the show. It became hard to see and I tripped on a rut in the shoulder.

She stopped, then sighed and headed down a sandy ravine that sloped away from the highway.

"Come on Q.T., let's get some sleep." She brushed an area clear and sat down on the ground, unsnapping the travel bag's shiny clasp. I sat next to her as she started removing various pieces of clothing from the bag, including her blue dress, a houndstooth blouse, and her black skirt.

She pulled me up close to her and draped the clothes over us, making a patchwork quilt. She flattened the satchel and slid it under our heads as a makeshift pillow. As we lay down, she curled around me.

"How much farther, Ma?" I could feel her breath against my ear.

"Not very," she said.

"Do you think we'll get there tomorrow?"

"Yes. Tomorrow."

"What's Gallup like?"

"Oh, it's like anywhere, I guess. A place." She squeezed me tight. "My little doll. What would I do without you? Huh? I'd be pretty lonely out here, I guess."

"Me too," I said.

"See you in my cheams, I mean dreams, I mean cheams," she whispered and giggled.

"See you in mine."

I drifted off to sleep then, finally swimming and falling into unconsciousness. I dreamed I was riding in my brother's car, Ma at the wheel, though I knew she didn't drive. She was laughing and waving out the window, hardly watching the road at all. "Isn't it lovely, Q.T.?" she shouted over the wind. "Isn't it just lovely?" I was wrenched awake by the tremendous roar of an eighteen-wheeler racing past. Light flooded the roadside, throwing long shadows against the earth, and the wind billowed dirt, making us sputter and spit. Then, in an instant, it was gone, leaving us with pounding hearts and gritty eyes.

She turned over stiffly, moaning through her arthritis, dislodging the precarious blanket. I replaced the pieces, carefully arranging each scrap to cover the two of us and draped myself over her the best I could against the cold. Throughout the night, she would groan as she moved in stiff pain. Trucks roared past on their way to Albuquerque or Flagstaff, hauling livestock or grain or maybe hay. Throughout the night, I kept vigil over the shifting quilt, waking to tug this bit here or tuck that bit there.

Slowly, the black of night receded and a thin ribbon of pink washed up the sky. I hitched myself up on one elbow and rubbed the sleep from my eyes, my hair damp with dew, a film of dust covering me. Ma turned over on her back and attempted to sit up.

I got to my knees, gripping her under the elbow and eased her to her feet.

She limped around a bit, testing the temperamental hip. After long nights working at the hospital, she'd get home as the early morning light sifted through the lace curtain in the kitchen. She would limp and grimace and sink into a chair, her white uniform thick with the smell of illness and antiseptic.

She pulled a bit of grass from her hair, glancing at me and chuckling. "Well, that was something, wasn't it, Q.T.?"

She shook out each piece of clothing, carefully folding and refilling the satchel. She rubbed her face and slapped at her clothes, sending dust to float on the morning chill. I pulled bits of grass and fuzz from the hem of her skirt, patting at a few stray patches of dirt. We brushed teeth with dribbles of water and she applied a fresh coat of lipstick, carefully lining her lips and dabbing at the crimson strays reflected in her compact mirror. She combed my hair, wiped down my face and neck, and handed me a tissue, instructing me to clean out my ears.

I passed inspection and we started up the ravine to the level ground of the highway's shoulder. She pulled the water bottle and a bundle of foil-wrapped tortillas from the satchel. She plucked one free, tore off a half, and handed it to me. We walked at a leisurely pace, eating the bread and taking in a morning, rare and unseen by many eyes.

We followed that stretch of highway the whole of the morning and on into the afternoon. I counted my steps for a time, until I got distracted by a bird that might have been a hawk or a vulture. I cursed the dot in the sky and started over. One, two, three… The sun was low in the west when a brand new, shiny red pickup truck pulled up beside us. An Indian man, Navajo most likely, and a woman who turned out to be his wife sat in the cab. I could feel the cool air wafting from the interior and Hank Williams crooned softly from the radio.

"Can we give you a lift?" he said, as he rolled the pickup slowly alongside.

"No, thank you." My mother kept her eyes on the road ahead.

"It's going to be dark soon. We're heading into Gallup. You don't want to be out here at night. It gets cold as hell."

Ma eyed him suspiciously and gave the truck a once-over.

"Please, Ma," I whispered. It was the music that made me say it. The music and that lovely, cool air, which smelled like a brand new pair of shoes. I was so tired that my bones hummed and I knew in my heart that if I had to watch that truck pull away, then I would actually have to lay down and die.

She looked down at me and back at the man in the truck.

"All right," she said. "If you're going into Gallup, we'd appreciate the ride. Q.T., you get in the back." I scrambled into the truck bed and she lifted the satchel in next to me. She pulled out a black suit jacket, with white brocade, and covered me to my chin, where I huddled against the back window. "You'll be okay back here," she said, and she touched my cheek before climbing onto the bench seat next to the woman. A sliding window separated the inside and the bed of the pickup. The man opened it and gave me a little wave before pulling onto the road. I could hear the mumble of conversation and the soft music over the wind and most of all, I could smell the newness of everything.

I watched the end of the sun paint orange over the desert speeding past. That red rocket never touched the ground as we raced through the beautiful evening and I laughed as I watched the shoulder turn soft and blurry against the blacktop.

Come on Q.T., wake up." She shook me awake in darkness and the man lifted me out of the truck bed and onto the sidewalk. The pickup was idling in front of a large brownstone building with wide steps, leading to a pair of wooden doors, light spilling from glass set at the center. The words "Catholic Indian Center" glowed in neon blue up above. My mother thanked the couple, offering to send them money for their kindness but the man shook his head and wished us luck as he drove away.

She watched them disappear into traffic and then looked down at me. "Well, we made it," she chuckled. We climbed the steps and my mother pushed a little white button just near the door. It seemed an eternity until a woman wrapped in a robe over layers of nightclothes appeared in the glass. She was very pale and her face was lined with years of seeing to the lost and the needy. She had clear, watery blue eyes and her head was covered with a white cotton hood. She let us in and my mother apologized for the intrusion, saying she had nowhere else to go.

The woman introduced herself as Sister Peter Julian and explained that there were no rooms available. There was a moment of heavy silence, uncomfortable and desperate.

"We can fix up the lobby for you, though," the woman said finally. "We'll not send you out this late at night, of course."

She led us through a plain, tiled entry and up a broad staircase. That's when I got my first look at that wild celestial clock. It was in the shape of a big golden star, splashy and slightly gaudy, so out of place in the lobby of a Catholic boarding house for young Indian women, fussed over and chaperoned by a flock of nuns.

The rest of the furniture was average and functional. A couple of couches, a scarred faux-wood coffee table, a bookcase lined with dusty religious and forgotten titles, and an old television. Nothing remotely resembling that beautiful clock. It was the kind of thing I imagined a movie star would hang on the wall, like Tony Curtis, maybe. You'd walk into Tony's kitchen and there, along with the groovy white bucket chairs and orange dining table, would be this very clock, making time seem glamorous and eventful.

I watched seconds tick around as sheets and blankets were brought out and makeshift beds were put together on the couches. I was sent down the hall to a bathroom with a toilet and a shower stall—all in emerald green tile—so I could brush my teeth and wash off some of the day's dirt.

I was suddenly so tired. I don't even remember making my way back down the hall or getting under covers, but when I opened my eyes, it was morning and I was startled by the sound of footsteps rushing for the stairs above a buzzing of voices.

Girls with long, dark hair and brown skin hurried past, on their way to their unfolding lives. I sat up blinking. Some of the women stared at me as they started down the wide staircase. The sheet and blanket my mother had used were folded neatly and stacked on the arm of the sofa.

She was nowhere in sight and I craned my head this way and that, uncomfortable with so many strange eyes on me. Then I heard her voice. She was explaining something in hushed tones beyond a doorway to the right of the stairs.

"I just need a few days," she murmured. "I can find a job and then we can find our own place. God watches out for us."

There were soft words in reply, though I couldn't make sense of them.

"Thank you, sister. God bless you."

I found it an odd thing to wish a blessing from God on a nun. If anyone was in good with God it was a nun, but I supposed every little bit helped.

She emerged from the side room with a woman wearing a navy blue habit with a crisp, short veil. Much younger than the woman who had welcomed us, she wore silver, cat-eye glasses and a stern, tense look. She gave my ma a smile that never quite got to her eyes. She glanced at me and withdrew behind a door to the left of where they stood.

My mother came over and sat across from me. "Good morning, Q.T. I brought you some breakfast." She pulled a banana and a carton of milk from a paper sack. She spread them across a napkin on the coffee table in front of me. "I laid some clothes out for you. Do you remember where the bathroom is? Do you have to go?" I shook my head and looked around to make sure no one was listening. "I have to go look for a job now," she said. "I want you to brush your teeth and wash behind your ears. You hear me?" She peeled the banana to the waist and folded the milk carton open. "Now, you are to stay here and don't wander around. You can watch TV, but don't give the sisters any trouble and don't touch anything."

All I really heard out of all of that was, "You can watch TV." The old television sat on a bookshelf, and it was much larger than the one we had back home. Also, this one appeared to have all its own knobs, and no coat hanger and tin foil antenna. "All right, then. Here you go. Come right back, please." She handed me my clothes and I tiptoed down the hall, where I washed behind my ears, dressed, and relieved myself in the muted humidity of the bathroom. I pranced to the mirror behind a row of sinks, kicking my legs behind me like a pony and trying not to step on any of the cracks between the tiles. I pulled at my lips and made a face at myself before splashing water on my hands to smooth my hair away from my face.

When I got back to the lobby, bedding had been folded up and piled on top of the previous sandwich of linens. The television was on, the volume turned down low.

She was dressed in her black skirt and yellow blouse with the black piping at the collar. My favorite. There was still a hint of dust here and there, and I patted at it. Her usual pearls hung down the buttery front of the blouse, a knot tied at the bottom of the strand.

"I'll be back early this afternoon and I'll bring you some lunch," she said, combing my hair. "What do you want?"

"Umm, hamburger."

"Okay then, I'll bring you a big, fat hamburger deluxe." She gathered my hair and pulled it back. "We should put your hair up once in awhile."

"Nooooo, no, no, no." I gently pulled away from her and slouched into the sofa.

She rolled her eyes as she shook her head. "What am I going to do with you?" She kissed me and took my hand, rubbing across each finger one by one, playing them like the keys on a piano. "I'll be back as soon as I can, so be good and don't go downstairs." She touched a finger to her eyelid and I did the same. Eye kisses.

I watched her back as it disappeared down the stairs behind the short wall that enclosed the staircase. I didn't want her to go. I wanted to yell out that she should let me come with her. "Good luck," I said instead.

My gaze slid toward the television. *The Price is Right* was on. Ma and I watched that show all the time, guessing the prices on the various fabulous prizes. We were swept away by the glitter, the pretty girls showing off merchandise, and the screaming contestants that occasionally got close to clocking Bob Barker.

The milk carton was sweating and the banana wasn't getting any younger. The banana was a little too ripe, but it was sweet and pleasantly mushy in my mouth. I drank the last of the milk, folded the banana peel, and placed the end of my breakfast into the metal garbage can near the bookcase.

I flopped back down on the couch and mentally took a guess at the price of a La-Z-Boy recliner in royal blue velour. It was quiet, except for the screaming of Bob Barker's adoring audience.

The lobby was situated in the corner of an L shape. The short end of the L was to my right. Here was the gaping maw of the staircase, the door from which my mother had emerged with Sister Stern-Face, and at the far end, the door the nuns came and went from. Their living quarters, I supposed. There was also a recessed nook off to the far right, with a door sporting a scrolled number 2. The walls and doors were trimmed in sculpted molding, and they were painted in shades of polite beige. The place must have been a hotel at one time.

The ceiling over the lobby had a huge, pyramid-shaped skylight, with black wire mesh throughout, to prevent anything unwanted from falling into the laps of *The Price is Right* viewers below. The glass was milky and uneven from years of rain and sun, but light still poured through.

The long end of the "L" to my left stretched into a spacious corridor, which was dimly lit, save for the window at the far end. Doors on either side of the corridor had the same ornate numbers. The green bathroom was set into an alcove, roughly halfway down. I could see that the corridor turned at the end, an inky-black opening, stretching further through the building.

A doorknob screeched, making me jump. I snapped back to the television screen. There was a commercial for toilet cleaner on. A very happy looking woman was wearing yellow gloves and smiling over the bowl.

A young woman walked into my line of sight. She was Indian, with the same long, glossy hair and wide, brown features. She was a little thick in the jeans and was wearing a peasant blouse, sandals, and a purse thrown over her shoulder. She slowed when she saw me and stopped a few feet from where I sat slumped on the sofa.

"You don't look Indian. Do you live here?" I concentrated on *The Price is Right* and shrugged. "Hey kid, where's your mom?" she said, raising her voice like I was hard of hearing.

"She went to find a job," I offered, without looking at her.

"Join the club," she muttered as she eased herself down on the opposite couch and dug inside her leather-stitched purse. It was a deep caramel, and it had an eagle hand-tooled on the front of it in splendorous color. Her face was shiny, a bit of acne on her forehead, and she smelled of vanilla.

"Want some gum?" she said, offering a pack of Juicy Fruit with a stick protruding from the sunny wrapper. I tentatively took it and folded it into my mouth.

The Price is Right had reached the part where the final two contestants were viewing the fabulous vacation showcases and bidding on the price.

"Five thousand, three hundred and twenty-five," she said to the screen.

"No way, we're talking about Hawaii here," I said. "Eight thousand...mmm, seven hundred and twelve."

"Eight thousand seven hundred and twelve?" She chewed her gum and gave me a dubious look. "Twelve? Where do you get twelve?"

I shrugged.

You could cut the tension with a knife. Everyone in the studio audience was on the edge of their seats. Bob was cool as ever, of course. "The actual price of the Hawaii vacation showcase is—"

Janice pulled the cover from the glittering figure. $9,350.00.

The crowd erupted. One of the contestants was bouncing around the set, her Cross-Your-Heart bra holding on for dear life while she yanked and pulled at poor Bob Barker.

"How did you know it was going to be so high?"

"I watch this show a lot."

"My name is Louise Begaye." Louise stretched out her hand. I looked at the neat nails–shining with clear polish–and the fine lines running through her palm.

"Deborah McCarroll," I said, as I took her hand briefly and turned back to the screen.

"Well Deborah, I'll see you around. Gotta go get into the world now." She sighed and slapped her knees before getting to her feet.

I nodded and watched as her head bobbed down the stairs and out of sight.

Three

CATEYES AND AGGIES, OH MY

How's your burger, Q.T.?"

"Mphhh." I nodded my head. She smiled and moved off to pour coffee into the cup of an Indian man reading a newspaper and wearing a stained John Deere cap. I watched her weave from table to table, dropping checks and picking up plates. She generally stared straight ahead, her eyes out of focus, her lips moving as ever. Occasionally, she'd smile and nod at nothing. The diners scattered around the dingy coffee shop, minding their own business for the most part, and rarely did anyone even glance at her.

She deposited the dirty dishes somewhere unseen and stood on the other side of the counter across from me, with the fist of one hand on her hip and a palm of the other flat on the counter top. Two stools down from me, a man got up and left money under his plate.

"You got a good appetite for such a little sparrow," he said.

I popped a fry into my mouth. My mother refilled my water glass. "Yes, she's always been a good eater, if it's something she likes."

"Your little one?" He cocked his head at me. She smiled and nodded. Shoving his wallet in his back pocket, he said, "She's gonna be a heartbreaker. You have a good day now. Both of you." We watched him lumber to the front entrance.

"We have to get you into school tomorrow morning," she stated, watching the door close.

"Aw ma, whyeeeee? I could just stay at the hotel. I won't make any noise, I swear."

"Don't say swear, and you have to go to school, you know that."

"You know, I'm not feeling so good. I think I'm coming down with something. Ma? Ma!" Her eyes were fixed on the horizon and her mouth had gone slack. She blinked and looked down at me.

"Tomorrow morning," she said, gathering up menus for the couple at the front register.

We had lived in the lobby of the Catholic Indian Center for almost a month, but when Mom got herself the waitressing job, we moved over to the Lexington Hotel.

The Lexington just happened to be on the same street as the Catholic Indian Center, two buildings north on Route 66, across from the Texaco station, where you could buy icy-cold Coca-Cola in little green bottles.

It was pretty easy to collect what belongings we had and walk the half block to the tarnished brass and glass double doors of the old hotel. I liked the Lexington, though I missed the girls at the C.I.C., and those evenings huddled up watching *Mannix* or *The Dean Martin* show. I could count on those good ladies to slip me a stick of Juicy Fruit or a Tic Tac or two.

The Catholic Indian Center looked just like what it was, but the Lexington still looked proud and fancy, even though it was kind of run down. It reminded me of that Barry Manilow song, "The Copacabana." *Still in the dress she used to wear, faded feathers in her hair. She sits there so refined and drinks herself half blind...*You could plainly see that the Lexington used to be a pretty big deal in its day. Now we could afford to live there.

It was nice to have a bed and as far as hotels go, the Lexington had pretty good ones. Ours was soft, with crisp white sheets and almost no squeak to the springs. The room had a small desk, with a note pad that said *The Lexington Hotel* in script at the top, and a padded chair that swiveled around and around. I was sitting in that very chair while my mother tied my shoes.

"Ma seriously, I think it would be better if I just stayed right here. You don't know what might happen to me out there. An airplane could crash into the school or I could get food poisoning from the cafeteria."

"Those new shoes are still stiff, huh? They look slippery, too." She was pinching at my toes and swiveling my foot around at the ankle. "Try scuffing them up when we get out on the sidewalk. And seriously, you have to go to school."

A nd where are her transcripts, exactly?" We were sitting in a small office across the desk from a woman with thin lips and waves of dark hair piled up on top of her head.

"Well, I don't know. Her last school, I imagine."

"Uh-huh. And how old is she?"

My mother looked down at me, trying to guess. "Uh, what grade are you in?"

"Second," I whispered.

"Right. Of course. She's in the second grade and she's eight years old."

"Mrs. McCarroll, I'd love to help you, but we really don't admit children without their transcripts. You can call or write the school administrator and they will send you the papers we need to enroll her. Otherwise, we have no way of knowing at what level she's learning or any special needs she may have, you see? Mrs. McCarroll?" Mother had gone away. She sat on the very front of her seat and she was very still. "Mrs. McCarroll?"

The woman sighed and looked at me. "What is the name of the last school you attended?"

Q .T., make sure you brush your teeth and wash your ears before you go to bed, okay?" She kissed me on my cheek and hugged me tight before buttoning up her coat and grabbing her purse. "Don't forget the room key if you go down the hall and don't let anyone in, no matter what. I'll see you in the morning."

Ma was working nights at a diner after losing the coffee shop job, so I was alone in the evenings now. Living at the Lexington meant there was no more TV, which was awful at first, but it was nice to sit at the desk, swinging around in the big padded chair and drawing pictures while the radio played soft and easy in the background. My favorite song was *The Candyman,* and when I'd hear those first twinkling notes, I'd run to the radio and turn it up so I could sing along. I'd picture that guy coming around with groovy lemon pies and bags of candy for all the kids that followed him, dancing and singing, sun shining on golden sidewalks alongside sparkling rivers. It's a great song.

Sometimes, I'd sit by the window as the sun went down, waiting for the first star so I could wish on it. I'd wish that she wouldn't have to go. That maybe she could stay and we could read the funnies or draw together, but in the end, she'd button up her coat and kiss me goodbye all the same.

I'd break out the puzzle books and stories from the school library about rabbits and frogs that went on terrific adventures. And of course, there were always drawings to be made in the big, pulpy pads that Ma would carry home under her arm as she crept through the door in the gray light of dawn. Smelling of bacon grease and coffee, she'd lie down on the covers next to me, stroking my hair and telling me about her night before I had to get up for school.

I walked blocks and blocks to school. It took forever. Up hills and down hills, along the cracked sidewalks that led through the city's retail district, and up into the tree-lined neighborhoods.

Along the way, I'd pass a house that had a wall made up of all kinds of different colored rock. Stone set into concrete, flat and smooth, with slashes of blue and red running through. My teacher, Mrs. Lewis, said that trees fell ages and ages ago and eventually became the rock in that wall. I imagined I could see pictures and alien landscapes in the surface. Sometimes, I'd see myself walking along jagged mountains and ravines, pausing to watch my two moon sunset. Then I'd collect my books and get moving again.

There were an awful lot of Indian kids at Lincoln Elementary School in Gallup, New Mexico. A whole slew of them. For every white face, there were a good ten Native ones. There was one blonde girl in the whole second grade class. She stood out in a crowd, and not just because of the yellow hair and freckles. Her name was Janine Pollard, and she talked just about all the time. In fact, it was hard to catch Janine without a bubbly twitter just pouring out of her. She had a very hard time with Quiet Period. Sometimes, I would picture Janine talking in her sleep, just chatting away in the middle of the night in her own little room, in her own little bed, with the plump pillows and the cowgirl sheets.

Janine pretty much drove me batty. I'd try to hide from her. I know that sounds mean, but she didn't seem to care, and she always found me anyway.

This one time, I tried to hide from her in one of the big, leafy trees way in the back of the playground, where kids aren't supposed to go. It wasn't a very tall tree, so I figured I'd be all right. Well, I ended up falling out of that tree and right into the dirt on a fresh pile of dog doo just as Janine came skipping over. All those times my sister stuck me up in that tree back home, and I never once fell. But the one time I try to be cute about it? Just goes to show you. Janine jabbered on about Easter and coloring eggs and her dress and I just sat there, refusing to get up so she wouldn't see the mess smashed into the seat of my pants.

Eventually, the bell rang and the teacher came out to wrangle everyone back to class. Janine tore off, windmilling her arms and screaming to no one in particular. Nobody even noticed that I wasn't there. I got to my feet, cleaned myself up the best I could with twigs and more dirt, and I walked home.

33

"Heya, Karl." I climbed down the first floor steps and took a seat on the Lexington's marble staircase. The air smelled of sharp pine and the lights hummed softly overhead.

"Heya," he shot back. Karl was my friend and the janitor at the Lexington hotel. He was good company in the evenings when Ma was working, though I wasn't supposed to be downstairs. He was Indian, not too tall, with bristly, short hair and black horn-rimmed glasses. He wore a uniform of faded green work pants and a matching shirt with his name stitched on the pocket.

"What's new in Youville?" he asked as he pulled a heavy mop back and forth in long strokes across the lightning forks of the marble floor.

I shrugged. It was black outside the big glass doors. Ma had gone on to work and I'd gotten awfully bored in that little room all alone.

"I got a bruise on my shin from dodgeball," I offered, lifting my cuff and pressing lightly on the tender green patch. He stopped mopping and looked through thick lenses at me.

He whistled. "Boy, that's a good one, all right. I hope you gave them something for their trouble." Karl was missing his two front teeth, so when he said an S, it made a sound like air escaping a balloon. He was grinning and I got a good look at his gums. I wanted to ask him what happened to those teeth, but I knew Ma would tell me it wasn't polite.

"I'm not so good at dodgeball," I said. He leaned on his mop and nodded. I took another look down at my injury. "Dodgeball is a lot like war, I think. Some kids like the war and they go out there to kill. You can see it in their eyes as soon as they get their hands on the ball. They got blood in their eyes. I don't got that, so I'm no good, but most of the time I can dart around pretty good to keep from getting hit." I pulled my pant leg down. "Not this time, though."

Karl nodded. "I guess you have to play, huh?"

"Yeah, everybody has to. I do better than some. Some of them don't move so good. The bigger kids, or this one boy that wears thick glasses with a black band to keep them on his head? I can see him trying to get hit when someone has the ball that doesn't throw so hard. Then he can just go sit it out. Sometimes some of them cry. I never have though." I noticed some scrapes and cuts on Karl's knuckles. "Looks like you got hurt too, huh?"

He looked down at his chewed hand. "Oh, that? I had too much beer and got into a fight. I guess there's all kinds of war, huh?" he said, and he grinned all the wider.

"What was the fight about?"

He shrugged and started mopping again. "Sometimes, when you're a man, you have to fight."

"I don't think I would. I think I'd run away," I said.

"Shoot, you can't run away. Not when you're a man."

I studied the wounds as his big hands worked the mop. Sometimes, Karl had angry gashes across his nose or on his forehead. Sometimes, his eye was blackened. He made me realize that the world beyond the doors of the Lexington was a mean place for some. I thought about the day my brother threw a bag over his shoulder and walked out to join the military. I wondered if it was hard for him to leave home, and I hoped it hadn't been too scary for him.

"I'm glad I'm not a man," I said, finally. He sighed and dropped the mop into the rolling bucket of murky water. "Yeah, I'll bet you are. It ain't all it's cracked up to be. Hey, wanna pitch some pennies?"

I dug into the pocket of my jeans. "I only got a nickel and a dime."

"I'll change them out for you. C'mon."

He pulled out a handful of change and picked out the pennies, laying them in my outstretched palm. We headed for our usual pitching arena, which was just inside the hallway next to the soda machine. He dug a toe line in the deep pile carpet with his index finger.

"Okay now, no crossing that line," he warned.

"I know, I know. Let's flip to see who goes first."

He tossed the coin in the air and I called tails. When it landed, Mr. Lincoln's profile gleamed in the soft light.

"Ah, dang," I said. He smiled smugly and shimmied his boot up to the scratch in the carpet as he gingerly tossed the coin. It landed a good six inches from the wall.

"Okay, okay, my turn." I toed the line and balanced the penny on my thumbnail. As soon as it was in the air, I knew it was a winner. Not a hair's distance from the baseboard. You couldn't ask for prettier.

He shook his head as I picked up the pennies. "You're good at the toss, that's for sure."

"Oh, I get a lot of practice at school."

His face clouded up. "Hey, no pitching pennies at school, you promised."

"Not pennies, silly. Marbles. When that circle is drawn in the dirt, and all the real pretty ones, or the scratched up every-day soldier marbles come out? That's when it gets good. Then it doesn't matter if I'm skinny or short or that I'm a girl. I can beat just about anybody."

"Ah, marbles," he chuckled. "Those boys must wonder what hit 'em."

"You said it." I stepped up to the line in the carpet again and searched my palm for a new penny. I didn't like to shoot the same coin twice in a row. It was bad luck. "I have a whole Pringles potato chip can almost full of marbles. Almost full up, I've won so many." I held my hands up like I was gripping the can at the top and bottom. "I have Cat eyes and Aggies. Big blue Shooters, Swirlies, those are real pretty, and, of course, the little Purees. Those are my work horses. If you throw them right, they get buried in the dirt. Very hard to hit." I loaded a penny onto my thumb and tossed gently. It landed a few inches from the baseboard. "The one thing I don't have is a Steely. A Steely is a big metal Shooter. A ball bearing is what it is. This kid James has one, but he never uses it. He just likes to roll it in the dirt while you're shooting. It's very distracting."

"Wow," Karl said. "It's a regular sport, huh?"

"Oh-ho, yeah. I've seen some guys almost cry when they loose their good shooters."

I heard the familiar shriek and ka-chunk of the front door. Karl and I both turned in time to see it close behind my mother. Her coat collar was up and she was carrying a paper bag close against the evening chill. She slowed on her way to the stairs when she got a good look at me.

"Hi, Ma," I said. "How come you're not at work?" Karl practically climbed up the wall trying to get around me.

"Evening, ma'am," he muttered, going back to his mop. She didn't even glance at him.

"Deborah June, what are you doing down here?" She'd use my full name when she was mad. Otherwise it was Debbie, or Q.T., of course. "Didn't I tell you to stay upstairs? Didn't I say that?" She had lowered the bag and she was holding it by one hand as her heels clicked slowly toward me.

I inched backward. "I didn't have nothing to do."

Her face was tight as a stretched rubber band. There wasn't a sound but the buzzing of the lights. Then she sighed and the weight of the day washed over her. "All right, Q.T.," she said. "Let's go upstairs. I'll read you a story."

She glared at Karl before laying a hand over my shoulder and ushering me up the steps. I took a quick look back at him. He had resumed his mopping in wide, sloppy swaths. He smiled his toothless smirk and waved goodbye with a two finger salute.

It was the Friday before Easter. Everyone in class was supposed to have a dyed egg for an Easter basket exchange. Ma never did get around to the shopping, so I was eggless and feeling kind of low and angry and sorry for myself as I shuffled along the sidewalk that eventually spilled into the school steps.

Mrs. Lewis specifically said that everyone should bring a hard-boiled egg. She'd said it twice. I think Mrs. Lewis was about the best teacher I ever had. When the afternoon sun was low in the sky, it would blaze in the classroom windows, turning Mrs. Lewis's hair from auburn to fiery red, and I was reminded of sugar cookies and new buds in spring when the hem of her dress brushed by my desk.

I was walking along, kicking a stone and keeping a good bit of dark cloud and gloomy thoughts hovering overhead as I passed the house of Kathy Martinez. I kicked my stone and glanced at that house now and then, studying the dark windows and the empty swing set.

Kathy sat next to me in class. She was almost as small as me. She had short dark hair, full of shine and curl, and her dresses were always crisp and pressed. She showed up every day looking like she was going to church. She had the best cursive writing of any kid in class.

She didn't talk to me too much. She had her own friends, but she gave me an apple from her lunch occasionally, or she'd sit next to me during story time.

I was invited over to her house once. She was a miniature version of her mother, and her house was just like the house on *Leave it to Beaver*. We played on her swing set as her mother looked nervously out the front window. I got the impression that she didn't think Kathy should be playing with such a shabby kid. That was the only time I got invited over, but I still had to walk by her house on my way to and from school.

The playground's jungle gym was in sight as I rounded the block and I took my time crossing the street. As I stepped up on the curb, I saw Janine and she saw me.

"Hey Debbie, look at my egg. It's a pretty one, isn't it?" We fell in to step together and I shifted my writing pad from one hand to the other. "I think it's the prettiest one I ever colored. I had a tough time picking though, there were so many good ones. See, I used glitter on the rings, see there? That was hard and some of it scraped off, but it still looks good, I think. My mom helped me, but I came up with what it should look like. I love to color eggs, don't you? I wish we could do it all year. Where's your egg? Don't you have one?" I sniffed and pretended to be very interested in my homework writing lesson.

"Oh," she said. "What are you going to do? You shoulda' told me. I would have brought an extra one. Maybe someone will have one." The classroom door was open and students were filtering in and showing off their handiwork. Janine trailed after me. "How come you didn't bring one?"

I squeezed around two boys who were pretending to throw the eggs at each other and I slunk into my desk. The bright yellow walls were crammed with construction paper rabbits and Crayola Easter baskets.

"Settle down, boys and girls." Mrs. Lewis sat on the front of her desk as kids shuffled and whispered loudly. "Please get out your paper baskets." I opened the lid to my desk. The lonely construction paper cone with the stapled pink handle wobbled inside. The cone had a sporty basket and daisy pattern drawn in crayon to help with the "basket" illusion. I laid it out on my desk.

"Did everyone bring an Easter egg?" Mrs. Lewis asked. Janine's hand shot up into the air. There was a soft knock at the classroom door. Mrs. Lewis studied the narrow window above the knob for a moment and hopped off her desk. She was nodding out into the hall and talking softly. Then she opened the door wide and my mother appeared out of thin air, like a magician's assistant popping out from a trick box. She came over to my desk and pulled a bright blue egg from the pocket of her raincoat. I looked at the egg. I looked up at her. Then I looked at the egg again.

"Well? Take it," she said. I couldn't peel my eyes away from it. "Take it, Q.T." She jabbed her hand in my direction. I gingerly lifted the egg from her outstretched fingers. Her painted nails blazed against the fresh sky color of the shell. "I also got you a little something extra," she said, producing a box from behind her back. The whole class was riveted. She laid the box on my desk and lifted the cellophane top. A grinning bunny, with holes where the eyes should be, stared up at me. She took the bunny mask out of the box and held it out. She pushed it at me again, but I didn't take it. She laid the mask on my desk and pulled a shimmery pink and white bunny onesie from the shallow box.

"Try it on," she coaxed. One of Kathy's friends whispered behind a hand. Janine was chewing gum and swinging her legs under her desk. I couldn't tell if the thump, thump, thumping was her heels hitting the front of her chair or my heart throbbing under my ribs.

"Go ahead." My mother held up the costume. It had red piping at the neck that tied in the back. I eased out of my chair and one of the legs screeched across the floor in the quiet classroom. She leaned over me and opened the back of the onesie wide, like a gaping mouth. She looked me in the eye and pointed her chin at the opening. I swallowed and stepped into it. She yanked the top up over the front of my shirt and tied the string at the back of my neck. The classroom erupted in laughter.

The pants ended mid shin and my jeans jutted below the hem a good six inches. The collar cut into my throat, choking me. The sleeves fell just below my elbows and the shoulders were pulling at the crotch of my pants causing my underwear to jam up my backside in a self-inflicted wedgie.

"Hmm, I guess it's a little small," my mother said, her hand on her chin. "But you look awfully cute." The box had fallen on the floor and her face brightened as she picked it up. "At least the mask will fit. You can have fun with that, huh."

She kissed me on my cheek and thumbed the lipstick off before leaving me standing at my desk. When the door had clicked shut, Mrs. Lewis faced the classroom.

"Well that was a very nice surprise, wasn't it boys and girls?" She resumed her place up front. Kids were still glancing at me and giggling. "But you know, since we're going to be getting to work now, you'll probably want to take that off so it doesn't get dirty, huh?" She smiled warmly at me.

We got fake grass for our paper baskets, and we drew names so we could trade eggs. I got a kid named Raymond who liked to eat paste. We had juice and Easter cake and we colored mimeographed sheets with black outlined Easter Bunnies on them. When the bell rang, I gathered my books, shoved my egg into my pocket, and smashed my cone basket into my jacket for the walk home. I left the costume under my desk and I never saw it again.

"Peace be with you." Father Connell's vestments spread majestically from his outstretched arms and draped to the floor behind the alter.

"And also with you," the small chapel echoed as the faithful turned to each other in greeting.

The priest did a brief curtsy and walked around the alter to shake hands, almost absentmindedly, with the nuns in the front pew. The greeting was mumbled and whispered throughout the room.

Mom gave me a squeeze and a kiss and said, "Peace, Q.T." The lady next to me put a plump hand out to me.

"Peace be with you," she whispered. I briefly gripped her fingers and muttered in return.

Every Sunday morning, I had to put on stiff shoes and a clean, pressed shirt, and we'd head down the street to sit through Mass in the little chapel just off the front entryway at the Catholic Indian Center. The church smelled of incense and candles and a smell I couldn't place. Furniture polish, maybe. Or maybe it was something too holy for mere mortals, something secret and ancient, known only to the priests and the nuns.

The collection plate was passed around and Ma pulled a twenty dollar bill out of her purse. Besides that bill, the patent leather clutch purse was empty, except for a lipstick and a squashed tissue. I watched the money travel down the row and back to the alter boy waiting in the aisle.

There were two clergy that said Mass at the Catholic Indian Center, but Father Silver was said to be retiring soon.

Father Silver was my friend. He was just about the nicest man that I had ever known. Pete was nice, of course, and I loved hearing his stories, but he was iron tough and gravel throated. Father Silver was calm and pink and he seemed to have a little smile threatening his face all the time. He had white hair that looked very soft and shiny, like corn silk, and he always smelled good with spicy-sweet aftershave.

The other priest was Father Connell. When Father Connell said Mass, he sounded just like Archie Bunker. He was thin, with wiry salt and pepper hair, and he would stare at me through the black rims of his glasses without saying a word.

He didn't say much to anyone, as a matter of fact, except Sister Daniel Ignatius. I'd come around the corner and there they'd be, heads together, speaking in hushed tones. Sister Peter Julian, Sister Marie Terese, all of them would come to attention when he'd walk in the room. I was a little scared of Father Connell really, and I got the feeling that he'd haul off and give me a pop if he thought he could get away with it. You can tell that about some guys.

"Go in peace to love and suv the Lohd." Father Connell waved his hand in the air, up, down, and over in the shape of a cross.

"Thanks be to God," we all answered.

My mother shook hands with the sisters and Father Connell and we strolled back toward the Lexington. We passed a barred doorway that smelled slightly of urine and stale beer. Splotches of blood smeared the sidewalk. It was always the same on Sunday mornings. There were quiet, shocking remnants of too much drink and bluster. I thought of Karl and hoped that none of the blood spilled in the glow of that neon had been his. Mother did not seem to see any of it.

"Well, it looks like it's going to turn out to be a beautiful day after all. It looks like the clouds are on the run," she said, her gloved hand over her eyes. "Maybe we should go to the park."

"Mom, did you put all our money in the collection plate?"

"Don't worry about it, Q.T. We'll be all right. There are always going to be those less fortunate than yourself. Little children that don't have shoes or anyone to love them. Women in need of a good meal and a kind word. The sisters do good work. What kind of people would we be if we didn't try and help them, hmm? Now, how about that park?"

It took a good while for everyone at school to forget about the bunny costume. Kids whispered as I walked by, and every once in awhile some dopey boy would dangle a carrot in front of me. But eventually things carried on as usual, and I went back to watching the tide of the classroom ebb and flow.

On this particular day, I was sitting at my desk, struggling with the dreaded arithmetic. Subtraction. A killer.

Mrs. Lewis had stepped out and a kid named Leonard was sitting in the desk behind me, jabbing the eraser end of a pencil into my back and howling like a hyena.

"Hey, hey, hey," he jeered as he poked at me.

I turned around and shot him a dirty look. He made a face at me.

"Hey, here's a joke." He was wriggling in his seat and leaning way out to the side. "Why did the chicken cross the road? Huh? He didn't, he was too chicken." He laughed and banged on his desk. He leaned back and the boy behind him thumped him on the head.

I slumped down in my chair and jammed my hands into my jacket pockets. My fingers closed around a pile of bird shot. Warm little BBs rolled around my palm, reminding me of a day miles behind me. A couple of soda cans, a BB rifle, and a lot of mud in my cousin Cindy's back yard.

Behind me, Leonard was screaming about his shoes being too tight and how his feet were sweating. I pinched one of the pellets between my thumb and forefinger and wedged it into my ear. The racket was cut in half. I shoved a second BB into the other ear. The world hummed and whooshed with a pleasant undercurrent. I could hear the in and out of my lungs. My heart played out a steady rhythm. I peeked over my shoulder at Leonard. He was having a pencil sword fight with the boy that thumped him. His mouth moved, but to me it sounded like long grass in the wind, peaceful and lovely. I leaned over my book and worked on moving numbers into place.

When the bell rang, Mrs. Lewis came around and collected our work. I gathered up my things and dug in each ear to pull the pellets free, but they wouldn't budge. I was still sitting at my desk, trying to pry the BBs loose, as the last of the students filed out.

"Debbie? Shouldn't you be getting home?" Mrs. Lewis was sitting at her desk, tamping a stack of worksheets. Her voice was muffled and the image of her swam through my welling tears. She knelt down by my desk with a sympathetic smile. "Hey, what's the problem here? Huh? School's out. Can't be that bad." Her teeth were very white and shiny. "Come on now, it's all right."

"I stuck BBs in my ears," I whispered.

She blinked, her smile frozen in place. "What's that?"

I reached into my pocket and showed her a fist full. "I can't get them out."

She turned my head and pulled my hair back. "I see. All right. Well, let's go see Mrs. Castillo. I'm sure she can help."

"Call her mother," Nurse Castillo said. "There's nothing I can do about it. They're too deep. Better to let a doctor handle it." A school nurse sees a lot of things, and she was neither surprised nor terribly concerned about my problem. She bounced back into her wool coat and reached for the door. "Good luck," she said.

Four

HOME SWEET HOME

It wasn't long before Ma lost another waitressing job, so she put on her coat and hit the pavement again. A dry cleaning place took her on to work the front counter, but she lost that one too. And another waitressing job after that.

Eventually, we walked our little suitcase right back to the Catholic Indian Center. The nuns took us in again and gave us a room just off the lobby. It was smaller than the one at the Lexington, with only a squeaky bed and a couple of chairs cozied up to a scarred table, but you couldn't beat the view. The trains in the yard across the way puffed and postured night and day, like lumbering dinosaurs.

I missed my grand hotel with the carpet and the fading wallpaper. I missed the good bed and pitching pennies with Karl, but what I didn't miss was the lonesome nights. Sometimes, there was shouting in the hallway or creaks and groans that caused me to bury my head under the covers, eyes wide and staring in the blackness.

Ma filled the night shift receptionist job at the C.I.C. She answered phones and let the girls know when they had a call or a visitor, but mostly she just sat downstairs all night in the little glass booth at the entryway so that I could go out to the lobby and watch TV or tromp down in sock feet and sit with her awhile. Also, I still got to see Karl when he'd bring his mother to play bingo every Friday night, which was great fun.

The bed in our little room was perfectly level with the third floor windowsill. I'd lie on my stomach, my chin on the backs of my hands, resting on layers of cracking paint, and watch the day hum by. There was a window screen at one time, but that was long since gone, with slats rusty and corroded, so you could lean way out and look straight down onto the tops of heads as people hustled by on the sidewalk below.

I was watching the trains creak and crash as they jockeyed for position in the sleeting rain. I pressed a spot just above my earlobe and the sound went dead. I tugged on my earlobe and the world came alive again. Rain, traffic, trains. Push, off. Pull, on.

After leaving the nurse's office, Mrs. Lewis had called my mother. She and I and the ticking clock waited until Ma showed up in a taxicab. A doctor looked in my ears and he said that he thought that the BBs would eventually fall out on their own.

Everything sounded like it was underwater for a long time, and then one day, pop! I could hear again. After that, I could turn the volume on and off with the push of a finger.

"Q.T., close that window, it's freezing in here." My mother was slipping into her tan wedgies. The bed bounced up and down as she struggled to get her heel into the back strap. Reluctantly, I closed the window and said goodbye to the boxcars.

"Why don't you come downstairs in a half hour or so and I'll give you some money so you can go out and get us some chicken at the KFC, okay?" I rolled over and she put both her hands on my knees and gave them a little shake.

"Okay," I said.

"Let's see your ears, they're looking a little red. How are they? Any sign of those BBs yet?" She turned my head and examined my ear.

"Not yet. I can hear okay, though."

She shook her head. "Honestly, what were you thinking?" She leaned in closer. "Uh oh. What's this, now? Why, I see cobwebs in there. We better get you a feather duster."

"Aw, come on." She gave my ribs a poke and I squealed.

"Now squeeze me real tight. It's gotta last me a good while."

"See you in a bit, Q.T." She kissed my palm before leaving. "You be good, now."

One day, I went to school and Janine wasn't there. She wasn't there the next day either, nor the next. Mrs. Lewis said that Janine had moved away. I was surprised to find that I missed her and sometimes I'd squint when I looked out onto the playground, pretending I could see her tearing away from the swings, her arms flying wildly away from her sides.

I found myself spending my lunch hours alone on the steps of the library now, slipping inside as soon as my sandwich had been wolfed down, settling in at one of the wide tables to read Laura Ingalls Wilder or Mark Twain or E.B. White for the rest of the period. This is not to say I didn't have friends. I had the best friends anyone could have. I had the Abbots. They just didn't happen to go to my school.

I met the Abbot kids last summer, after stopping to catch my breath at the top of a big hill in front of their house. They were making chalk drawings on the sidewalk and I had laughed at a picture of a terrific pink alligator devouring a spaceman. There are nine Abbot kids in all, but only three near my age. Paula, Chris, and Daniel, who is a year behind us and can be a royal pain at times.

"How's this?" Paula held up a Coke cap.

"No, that's too small. Do you have anything a little bigger?" She rummaged around in the refrigerator and produced a juice bottle with a wider mouth. She twisted the cap until it sneezed. I examined the cap and pressed it into the slice of Wonder bread on the counter in front of me, cutting out a neat circle. "Oh, that's perfect," I said. I smashed the wafer between my palms and pressed the crucifix from my necklace into the bread, making a clean impression. I held up the make-shift Eucharist triumphantly.

"Wow, cool," she said.

We made a dozen or so Wonder Bread bodies of Christ and spread them out on one of Mrs. Abbot's good silver plates. We carried the sacred bread into the front room, along with a fancy wine glass and a bottle of grape juice.

"Ready," Paula said, showing off the wafers.

"Okay, where's the robe?" Daniel pulled a white terry bathrobe from the back of a chair.

"I wanna be the priest." He held the robe behind his back. Paula looked at me. "Do it," she said.

I plucked one of the Eucharists off the plate and held it high with both hands. "On the night he was betrayed, our Lord took bread, and gave thanks. He broke it, gave it to his disciples, and said, "Take this and eat of it. This is my body, which has been given for you and for all men, so that your sins may be forgiven. Do this in memory of me." Yeah, and then you have to ring the bell."

She looked at Danny. "Can you do that?" He handed the robe over and I put it on backwards, smoothing the front. Paula draped one of her mother's scarves down either side of my shoulders and the illusion of a priest's vestments was complete.

We solemnly lit the candles I had brought and I began to say Mass over the towel covered television set/alter. My congregation stood, knelt, and sat in all the appropriate places until it was time to line up and take communion.

"How do you remember all that stuff?" We were draped around the living room, enjoying the last of the body and blood of Christ.

"You kidding? I've only heard it like a thousand times. I might not get to school every day, but I always, I mean always, have to go to church. Heck, I live over a church now. Sister Marie Therese says they might even let me be an alter girl."

"There's no such thing as an alter girl. Only boys can do that," Danny said.

I shrugged. "Take it up with the nuns." I got up to leave before Mrs. Abbot got home from work.

Forgive me father, for I have sinned. It's been a week since my last confession." The thinly padded rail I was kneeling on made my knees ache. "I was disrespectful to my mom...I, uh, lied and I stole..."

"What did you steal?" Father Connell's voice shot from behind a patterned partition.

I had to go to confession every week. Most of the time, I had to make bad stuff up just to have something to say. Today I had barely been paying attention, being hot and bored and worrying about my knees and the cramp beginning to snarl up in my calf.

"Gum..." I whispered, my voice ragged and dry.

"Is that all?" Obviously, he was missing those candles.

So okay, yes, I swiped the candles from the rectory. What kind of a Mass doesn't have candles? It would be sacrilege. So the way I figured it, God and I had an agreement. He understood. I had to have the matches too, though really I don't count that as stealing, since those are free for the taking in restaurants.

But as I knelt sweating in that confessional, I knew that I could never make Father Connell understand any of this. He was what my mother called a "cold fish," and you can't tell a cold fish anything.

I did get caught stealing for real once, when I was very young. My mother had taken me with her to the drugstore to buy aspirin or foot powder or maybe ear swabs. As I followed her down aisles full of cold remedies and shampoo, we passed a display of play money hanging in plastic bags between decks of Bicycle cards and a bin of rubber balls.

So much money. The want burned in me like a fever. I suppose you could call it greed, and it was all-consuming. As it happened, my slicker had a big hole in the pocket, so while my mother was busy deciding which peanut butter to buy, I slipped a pack of that beautiful cash into my pocket and worked it around to the back through the lining.

When we got home, my mother insisted on hanging my jacket up on the hook by the door. I believe I had already started crying by the time she'd pried it off me.

We marched right back to the store and the manager was called. He turned out to be a well-fed man, with a shiny scalp and a little mustache. She made me tell him that I swiped the money and that I was sorry and she made me hand it over.

He looked embarrassed, and I was terrified, and on the whole it was awful. It probably wouldn't have been so bad had he not known where we lived and who we were. What do you say to a dirt-poor kid stealing play money?

Father Connell seemed to be debating whether he could pry more information from me. Finally, he coughed a little and said, "Say twelve Hail Mary's and five Lohd's Prayers and stay out of trouble. Go in peace to love and suv the Lohd."

"Ma, isn't it true that God is everywhere?" I said, later that night.

"Mm-hmm." She was filing her nails at her usual perch in the little glass booth at the Catholic Indian Center entryway.

"And when you pray, you talk directly to God, isn't that right Ma?"

"Yes, yes, that's right," she said, distracted.

"Then why do I have to talk to Father Connell? I don't want to go to confession anymore. Can I just talk to God directly?"

She stopped filing and looked at me. She was so still I began to think she hadn't heard me. "I don't see why not," she said, finally.

Hey, Louise Begaye," I said.
"Hey, kid." She had been reading a paperback and she laid it–spread open, pages down–on the desk in the C.I.C.'s reception booth. People were milling in and out of the big hall under the flimsy garland and plastic evergreen branches, waiting for the Bingo games to begin. The regulars shuffled in, carrying ugly Troll dolls, rabbit's feet, or elephant figurines for luck. Somewhere, *Away in a Manger* tinkled over the din.

I stepped on the guest chair that was squeezed between the wall and the desk and I planted myself on the corner.

"How's the reception game treatin' ya?"

"You are the strangest kid I've ever met, you know that?" She finger-raked her hair back from her forehead. "Work's boring. Like always. That's why they call it work."

"Is that true? Work's always boring?"

"Yeah, kid. Always boring."

"Some people must like their work. Sonny and Cher? They like their work."

She snorted. "That ain't work. That's fantasy. I'd like it too if all I had to do was sing songs and tell jokes. That ain't reality."

"How about the nuns? Does that count? I mean, is that a job?"

"Naw, that's a calling. It's more than a job to them. They don't do it to make money, so I don't think you can say it's a job." She leaned closer. "Not that it matters, most of them are such sourpusses anyway."

"Yeah. Why do you suppose it has to be like that?" I said. "I mean, it's people that invented work, and yet it's people that hate working."

Louise Begaye's eyes were black, like strong coffee, and when she looked at me, I could see tiny pictures of myself in them.

"It doesn't matter. What matters is that when you get in the world, you're going to find out that there are those that get and those that give," she said. "You just make sure you end up on the right side of that equation."

I picked at a hangnail and she thumbed through her paperback. "Do you believe in aliens?" I asked.

"Huh?"

"Hey, it's the gambler!" I looked up and Karl was grinning through the glass. He was wearing his false teeth, so the hole in his mouth was paved over with a white partial.

"Karl!" I hopped off the desk and he stepped in the doorway to shake my hand very formally. "How's the Lexington? Anything new over there?" I said.

"There's a serious penny epidemic since you left, Debs. They're clogging up the toilets and piling up in the lobby cuz there's no one to clear them away. We can't find one of the guests and I'm afraid he's buried under all those pennies, a goner by now," he said, and he winked at Louise.

"No, sir," I said, and I gave him a wap on the back of his hand. He was looking at Louise.

"Oh. Karl, this is my friend, Louise Begaye. Louise, this is Karl."

He stepped in and touched her fingers briefly. "Nice to meet you," he said. Louise went back to her book.

"Well, I should get back to my mom. It was good to see you, Gambler. Bye, Louise." He said it in a little singsong and he wiggled his fingers at her.

Louise had the paperback open, but she watched him as he walked away and disappeared into the Bingo hall.

"You like Karl?" I said.

"Kid, I ain't made the best decisions in my life. I'm just now trying to scrape it together and keep it clean. The last thing I need is that kind of guy wading in and muddying up the waters." She took one more look at the door and then went back to her book.

Merry Christmas, Q.T."

"Merry Christmas, Ma." I was unwrapping the large box she had pulled from under the bed. "Oh Ma, it's beautiful!" I pulled the box top off to reveal a small guitar, blonde finish, black strap included. I couldn't help jumping around in my bare feet and pajamas. After seeing John Denver on the *Sonny and Cher* show, I had realized that it was my destiny and calling in life to play the guitar. Ma had said we couldn't afford it. Pretty sneaky, really.

"The sisters know a girl who can give you some lessons," she said. I had one arm around her and one around my brand new guitar.

"Aw Ma, thanks. All I got you was that stupid old rock." I had stayed after school to paint a sunset on a smooth, round rock I'd found. It was a little lopsided, but I thought the color turned out.

"Oh no, I love it. I'm going to keep it on my desk downstairs so I can see the sunset every day."

All week at school we had drawn pictures of Santa and reindeer and twinkling evergreen trees, and I had taken the liberty of pasting them all over our room. Ma had a little red poinsettia sitting in the middle of the table, and I thought it looked very festive. Somewhere along the line, she'd brought home an old radio and it was playing softly in the corner. There was a knock on the door.

"Merry Christmas, Mary." I stepped around Ma and opened the door wider. Sister Marie Therese was standing in the hallway with a big basket wrapped in cellophane. "And Merry Christmas to you, Deborah. This is from all of us. We hope you enjoy it," she said.

"Oh my goodness, thank you." The basket had a canned ham, lots of candy and fruit, a bag of nuts, and a doll with eyes that fluttered when you bounced her.

"It's our pleasure. We enjoyed the chocolates very much and we appreciate the work you do here. I realize that isn't an easy shift," she said. "Oh, also you have a phone call. It's your daughter, Isabelle."

Chapter 5

YEAH, BUT HOW WAS THE RECEPTION?

Ma! Ma! They're gone! You gotta do something! Somebody stole my marbles!" I rushed into the room and hurled myself onto the bed beside her. She was just settling in to sleep after her long night shift.

"What, why aren't you at school?"

"My marbles. Somebody took my marbles. My Pringles can in the secret safe. You know, my marbles! I had a whole can packed full. I kept them in that old fuse box in the hallway! AND NOW THEY'RE GONE!"

"Oh, that? I threw those away. You're too old to be playing marbles with the boys. Now get to school, you're going to be late." She shifted away from me on the groaning bed.

I sat in the lobby, eyes closed, feeling the smooth weight of glass in my hand, feeling them clack against each other. I opened my eyes and tears spilled onto my empty palm.

I found myself on the sidewalk out front. I turned the opposite direction from school and started walking. I walked all day, finally ending up on a curb behind a 7/11. My nose ran continuously in the cold and I was stuffed up from all the crying. Also, I had developed the hiccups.

My cousin's rooms had been stuffed with the newest, shiniest toys. Etch-a-Sketch, Easy Bake Oven, all that. Eventually, they all broke and they'd end up half buried in a garbage heap at the dump. They were just things. My cousins didn't love those toys. Not like this.

I had been building that collection for years. Knees in the dirt, one marble at a time. I had won them. I had EARNED them. My very blood colored the glass and it was my breath, trapped and frozen, in those tiny bubbles. Now my blood was cold, and I could hardly draw a single breath. How could I with all that was missing? Why would she do it? Why? She knew what that bunch of glass meant to me.

As I sat alone with my misery, a blue pickup truck pulled into the lot and slowed as it passed. I pretended to scrape something off the sole of my shoe.

It seemed to me that my mother had a lot in common with that ole rock I painted for her–just sitting in that little room downstairs, nothing more than a picture on the outside and solid stone on the inside–and I wondered if she would even bother to eat or breathe if she didn't have me to drag around with her every day.

My feet were stiff and cold as shadows turned icy black. A chill ran through me and I shuddered at the orange and purple in the sky. I stood up, wiped my nose, and headed for home.

The satchel sat on the bed, top open like a wide mouth, ingesting unsuspecting socks and trousers. Powder and lipstick perfumed the air.

"Q.T., did you give your teacher the note saying that you weren't going to be in school?" She was folding her hound's tooth skirt. An open tortoise shell case rested on the table. When I peered inside the box, her cologne tickled my nose and my round face stared from the neat mirror mounted on the lid. Inside were all sorts of fascinating gadgets and products. Tubes of foundation cream, bobby pins, lipsticks, and a tiny pearly-pink brush that clicked out like a ball point pen to apply color. There was face powder, sturdy razors that opened their shiny jaws when you twisted the handle, and of course, there was the prerequisite jar of Pond's cold cream.

"Uh-huh," I said. I was still stinging from the loss of my Pringles can marble collection, but I had secretly started to re-build my stash. At this time, I had exactly four marbles–none of them particularly special–in a gym sock stuffed way under the mattress.

I plopped down onto the scuffed kitchen chair at the kitchen table and pushed one of her black pumps around with my toe. She picked up the shoe and fed it to the satchel. My clothes had already been neatly folded in the bag.

"Where is Houston?" I asked, picking at the peeling chair.

"It's in Texas," she said.

I didn't know what Texas was, but I knew that I was getting on an airplane and that set off such a fluttering in my stomach. I also knew I was going to see my sister, Isabelle, again. Sister. It's a word so full of closeness and comfort, yet I couldn't seem to so much as focus a picture of her in my mind. I could see her pretty orange and blue cheerleading uniform, the thick rug of embroidery in the letter sewn on, and the shiny pins that punctured the sweater front. Her fluffy mum corsage, still full of its delicate scent–if slightly sad–the morning after the Homecoming dance. But I could not make my mind see her face or hear the timber of her voice. It had all been so very long ago.

I had a hard time getting to sleep that night. I lay in the dark, listening to my mother's breath come and go. She skipped her shift because we were leaving early in the morning. She had whispered to herself for a while, sometimes giggling and gesturing in the dark, but soon her breath came and went evenly.

I watched the lights from the passing cars chase striped shadows across the ceiling. Eventually, sleep pulled me down into blackness and I dreamed of walking the same familiar route to school, but the color was washed out and the sound echoed, as if in a cave.

A cardboard box lay in the road while the traffic hummed all around. As I got closer, I saw that the box was full of kittens–no more than a few weeks old. Some black, some gray or white, the soft, big eyed balls of fluff scampered playfully out of the box and into the street. I scrambled to collect them and get them back into the box as the sound of passing cars got louder and louder. I felt a whoosh of wind as a sedan streaked by. I reached for one of the kittens and something pulled at my shoulder.

"C'mon Q.T.," my mother said, nudging me awake. "It's time to get going."

It turns out airplanes smell a lot like buses. Old, stale cigarette smoke mingled with aftershave and perspiration. But that's about where the similarity ends. On an airplane, there are powdered ladies in uniforms to help you get to your seat, or bring you a blanket, or a small cushy pillow. They smile and move with silky efficiency, closing bins and wheeling carts around. You won't see any of that on a bus.

"You're going to have to fasten your seat belt, if you please." One of the uniformed ladies with the thick eyelashes and painted lips smiled sweetly at me. "And young lady, I have something for you." She gave me a lapel pin of little tin wings and a glass globe at the center, very shiny and official looking. I pinned it to my jacket.

"Here Ma, like this." I buckled her seat belt with a satisfying click and handed her the strap to pull tight. She had been jamming the tongue part into the back of the lap belt lock. She squeezed my hand and smiled nervously. Pretty soon, she was whispering to herself and out of the corner of my eye, I saw the woman seated next to her glance in our direction. I looked straight at her and she busied herself with a magazine.

I had a window seat and once we had left the ground, with a tremendous roar and me all pushed into the back cushion, I was able to look through the thick glass down onto the clouds below. Fantastic giant, puffy cotton for bouncing and tumbling, with no corners or hard surfaces on which to bonk your head.

Pretty soon, we were served sodas—absolutely free—and peanuts. It was all very exciting, and I found myself absentmindedly kicking the back of the seat in front of me. My scuffed shoe thumped against the pocket containing magazines and barf bags. The man in the seat in front of me was large and pink and had a tie that bit into his fleshy neck. "Would you mind not doing that?" he said, through gritted teeth as he craned around to get a look at me. Startled, I concentrated on my thumbnail. The seat groaned as he eased back into it.

I looked at all the magazines and counted all the chairs in the plane. I took inventory of everything in the pocket and put the tray table up and down. I was pretty tired of this ride by now. The man in front of me turned around and glared again. My foot had a mind of its own and it had resumed the thumping. I put my feet up and crossed my legs. He gave me one lingering, dirty look and faced forward again.

We got off the plane in Dallas to get on another plane that would take us to Houston. We headed through the airport and finally sat down in one of the rows of black vinyl chairs for the wait until our next flight. I went to the window and looked out at the men in coveralls and ear protectors slinging brightly colored luggage into the belly of an airplane.

As I looked up at the board behind the counter, I saw white plastic letters that read "Flight 1420 to Houston - On Time 9:15." I checked the big silver clock over the windows. 8:10.

The lights from a number of planes hovered and descended onto glittering runways. People drifted in and out of the area. Tired looking men in ties, women with babies. Some took seats and read. Some walked slowly up and down the corridor, looking pale and restless. Through it all, Ma sat in the same chair, staring, whispering.

A woman's voice crackled from the overhead speakers. "Attention ladies and gentlemen, at this time we would like to begin boarding flight 1420 to Houston Intercontinental Airport at Gate 2B."

I turned and looked back at my mother. She sat staring blankly, hands resting in her lap. I walked back over and stood in front of her. "Ma, I think they're calling our plane." I said. She looked right through me. "Ma. Ma!" She reached out and grabbed my arm, yanking me into the seat next to her.

"Sit down!" I sunk into the chair and blew on my stinging arm. The voice droned over the intercom twice more.

"Mom, that's our plane." I pleaded. She continued to work her lips, her brow furrowed in concentration, her eyes soft and unfocused.

"Ladies and gentlemen, this is the final boarding call for flight 1420 to Houston Intercontinental Airport at Gate 2B."

One by one, all the people disappeared through the door. Some wandered off to other gates until there was just the two of us. I watched the plane pull away and taxi into the darkness as I sat next to her. I pulled my knees up to my chest and hugged them tight, biting my lip so I wouldn't cry. Now what?

We spent the night in that very spot, the steel arms digging into my back and neck, causing me to wake throughout the night, knotted and cramped. The terminal was too cold and everything swam and burned red when I closed my eyes against the bright lights. I woke once and watched a janitor buff the floors until my head wobbled on my shoulders and fell back onto the chair.

When the scenery behind the big windows reappeared, soft and blue, I sat up and stretched. My mother's lipstick had faded and there were dark circles under her eyes.

"Mom, are you okay?" I touched her hand.

"We better find your sister," she said. "Are you hungry?" I wondered if she realized what had happened, if she felt as if she'd been tricked in some way, distracted and preoccupied by mischievous spirits playing a petty joke on her. I looked for signs of anger or frustration, but she just sighed way deep in her chest and rubbed her tired eyes.

A coffee shop opened its steel mesh curtains and we had a seat. I ate a donut and a banana with my orange juice. Ma had coffee and some kind of Danish sweet thing.

"Paging Mrs. Mary McCarroll, white courtesy telephone. Mary McCarroll, white courtesy telephone, please." She'd heard it. It registered in her eyes, sharp and clear.

"You wait here Q.T., I'll be right back." She disappeared down the corridor. I had finished everything in front of me and snuck a few tastes of her coffee by the time she got back.

"Let's go, we have to go." She gathered up the trash on the table and dumped it into the garbage can on the way out, pulling me behind her.

We lined up behind a man smelling of cigarette smoke who was holding a brown briefcase and wearing matching brown shoes. The woman at the door smiled as she tore the sheet from our tickets.

Once we were in the air, Mom drifted off to sleep in her seat. I studied her as she dozed, head to the side, mouth slightly open. I reached out and ran my fingers lightly over her brow. Her skin was smooth and cool to the touch. I hardly ever saw her sleep. I was usually dead to the world by the time she got to bed, and she was always awake by the time I opened my eyes. There was a time when I wondered if she ever slept at all. Looking at her, she reminded me of the wide, still desert, so empty and quiet and heavy, with the feeling that so much more was happening just out of sight.

Isabelle was waiting as we streamed out of the jet way doors with the other anxious passengers. She smiled and threw her arms around my mother. There was a lot of fuss made and a lot of oohing and ahhing. My sister fairly shimmered with relief.

When I saw her, I couldn't believe that I had forgotten so much of her, her smile and her wink and her lilting voice. My mind could see her clearly now as she had been, practicing elaborate cheers or sitting quietly in her bedroom in our little house across from the school. I was happy, and a little sleepy, sitting in the back seat of her car as it threaded through the city.

"What happened to you, Mother? I thought I'd lost you," Isabelle said, from the front.

"Oh, I got confused. There was so much activity, so many people. I don't know how anyone can ever keep any of it straight."

I looked out the window. Houston was lush and green, even though the last of winter still hung on the calendar. It was so completely different from the dry hills of Gallup. I was astonished at the long grass growing right on the side of the freeway, with no care or hosing down from anyone. There were palm trees everywhere and everything was huge, billboards towering high in the air and buildings, seemingly no top to them, sparkling in the sun. Flying down that highway was like suddenly waking up in the future. All that was missing were the hover cars zipping overhead. I did a double take out the back window just to be sure I hadn't missed them.

Isabelle lived in a white brick apartment complex wrapped around a swimming pool in the shape of three circles joined together end-to-end. There were two levels to the building and iron hand rails alongside pebbled concrete stairs. I wondered what it was like to live like you were on vacation all the time, everything bright and big and new.

Her apartment was on the second floor. It was cool and quiet, with chocolate brown carpet and white stuccoed walls. A large television sat in the corner on a pedestal. A balcony overlooked the crystal blue pool.

Other people's houses were usually stuffed with knick-knacks and photos, mismatched furniture, and religious pictures. Isabelle's was not at all like that. It was sleek and sparse, with splashes of color and everything matching. Here were rooms dressed up with thought and care, and it made me feel good to just stand and smell the brand newness of it all.

I awoke not knowing where I was. I sat up in a room with fresh walls and lacy curtains. A patchwork quilt was draped over the bed, and the biggest Raggedy Anne doll I had ever seen stared at me with shiny, black button eyes. I climbed down from the bed and tiptoed out into the living room. My mother was sitting on the sofa, a coffee mug hovering on the chrome and glass table in front of her.

"Well, good morning sleepy head." Isabelle emerged from the hall, tightening the clasp on her watch. "We better get going. We have a full day ahead of us," she said, brightly. "There's toast and juice on the bar. Have some breakfast and then go get dressed. We have some shopping to do."

H oney, this is my little sister, Debbie." Isabelle smiled at a quiet man with dark, wavy hair and a lazy eye. "This is my fiancé, Mark. This is his family's shoe store," she said, slipping a hand under his elbow. Mark Cooper had hair below his ears and sideburns that trailed down his cheeks. Add a green knit cap, and he was the spitting image of Mike Nesmith from the Monkees.

"Nice to meet you," he muttered. I met his father and his brother, who was fetching a pair of brown buckled heels for a woman in a loud print dress. Boxes and boxes of shoes were stacked in ragged piles on the floor around me while my foot was measured with a metal plate.

There were sandals and sneakers, dress shoes, and something called deck shoes, with leather laces, that smelled like the inside of a new car. The top was flipped off a box and a pair of blue suede boots, with shiny black rivets, was slipped onto my feet. It was like Christmas and my birthday all rolled into one. I looked across the store and Ma was slipping one foot into a white sandal. She stood and took a tentative step, looking a little sheepish about the whole thing.

I thanked the Coopers and climbed into Isabelle's back seat between a fortress of shoe boxes. As we slid down the highway, I couldn't help peeking under the lids to run a finger along the stitched leather.

We ended up at a giant mall with an ice rink at its center. For hours, we crawled in and out of brightly lit stores with piped-in music as throngs of people chatted and drifted along like leaves in a lazy stream. Isabelle bought Mom skirts and slacks and a sweater that was soft as a kitten to the touch. I got blue jeans, t-shirts, turtlenecks, and some cotton underwear with the days of the week stitched in pale colors. As we circled huge racks of items, Isabelle would say, "See something you can't live without?" I would shrug as she'd pull a hanger from the tangle and hold it up against my shoulders. I was grateful for it all, but something in my stomach tugged and burned, making whole a reflection of myself, greedy and begging.

I had to try on about a million dresses for the wedding before Isabelle was happy with a long, flowered flimsy thing in light purple and white. Trying on clothes is just plain boring, and I don't care for dresses as a rule. It's hard to run in them, and they make it tough to play anything that's any good. You can't climb trees or sit on the ground. You just have to sort of look good in your dress. I did used to have this one red and black-checkered skirt that I just loved, though. I'd wear it with everything, even over my jeans. Looking back, I must have looked completely nuts.

It was a huge brick house set back behind a sprawling lawn. The sidewalk, which was puddled with morning rain, reflected a gray sky. I saw my aunt Charlene's face ripple through the leaded glass windows before the door swung open. She was wearing heavy false lashes under peacock green eye shadow. Her blonde hair sat high on her head like a toasted pan of Jiffy Pop popcorn. She wrapped her arms around my mother and smashed her face into Ma's cheek for just an instant, and then she ushered us all into an open air entryway and down to the sunken living room.

"My god Mary, you look like a million bucks. I'm not kidding. My god, how long has it been? Unbelievable." My aunt Charlene took a drag off an impossibly long cigarette and eased into a gold velveteen chair, gesturing at an equally splendid sofa buried under pillows. I waded through deep, orange carpet and took a seat. "Debbie, I swear you've grown a good two feet since I last saw you. Paul! Where the hell is that boy? Paul!"

"What!" Paul appeared on the stairs. His blonde hair was shaggy and his bangs fell over his eyes, causing him to rake his fingers through them after every few steps.

"Get down here and say hello." She raised an eyebrow at him and cocked her head in our direction. He dug his hands in his pockets and skipped down the stairs.

"Hi, Auntie Mary. How's it going, Lil Debbie?" He grinned at me, mussing my hair. His dimples creased his face high on his cheeks.

"Show her your room. God, where did you get your manners?" My aunt Charlene lit another Salem 100 and blew a stream of smoke at the match flame.

"Well, I got my manners from you of course, Mommy." He smiled at her sweetly. She narrowed her green eyes.

"Don't. Be. Smart." His smirk evaporated and he pretended to stretch.

"C'mon, Lil Deb."

His room was immaculate, decorated in dark greens and blues. His shelves were lined with spotless toys, some still in boxes.

"Wow, don't you ever play with any of this stuff?" I picked up the Rock'em Sock'em Robots.

"I guess so. Some of it." He dropped down on the bed. I put the toy back on the shelf. A skateboard of clear red plastic was propped up in the corner. It looked like a long, flat plank of red hot hard candy, flawless and sporting transparent rubber wheels the color of corn syrup.

"Whooooo," I said, as I ran my fingers over the smooth surface. "Can I pick it up?"

"Sure. Knock yourself out." I held the board and gave one of the wheels a spin. It made a smooth ticking sound as it whirred, silky and musical.

"Holy cow, haven't you ever ridden on it?"

"I took it out when I first got it. I like my bike better," he said. I couldn't take my eyes off of it.

"C'mon, this is boring. Let's go for a walk. I'll show you the neighborhood." I used the tail of my t-shirt to rub away any fingerprint smudges and put the skateboard down, wanting with all my heart to stuff it under my jacket and make a run for it.

As we skipped down the stairs, we heard shrieks of laughter from what I took to be the kitchen. The rain had stopped, though the clouds overhead were still thick.

"So Lil Debbie, haven't seen you in awhile. Where do you live now?" He had picked up a stick and he was dragging it in the street as he walked with one foot on the curb and one in the gutter.

"We live in Gallup. Across from the train yard," I said. He nodded.

"Uh-huh. You ever see Gramma or any of them anymore?"

"No, not for a long while. You?"

"Naw."

We ended up at a construction site. There were several houses that looked just like Paul's, all in various stages of undress. Some were no more than a foundation slab with pipes jutting up from glassy puddles of water. Others were nearly complete, stickers still on the new windows. Paul left the sidewalk and tramped through the fresh mud past stacks of lumber and brick.

"I don't think we're supposed to be here. We're gonna get in trouble," I called after him.

"Don't worry about it. I come here all the time. It's Sunday, nobody's around."

I trotted after him, trying to find patches where the mud had been packed down. I followed through a door frame and into a structure of skeletal two-by-fours and drywall. Something dripped in the quiet and the room smelled of wet sawdust. He picked up a board and swung it against a post. The sound shattered the quiet.

"Paul! Somebody's gonna hear you."

"So? Let 'em," he said. He looked around and leaned on the plank in his hand. "Let's build something."

I took in the piles of boards and pipe. "Like what?"

"There's plenty here. Let's build a fort." He dragged a saw-horse, scraping it across the new concrete. "We can set these up for the walls. Go grab that one."

We worked through the afternoon and eventually, there was a precarious structure of lumber and plywood. We sat together in the heavy smell of pine. He pulled a tin box from his pocket and produced a half smoked Salem 100. He struck a match and tendrils of smoke curled lazily through the murk. It smelled like someone was burning a peppermint candy.

"Here, try it," he said, handing it to me. I expected it to taste sweet, but it didn't. It was sharp and when I sucked in my breath, my mouth felt cold.

"Hey, you remember that time we made those mud pies in the back at Gramma's?" he said, as he took the cigarette.

"Yeah, that was fun."

"Everybody got all mad because we opened the new feed sacks and used the grain on the top of the pies. I thought my mom was gonna kill me," he said, puffing.

"Really? I don't remember that."

He scoffed. "Sure you don't, because you never got in trouble. Auntie Mary never said a word to you. Do you ever get punished for anything?"

I thought about this. "Not really. I help her and she helps me. We stick together."

He stared at me until I started to fidget. He passed the butt back to me. "Yeah, you get punished in other ways, though."

The wedding rehearsal was long and dull. A lot of talking, standing, kneeling, and sitting. Why anyone would want to get married is beyond me. It's so much work.

My brother took a leave from the Marines to be in the wedding. His hair was cropped to bristles and he was wearing the most beautiful suit in shimmering olive green. The fabric whispered when he pulled me up into the crook of his arm. His shirt was ruffled gold, pinned with jeweled cufflinks, and I couldn't help touching them when he wasn't looking. Judith stood off to one side, rubbing her hands together nervously and looking like she was about to say something, but she never did. Her hair was lighter in color, with a single blonde streak framing her face. Very mod, as Ma would say. She had recently moved to Houston, leaving the dirt roads and Bob and his Green Machine far behind her.

That evening, we gathered for dinner at a fancy restaurant around a long table covered in white linen. There were stories about the happy couple and loud laughter until the wee hours. Chairs were cleared and couples got up to dance. My brother plucked me from my chair and I stood on his feet as he whirled me around the room.

I awoke early the next morning and tiptoed out to watch cartoons with the sound turned down low. My new pajamas itched and chafed around the knees. I missed the big, soft t-shirt I usually wore. Ma's always trying to get me to wear a nightgown, but they get twisted up and wrestle with you in the night. Just between you and me, pajamas aren't much better.

Isabelle slipped in and sat on the floor next to me in a white silk robe, her hair a messy pile on top of her head. From behind her back, she produced a pickle jar that was crammed to the top with coins.

"I've been saving this for you," she said. "Every time I have spare change, I put it in the jar and think of you."

"Thank you," I breathed, feeling like my eyes were going to fall from their sockets. I'd never seen so much money. I screwed off the lid and pulled a fistful of treasure from the opening. She smiled and hugged me sideways, kissing me on the top of my head.

"I've missed you, Debbie. You've gotten so big since I last saw you." Everyone was very concerned about how big I'd gotten, but I didn't feel any bigger, and I was still the shortest in my class.

"How do you like living in Gallup?" she asked.

"I like it okay. Sister Marie Therese is teaching me to play tennis."

"Really? There's a court just down the street. Maybe we can play while you're here. Is that what you want to be when you grow up, a tennis player?"

I was dropping streams of coins into the open mouth of the jar, enjoying the musical sound they made. "Naw, I'm not very good."

"Well, you can be anything you want if you put your mind to it and work hard, you know. What would you like to be?"

I shrugged. "I like to draw, I guess."

"Ah-ha, an artist. I used to draw when I was in school. You remember?"

"Yes, daisies," I said.

She laughed. "Oh yeah, the orange daisies on the wall. Not my best work." She gave me a final squeeze and got to her feet. I poured a river of silver and copper onto the carpet and held a mound of it in my two hands. Dimes and pennies spilled through my fingers. I felt lightheaded.

"Would you like to go swimming today?" she asked, busying herself with the scooping and pouring and all the other rituals of coffee. I didn't know how to swim, but I said that I would like to go.

The water was cold at first, especially around my belly, but after moving around, I forgot my stiffness and chicken skin. So much cool, silky water. It pulled me, like gloved hands holding me everywhere, making it hard to walk or run, and yet I could bounce with no weight to me at all. I was on the moon's surface, searching for good rocks and golf balls and flags left by men in bulky white suits.

Mom sat at a table under a big umbrella at the far end of the pool. Isabelle came down from the apartment carrying a couple of splashy beach balls with loud flower patterns. She threw them into the pool, laughing when the slap on the water sprayed my face, which made me sputter. I hoisted myself up on one of those balls and floated around for a long while. Isabelle sat with Ma. They talked in low tones and Isabelle put one hand over Ma's, and then she got up and went back upstairs.

The wedding was even longer than the rehearsal had been. It was a very serious affair, without the jokes and light mood of the rehearsal, and people were crying all over the place. Judith was a bridesmaid, dressed in a sunny yellow dress and matching floppy hat, and she bawled her head off, her nose drippy and her breath coming in sputtering hiccups. She would smile at me while tears poured down her face. The Marine dress uniform my brother wore was a borrowed one from a buddy. Ben is tall and lean, but his friend was thick in the chest, so Isabelle, all white and fluffy with pins in her mouth, fussed at his sides until the coat fit. He looked handsome and very brave walking her down the aisle.

Water leaked from my mother's eyes, and she dabbed at the tears with limp tissues. I hadn't ever seen her cry before, and I kept stealing glances, hoping she wouldn't catch my eye.

I suffered through the dress and the silly banana curls inflicted upon my poor head. The new shoes were slick and stiff and too tight, and I think I fidgeted too much, but no one said anything about it. Then the couple kissed and the music started and everyone stood and clapped. As she was whisked down the aisle, Isabelle smiled and winked at me as she passed.

Before stepping into a gleaming car, cans knotted to the bumper, Isabelle muttered to Ben and handed him a set of keys. There was a commotion as people happily threw rice and snapped pictures. My brother gathered up my mother and me, folding us into Isabelle's cramped Mustang, and we followed the wide back end, "Just Married" written in lipstick in the rear window.

We trailed that long car, through the warm Houston evening, over countless unfamiliar streets. We pulled up to a stoplight that turned from yellow to red. It was then that Isabelle and her new happy husband and the car with the "Just Married" in the window and the bouncing cans dragging along glided right through, leaving us behind.

My brother said Isabelle's car needed a clutch. Actually, he gritted his teeth and pounded his fist and shouted, "This damn clutch!" The poor machine would grind and grind like the whole center of it would drop to the pavement at any moment. After a while, we were good and lost and I thought my brother was going to have a stroke and bleed from the ears. We rode around for hours. My legs were tired of their crimp and angle and my head had begun to loll on my shoulders. We stopped at a gas station and I pried myself from the back seat.

"Get back in the car!" he growled, as he circled the gas pump.

I bumped my head and cowered in the back, choosing pins and needles over murder. Mother sat calmly in the passenger seat, her hands resting in the lap of her long, blue dress. She had a big white flower pinned to her chest and it was listing unhealthily to one side.

Ben got back in the car and ripped off his white gloves, the fingers smeared with red lipstick. He crammed the stick shift into first. The engine whined and gears slipped, chewing metal on metal. There was language from the driver's seat that I knew I was never to repeat. Through it all, Mom stared quietly through the windshield.

We drove until the small hours, finally finding ourselves back home. Everyone said it was a lovely reception. The cake was beautiful, the photos looked great, and I finally got to kick off those pinching, white patent leather shoes and crawl into bed.

The trip back to Gallup and the C.I.C. took an eternity. Isabelle put us on a bus before heading off to Mexico for her honeymoon. "You take care of her for me," she'd said, as I'd stepped up onto the bus. I suspect she was afraid to put Ma and I back on an airplane, so she'd traded in the plane tickets for Greyhound, which I thought was a pretty good idea, even though buses make me queasy.

We stopped a lot along the way at diners and rest stops. People climbed on and climbed off throughout. I watched the world go by, coloring in books and reading and imagining I was an explorer on the dry Martian landscape out the window. I slept in the big high-backed chairs and had snacks of chips and Cracker Jack.

"Hey Ma, how come you're not still married?" I was flipping through an old Life magazine, not really paying any attention to the pages.

"Oh, that's ancient history," she said.

"What's "ancient history" mean?"

"It means it isn't worth talking about."

"How come?" I closed the magazine and folded it between my leg and the arm of the seat.

"Because all that matters is that you and I are together, that's why. When you're sitting right here next to me, with those gorgeous brown eyes and that sweet freckled face, what else on Earth could possibly matter?"

I was very happy to be back in our little room with the shabby furniture and the dingy hot plate. That evening, Ma and I laid around and listened to the trains roll on by. She read the funny papers to me and we laughed at Prince Valiant's haircut. We compared our hands, lying on our backs and reaching for the ceiling. She sang a song about it. She makes up songs and sings them to me. Mostly she just says the same words over and over to the same notes, but they're funny little songs and I love them. I think she was happy to be back too. I told Sister Marie Therese all about the big freeways and the skyscrapers. Sister Daniel Ignatius nodded at me and actually crooked a smile on her way down the stairs.

That night, I laid under the covers and watched those striped shadows run across my familiar ceiling, drifting off to sleep in a creaky bed to the music of the creaky box cars, just happy to be me and happy to be home.

Chapter 6

AND I'LL ALWAYS HAVE THAT

I was sitting on the front stoop, a notebook on my lap. I was working on a picture of a horse, but I'd misjudged the bigness of the horse and the smallness of the page. Now there was no room for his head. I was thinking I'd maybe keep going onto the back when Ma swung open the big front door and peeked around at me.

"I have a surprise for you, Q.T." Most of her disappeared while she propped the door open with one foot. The foot jiggled a bit and a bicycle rolled out. It was sparkly red, dripping with chrome, and finished with a tufted-black banana saddle.

She lifted the bike and bumped it down the stairs until it came to rest in front of me. It was gleaming fire in the morning sun. There were still little spurs in the tires where the fresh rubber had pressed out of the mold.

I stared at it and looked up into my mother's face. She was smiling, one hand on a handle bar grip. She leaned the bike my way. "Well, try it out!"

I took hold of the bike and swung my leg over. I eased up onto the seat and rolled the bike back and forth, turning the front tire side to side. "It's so beautiful, Ma. I love it!"

Her shoulders loosened and she smiled wider. "I knew you would." She laughed and leaned a hand on her hip. "Every kid should have a bike, you know." Her eyes got soft and she turned, as if she was listening to something. "You have fun, Q.T." She started back up the stairs. "Stay out of the street." She gave me a wink and the door closed behind her.

I sat there, straddling the bike, alone on the walk. The thing was, I didn't know how to ride a bike. Oh sure, I'd been on the back of one plenty of times, even taking a bruising ride on my cousin's handlebars, but I'd never been on the business end of one before.

I hopped off and set the kickstand. I grabbed my notebook from the stoop and jammed it into the waistband of my jeans. I walked the bike around the building to the side parking lot. It made a soft clicking as it rolled along. As soon as the gate was shut behind me, I scanned the lot for any movement and climbed on the bike. I put one foot on the pedal and stepped down hard. The bike lurched forward and my other foot turned to lead, dragging on the pavement. The front wheel spun around and I was on the ground, the bike a heavy tangle on top of me. I sputtered, pulling free from where it lay, twisted and glinting.

I squatted against the wall and looked down at my horse drawing. Poor old headless horse. My elbow hurt where I'd hit the blacktop. I craned my neck over the arm. No blood. Things were looking up.

I righted the bike and slid onto the sun scorched black seat. I leaned over the handlebars and rolled forward, kicking rocks with my baby steps. The bike would pick up a little speed and I'd get one foot on a pedal before feeling the tip, tip, tipping and I'd have to touch a toe back to solid ground.

It went like that the rest of the afternoon. I was breathing heavy and my shirt was damp at the back of my neck by the time I threw the bike down and gave it a good kick. Stupid bike. It was impossible. How could it ever work? That skinny frame, on those skinny tires, with skinny me on top, all up-right, all moving in the same direction? Impossible.

What was Ma thinking, buying this thing? I sat with my knees up, head on my folded arms. "Every kid should have a bike." That's what she'd said.

I knew it would never have occurred to her to wonder if I could ride the thing. Ma just didn't think like that. To her, things just were. They just happened. She didn't question and she just kept going. She always kept going.

I picked up the bike and got on. It was like dancing. Pedal, step. Pedal, step. And then, all at once, I was doing it. It was wobbly and I wasn't going to win any prizes, but I was riding a bike. I braked, nearly falling, and a feeling washed over me like I'd never felt before. At that moment, I could have lifted off and soared over the Catholic Indian Center. I could have lifted that bike over my head and spun it like a pinwheel. I could have done anything. But what I chose to do was ride my bike.

I whooped and laughed, riding in circles and racing a straight away, feeling the happiness of smooth gears and tires on pavement until the sun was all gone and the moon climbed over the blue night.

Ma was at the desk when I wrestled the bike in through the door. She beamed at me. "Did you have fun?"

I rolled over and expertly set the kickstand. "Lady, I sure did." She started to say something, but I threw my arms around her and hugged her tight, burying my face into her perfumed neck. "I love you so much, Ma."

She squeezed my waist and rubbed my arm. "I love you too, kid."

I looked her in the face, smiling. She touched my hair. "Time to cut those bangs again, I think. Now, go on upstairs and get cleaned up. You look like an orphan."

"What about my bike?" My bike. My face was starting to hurt from smiling.

"We'll keep it in the office for now. Nobody will mind." She stowed the bike and I took the stairs, two at a time.

The next week, I left the bike at the front curb while I went in for a drink, and when I came out, it was gone. At first, I'd run up and down the block, panting, my heart in my throat. Then I'd sat and cried my guts out for what seemed like days.

Ma never did ask about the bike again. It was like she'd forgotten she'd ever bought it. Like the whole thing never happened. Except now I know how to ride a bike. And I'll always have that.

I was deep asleep, but I could feel it. Slowly, very slowly, I realized the bed was shaking. The room was completely dark but for the light from the street lamps outside, and it was quiet, with very little sound from the street, so I knew it was late. The bedsprings shrieked and the mattress bounced again. Mother had climbed up on the bed and she was standing unsteadily over me, holding a belt.

"Leave her alone!" She screamed at the wall and swung the belt, hitting the plaster above me with a loud snap. "You get away from her, you son of a bitch!" She braced herself and swung again. I was frozen under the blankets, every muscle tense, cringing at each blow.

"No, you will not. You can go straight to hell. No. No, you won't." She stepped off of the bed and dropped the belt. The lights blazed on and she rummaged around, muttering to herself.

"C'mon, Q.T., turn over." She pulled the covers back and lifted my shirt. She had a jar of Vicks Vapor Rub open and she spread a sticky glob across my chest. "This will protect you. They can't hurt you now." She smoothed my shirt back down and it stuck to my chest. She got heavily to her feet and snapped off the light, plunging us both into blackness. The Vicks was so strong that I was sure I could see clouds of it, hovering hot and white, in the darkness before me. Oh, how I hate Vicks Vapor Rub.

She climbed back into bed and pulled me close. "We're going to be all right now, Q.T. Everything is going to be all right."

Keep your arm up. That's it. Nice one!" The tennis ball echoed off of the white cement wall in the deserted bingo hall. Sister Marie Terese wound up and hit a smooth backhand, sending the yellow ball hurtling back. It hit the surface again and took a bounce. I stepped in to meet it but flubbed the stroke, catching it on the racquet frame. It made a lazy arc and hopped crazily under one of the pallets of stacked folding chairs.

"Aw, man!" I swung the racquet and let the momentum spin me around.

"That's okay. Good job. Your serve has really improved." The Sister was pale and thin as a bird in her dark blue skirt and short habit. She pulled a tissue from her pocket and removed her glasses to polish a lens. Every Sunday afternoon, after my church clothes had been put away and Ma and I had had our lunch, Sister Marie Terese would show up at our door with two tennis racquets and a can of balls. Occasionally we'd catch a match on TV, and slowly I'd figured out the scoring and the rules, even getting to where I had my favorite players to root for.

I got down on my knees and pulled the stray ball from under the chairs. I handed it to her and she dropped the ball into a canister, snapping the plastic cap shut. She gathered the racquets and we walked back to the entryway.

"You're doing really well. I think you're going to make a fine tennis player. We should get out on a real court pretty soon here," she said, leading the way to the door.

"You think so? Sometimes I feel like I've got the hang of it, and then something goes all kerflooey."

"It just takes practice." She playfully hip checked me on the way out. As we started for the stairs, Louise Begaye appeared on the landing. Her hair was pulled back and she had purple eye shadow on.

"Woo-hoo," I said.

"Hello, Louise. You certainly look nice this afternoon." The Sister smiled at her.

"Thank you, Sister." Louise hugged herself and looked nervous. "Uh, well I was just heading out, so..."

She had reached the first floor when the front door opened and Karl walked in. Sister Marie Therese and I both looked at him and then turned around to look at Louise.

"Hi, Karl," I said finally. I glanced back at Louise, and she eyed me and shook her head the tiniest bit. "You here for the charm your mom left at bingo, Karl?" I asked. The Sister was watching him with interest. She walked over and put out her hand.

"I don't believe we've met. I'm Sister Marie Therese."
She wedged the can of tennis balls under her arm. He looked
down at her hand and wiped his palm on his pants before
gingerly taking her fingers.

"Karl Zhonnie," he said. Louise walked past him and out
the door. He watched the door close behind her.

"What is your business here?" the Sister asked.

"My mom comes here for bingo. She...she forgot something. Forgot something here." He wiped his hands on his
pants again.

"Here, Karl. It's in here," I said. My mother was sitting at
her usual post behind the steel desk. "Hiya, Ma."

"Hello, Q.T. Did you have a good lesson?"

I opened the side drawer and removed a ceramic horse
wearing a straw hat. "Pretty good. Sister Marie Terese says my
serve is getting better. I like your nail polish. I like that better
than the red, I think."

"Really? You think? I don't know..." she trailed off, examining the pink polish.

I closed the drawer and walked back to Karl. I placed the
figurine in his hand. He looked at it for a second and then
slipped it into his pocket.

"Well...thanks," he said, and he turned to leave.

"Say hello to your mother," Sister Marie Therese called,
shifting the racquets to her other hand. We turned and started
up the stairs. "Do you know that man well?"

"Karl? Oh sure, he works at the Lexington. He's all right."

I was slouched on the lobby sofa, watching *Kojak,* when Louise Begaye plopped down opposite me. "So, how's Karl?" I
asked, smiling.

"Oh, so you think you're pretty smart, huh?" I shrugged.
"He was supposed to wait outside. I told him to wait outside.
The nuns would skin me if they knew he was coming around
here. Male visitors are strictly forbidden," she said, in a high,
nasal voice that was a dead ringer for Sister Daniel Ignatius.

"I knew you liked him."

She gave me a look. "I don't like him. I think he's...interesting. Funny. Crazy." She shook her head. "Anyway, thanks for covering like that. Where'd you get that horse? Karl played with that thing the rest of the night. He thinks it's his good luck charm now."

"Oh yeah? I hope so. Hope it's better luck for him than it was for the last guy who had it. People leave all kinds of junk after bingo. Once, I found a gold tooth on the floor. I think it's still in the drawer downstairs. I thought the last thing you needed was a guy like Karl."

She sighed. "You know, one minute I think I got it all figured out, straight and narrow. I know just what to do. And then this guy smiles at me and he says all the right things and everything turns upside down again." She rubbed her eyes and let her fingers rest on her temples.

"It's because he likes that beer, huh?" I said. "You don't want him?"

She looked at me. "How do you know he likes beer?"

"He told me." I hitched myself up to better see her. "Maybe he'll like you more than that beer."

"Yeah and maybe the sky will open up and money will rain down from heaven. Solve all our problems."

"You know, Karl, he probably doesn't know what to do either. Could be he gets kind of mad about it and then he goes and drinks beer and fights. It's a man thing, he says. Maybe you two guys can decide what to do together." Louise looked back at the TV.

"Maybe, kid. It don't usually go like that for me, though."

I pulled a faded pink towel from the pile waiting to be folded. One corner was fraying, and a single long thread had wound itself through the laundry. I untangled the string and bit off the length with my teeth. The overhead lights flickered in the sparse Cleen-n-Cleer Laundromat. I don't care for those places, having spent a very uncomfortable night in one. It's that particular smell of detergent and hot clothes. I do like socks right out of the dryer though, and I slipped a toasty pair onto my hands and held them to my cheeks.

Three dryers down, a woman was loading wet sheets into a machine while two grinning kids giggled and hung onto the basket as it rolled crazily along. She looked to be about my sister's age, with dark hair and blue jeans. I made my eyes go all soft and pretended it was future Louise Begaye, married to Karl and toting a couple of dopey kids.

Ma bundled up the last pair of socks and closed the drawstring on the laundry bag. "Grab the soap, Q.T.," she said, and I hefted the box of Tide for the walk home.

Back in our room, she distributed the clean laundry into piles in the closet, gathering clean undies and wrestling some items onto hangers. I was opening and closing the eyes on the doll I had gotten for Christmas. I had named her Sweetie Pie.

"Hey Ma, is laundry soap made up of the same stuff as bar soap?" She closed the closet door and chuckled to herself. "Ma?" She went to the shelf and started to open a can of tuna. "Ma!"

"What?" She slammed the can down and faced me.

"Nothing," I said.

She continued to work the opener and she dumped the tuna into a bowl with some mayo. I took a seat across from her. She reached for the bread.

"Can you chop up the tuna a little more? I don't like it so chunky. It tastes fishy," I said. She put the spoon down.

"You've always liked it chunky before," she said.

"Nah-ah. It's fishy," I replied.

"They're telling you to say that. Don't do what they say."

"Ma...Ma, how come you have to be this way? How come you have to talk like this?"

"What do you care what I'm like or how I talk? What business is it of yours?"

"Ma, I gotta live here too. I'm right here. All the time. And you know, I'm not doing what anybody says." I could hear my own voice gaining strength and fury, like a gathering storm.

"There's nobody telling me anything and there's no such thing as "they!""

She slapped me hard across my face. I blinked, feeling my cheek heat up. She took two slices of bread out of the bag and started piling on the tuna.

I ran out of the room and ended up at the train yard. I sat on the switching station curb, rubbing my raw cheek. She'd be sorry, boy. I could just get on one of these trains and beat it out of here. I could just keep going. Then she'd be sorry.

She had only ever hit me once before. A lady selling something in a suitcase had come to the door while Ma was reading to me. I had pulled and fussed while she was talking. When the sales lady went away, I got a spanking. That was the only other time she had ever raised a hand to me. This was different, of course. This was no spanking. She'd slapped me. And it felt like she didn't like me. It felt like she wished I weren't around, and I had never felt that from her before. We were a team, The Deb and Ma Show. I didn't know if it was because I had sassed or because of what I had said, but I knew one thing. I was never gonna argue about tuna fish with her again.

You can't do that," Paula warned. "That's the road, it's not the moat. You're putting a bridge over a road."

"You never heard of an overpass?" I said defiantly.

She crossed her arms. "An overpass is one road crossing over another road. You don't have a road, just a bridge." We had built an extensive city in the front yard of the Abbot house. Tonka Toys, Lego pieces, and various other scraps, including buttons, bottle caps, and toothpicks littered the yard.

It had been a hot day for early spring and the sun was beginning to sink, turning the light to gold.

I relented, finally removing the cardboard bridge, and Paula went back to working on a wall she was constructing by mashing damp mud between the meaty parts of her palms.

"Do you believe in extraterrestrials?" I asked.

"What's that?"

"You know, aliens, like from another planet."

She shrugged. "I don't know, I guess. Why?"

"Sometimes I think I'm an extraterrestrial."

"No kidding. How come?"

I picked at the dirt under my fingernails. "Just seems to be the way it is."

She sat back and clapped mud from her hands. "You seem just like anybody else to me."

Chris craned her head out from behind the front door. "Paula, Mom says dinner in a half an hour, so come wash up." She disappeared back inside.

Paula sat back on her heels and looked at me through her Hershey brown eyes. "You wanna stay for dinner? I'll go ask."

"Naw, I oughta go. My mom will wonder where I am." I doubted Ma had even noticed I was gone, she was so distracted lately, but I didn't feel up to sitting around the dinner table with the Abbot clan. I stood up and knocked the caked dirt from the seat of my pants and examined my grimy hands. I did my best to wipe them clean on the front of my shorts.

"See ya later," I called, heading for the sidewalk.

"Okay, come back tomorrow and we'll finish." Paula was engrossed in scraping junk from under her fingernails as she slowly turned to go inside.

I walked home, soaking up the evening sounds and smells. I passed the stone wall and stooped to examine the smooth rock, as I'd done a hundred times before. It made me feel safe, somehow, to look at that rock. At least something was always the same. Solid. I gave the surface a rub with a grubby finger and then continued on my way.

By the time I got home, the sun had sunk behind the puffing trains and it was nearly dark. I stomped my feet on the mat outside the C.I.C. and pushed through the front door. I could hear the TV on upstairs. Mom was already at the desk behind the glass window in the reception box.

When she'd hit me–after what I've come to think of as "The Tuna Incident," I'd felt very sorry for myself and considered actually jumping on that boxcar. But I couldn't think where I'd go, and life without Ma kind of scared me, so eventually I'd shuffled home. She'd saved my sandwich for me, and when I came through the door, all hurt feelings and sniffles, she just put her arms around me, unwrapped the plastic on the sandwich, and popped the top on a can of soda.

"Hi Mom," I said, as I sauntered up to the office door, hands in my pockets.

She was sitting at her desk, whispering. I gave her a kiss on the cheek before heading out and up the stairs. When I got to the top landing, I glanced over at the couches. Young women were lined up like birds on a wire. They were concentrating on the television, some mini-series most likely. They loved the mini-series, anything with a lot of kissing and dramatic music. No Louise Begaye, though. I wondered if she was with Karl.

I banked left and turned the knob to our room. I hit the light and took a Superman run at the bed, getting good air and hitting the mattress flat on my belly with a bounce. The window was open and the traffic sounds rose and fell as cars whooshed by.

I turned over and examined the scab on my shin. It was nearly healed now, and the angry purple bruise had turned to greenish-yellow and was fading.

The nurse had said I was lucky I hadn't broken my leg. My fourth grade class had been assigned to build a garden alongside one of the portable buildings. A pudgy girl by the name of Margaret and I were carrying rocks from one end of the school yard to the garden area. It was our job to build a neat border around the plants. The boulder we were lugging was a killer, a couple of feet long and about half that wide. I had one end and she had the other, and I was walking backwards, grunting and sweating under the bulk, when my heel caught on a root and down I went, with that big rock crashing right down on my shin. The blood had gushed and a welt had formed almost instantly. I screamed and my carrying partner had turned pale. Our teacher, Mr. Hornbuckle, was nowhere to be found. Kids gathered around and gawked at me while I sat on the ground bawling.

Suddenly, the ring of staring fourth graders had parted and Cora Feldman had appeared. Cora was the biggest kid in our class. She was a tall, blond girl, with buckteeth and large feet. That Cora came right over to me, bent down, and scooped me up. She pushed through all those kids and trotted into the main building and all the way down the long hallway, carrying me and my bloody leg like we were in some kind of John Wayne war movie.

In my mind, I can still see the side of her face as I clung to her, with my arm around her shoulder. Her jaw set as she stared straight ahead, snorting through her nose like a bull.

By the time we got to the nurse's office, Cora was pretty much done. She dropped me down on the examining table, sweaty and out of breath. The front of her dress had little cherries on it, wrinkled where I had been pressed against her, and some of the cherries were hemorrhaging freely. The startled nurse examined my leg and questioned Cora about what in the world had happened.

It's funny, huh? I don't think I had ever even talked to that girl before that day, but she just ran me on down to the nurse like she was some kind of crazy hero. After that, whenever I saw her, I felt so embarrassed I couldn't even look at her.

I guess when something like that happens to you, you either become fast friends or it just reminds you that you were way too close for any kind of comfort. Way too close.

She saw my pain. Saw me with my feelings all spilled out. And me? I had looked right up her nose. Seen the fear in her eyes, felt her sweat, and her breath heave in and out as I was mashed in her arms. It all mingles together in my memory to make one painful, embarrassing stew.

I can't say what Cora thought about it. She never tried to talk to me any more than she did before. She still ate lunch with her friends and I still spent lunch period in the library. What can I tell you, no touching After School Special ending, just a kid with a scab on her shin and one heckuva bruise.

I pulled a dog-eared shoebox out from under the bed and laid it on the mattress with me. I lifted the top off the box and took a good look at the hodgepodge of stones inside. Blood-red smooth jasper. Jagged obsidian, deep and black as ice on asphalt. Feather-light pumice that smelled like the head of a match.

All kinds of rocks, gritty and just this side of sand, or ones with bright colors hiding under dull coats. I picked up a piece of quartz and wet it with a licked finger. The inside sparkled and danced in the light. Someday, I was going to get one of those polishers that tossed the stones over and over for days until the color shone and the rock was smooth as glass. I'd help each stone turn into that pretty butterfly hiding in each dull cocoon. For now, a bit of spit gave me a peek at the true creature inside, and that was pretty good.

Some of the rocks in the shoebox I'd picked up here and there. Some had been given to me by teachers, and one of them I had pried loose, one rainy day, from the rock wall that I passed every day on my way home from school. It was just a chip, really, and I didn't think it would be missed.

Still, looking at it now, I felt a pang of guilt. My heart had beat like a rabbit as I had jimmied that little rock back and forth in the concrete until it had come free. When I pocketed it, I had crawled on my hands–butt in the air, like a crab–until I was out of sight of those accusing windows, which was nearly a whole block later. Then I'd turned it over in my hand all the way home, admiring the melting colors and the woody texture.

As I returned the stone to the box, my stomach gurgled, reminding me that I hadn't had anything to eat since my morning PB & J. I hopped up and grabbed the can opener out of the plastic box that served as a drawer. I yanked a can of SpaghettiOs off the thickly painted shelf and clamped the jaws of the opener down on the rim of the can. The thin rod of a handle bit into my palm as I wrestled with the crank, banging the can around on the table. I finally got the Os free, and the smell wafting up at me made my mouth water. The thick goo of orange sauce and O-shaped pasta dropped into the dented pan with a lovely little plop. I put the concoction on the hot plate and turned the knob to medium. The red power light jumped on and the coils started to glow.

I picked up my guitar and strummed while the SpaghettiOs sizzled, stopping between chords, carefully positioning each finger on the correct string and fret, and then I'd strum again.

The SpaghettiOs were making a racket, bubbling and popping in the pan. I spooned some out and polished off my meal with a cup of cold water in a sweating metal cup and a slice of Wonder bread. When I was done, I dumped the rest of the uneaten Os from the pan into a plastic "I Can't Believe It's Not Butter" container. I wedged it between a package of baloney and someone's shriveling apple in the tiny common refrigerator down the hall. People cram a lot of food in that fridge, and sometimes they leave it when they move out. The nuns go nuts when that happens. There are lots of taped signs on the fridge about being responsible for your own stuff and being considerate. They throw everything away once in a while, so you gotta make sure you know when they're going to get it in their heads to do that, or you can kiss your stuff good-bye.

I rinsed out my dishes in the sink near the fridge and left them to dry on a dish towel draped over our little dinette.

I narrowed my eyes and looked slowly over my shoulder. The room was quiet. I was deep in enemy terrain. I turned around and karate kicked the mattress. Then I gave it a good chop with a "hi-yah!" and swung around, ready for more action from the flank. I did a sideways flip and landed on the bed belly up, rippling muscles tensed for battle.

The Abbots and I like karate movies. Sometimes there's a double feature, and we can lose ourselves in the dark theater almost all day. Those movies are crazy. People fly into trees and blood gushes from sword wounds. Muscly men in black pajamas beat the tar outta one another, chopping and kicking on stairs and furniture. Their heads jerk and they make a lot of noise, yelling and carrying on. It's fantastic.

After the movie, the Abbots and I re-enact the whole thing at their house, so I practice my moves whenever I can.

What are you doing here?" I was standing in the light from Paula's bedroom window as she whispered from above. I had thrown a good seven pennies before she'd appeared.

"Can I come in? Don't tell your mom."

"Go to the back door. She's in the den watching TV."

I snuck in through the kitchen and we went upstairs to her room.

"What's going on?" Chris and Danny ran in from down the hall.

There were muffled footsteps on the stairs. We all looked at the door. "Come on." Paula grabbed my hand and we all crowded into the bathroom that she and Chris shared.

"Why are you here?" Danny asked.

"My mom is gone. She didn't come home last night, and I don't know where she is. I looked for her but I couldn't find her anywhere. She doesn't usually go anywhere. She works right there downstairs. She doesn't go anywhere." I had started to cry and my nose was running. Paula put her hand on my shoulder. Chris pulled tissue paper from the roll and handed it to me.

"We should tell Mom," Danny said.

"No! Please, don't do that."

"Why not?" Chris chimed in. "She can help. Maybe she can find her."

"If you tell your mother and she calls the police, which she will, then they'll find my mom and they'll lock her up."

"Why would they do that?" I sniffed. "Deb? Why would they lock her up?"

"She's sick," I said, starting to cry. "She hears voices and she yells in the night and she swears sometimes, but she can't help it. She loves me and she takes care of me and I just want her to come home. That's all."

"It's okay." Paula put an arm around me and Chris handed me another tissue. "It's going to be okay. You can stay here tonight and tomorrow, we'll skip school and all go out and find her. Don't worry, it's going to be okay."

That night, I laid on the floor in their room, zipped into Paula's sleeping bag, with the sound of the television leaking through the floor from Mrs. Abbot's bedroom. My stomach was twisted up and I couldn't sleep. Water leaked from my eyes and into my ears. Finally, when my friends were asleep, I crept downstairs, quietly turned the doorknob, and stepped out into the cool night. I walked home in the shadowy dark, past the rock wall, now all pitch black and sleepy. I went back home. Back to the C.I.C.

An Indian girl I didn't know was in the little reception room. She smiled at me as I slunk past her and up the stairs. The TV was silent, and there were no birds on the wire to-night.

I got back to the room and the air was cold and stale. I took my shoes off, shut the window, and crawled into the freezing bed. I prayed for God to bring my ma back. I prayed for her not to be sick anymore and I made all kinds of prom-ises in return. No more stealing. No more lying or talking back. Promise.

I don't remember falling asleep, but the next thing I knew, it was morning. I got up and put my shoes back on. I knew the Abbots were probably in school. Mrs. Abbot dropped them off every morning. I knew I couldn't stay there. Knew it would be hard for them.

I walked around town most of the day. I went to all the places she had worked, down streets with rows of shops, where she'd held my hand and pointed at the shiny things. Those streets were bustling with all kinds of people, but not my ma. Once I thought I saw her in a store, but when the lady turned around, she didn't even look much like her.

The sun was sinking and my shadow stretched down the sidewalk before me. My stomach felt sour and flat. When I got home, my feet were tired and my legs were heavy as lead. I let myself into our room and pulled a slice of bread out of the plastic bag. I sat down and watched the trains roll by in the falling gloom as I chewed on the crust. I could hear heavy footsteps and muffled voices in the corridor. I peeked around the corner in time to see a blue nun's habit disappear down the stairs. I followed at a good distance, tiptoeing quiet as a mouse in my sock feet. I crept around the second landing and on down toward the lobby, still clutching my mangled piece of bread. I peered under the first flight ceiling and saw a tall man talking to Sister Daniel Ignatius.

A few people were chatting as they made their way to the side door for Thursday night bingo in the hall. I turned to go back upstairs when the man called my name. I turned around and realized that my brother was standing in the lobby of the Catholic Indian Center.

Seven

A PILE OF SHINY, BLACK FEATHERS

His teeth flashed under a mustache that crawled down either side of his mouth. Tall and lean, his broad shoulders bulged beneath a faded black t-shirt, and blue jeans had replaced the beautiful shiny suits. His hair had grown out from the military stubble and sideburns trailed down his jawline. I glanced behind me and took a step back. He came over and scooped me right up off of the step where I stood.

"Oh god, you're so heavy. And you must grow a good inch a day. Do you?" he said, bouncing me in his arms. His voice was deep, and it hummed in my rib cage.

He said Ma had gotten very sick and that she'd been sleeping in a ravine outside of town. He said she was fine, that she was safe. The police had found her and they'd called the nuns. Then the nuns had called Isabelle, and she'd called my brother. Mom was in the hospital, he said. I'd be staying with him until she was better. Well, him and his wife.

He swung around so that we faced a tall woman standing near the door, all wiry black hair and white teeth. She was thin and nearly as tall as my brother. She blinked behind thick glasses.

"This is my wife, Elandra," my brother said.

"Hi, Debbie. I've heard a lot about you." She smiled and offered me her hand. I stared at it and then transferred my mashed slice of bread from the right hand to the left. Her palm was moist and the fingertips cold.

I wondered, for an instant, if I was dreaming. If it were all only a dream, and I'd wake up to find Ma reading next to me. She'd yawn and look at me with sleepy eyes before rolling over to turn off the light.

As it was, I was about to be abducted. Abducted by tall, slouchy beings from a faraway place. And they were introducing themselves to me.

Everyone stood around then, not really knowing what to do. The usual bingo crowd continued to stream in around us, looking forward to a good night. Maybe there'd be prizes to take home or a little money. I scanned the faces, hoping I'd see Karl. He'd ask just what the heck they thought they were doing, and then he'd punch my brother in the gut and we'd beat it out the door and down the street.

Sister Daniel broke the silence. "Well, we'd better get her things together." She turned to my brother. "Men are not allowed upstairs, so I'm afraid your wife will have to supervise."

I frantically looked around for Karl. The lady with the wild hair and the big teeth was going to go upstairs. She would walk into our room and she would touch our things with her hands and with her eyes. She would see where I dressed for school and where I ate my dinner, and she would run her long, cold fingers through the whole of me.

My brother lowered me onto my feet. Sister Daniel started up the steps and turned to look at me. "Come on, Deborah. It's going to be all right." But I was very sure that it wasn't going to be all right for a very long time.

The window glass was cold against my cheek as I stared, for hours, up at the stars from the dark back seat of my brother's Chevy Vega. They were twinkling and brilliant, like glitter shaken onto a black quilt. They made me feel kind of peaceful, even though I was sad and scared. I wondered if Mom could see them.

I thought about Gallup and all of the things that filled up my life there, from the time I first saw the place to this very minute. I thought about Louise Begaye and Karl and Kathy Martinez. I thought about the Abbotts and about Wyatt.

Wyatt was a long time ago, and I hadn't thought of him in ages. He and his mother lived at the Catholic Indian Center for a short time when we first moved in. He was an Indian kid, a little younger than me, with very short black hair and a huge head that made him look a little like Charlie Brown. He was the only other kid I ever saw at the C.I.C.

Wyatt was a good friend, though he didn't talk much. He would just smile and follow me around. We would color together in the Jesus color books the nuns gave us or watch *The Price is Right*.

We even took a shower once in the big green bathroom, wearing running shorts and sopping tank tops. His was white, with a dark blue number five on it. I think mine was yellow.

It was fantastic, like splashing around in a warm rain. I can still see his tiny spaced teeth set into that big head of his, water clinging to his lashes and dripping off his nose.

His mother came and yanked him out and complained to the nuns, who threw a tremendous fuss. I didn't have a clue why at the time, but now I think they must have thought something sexy was going on. Ma just shook her head at them and helped me into dry clothes. She was like that. As crazy as they say she is, she usually seemed the sanest one in the room to me.

Wyatt only lived at the C.I.C. for a few months. One day, he was just gone. His door had been left open just a crack. His room was neat and barren, the bed made up and waiting, like our room will be. Pretty soon, I'll be just a shadow to the people there, hardly anything to remember at all.

I'll never see Wyatt again, of course. Or Paula, or Chris, or even Louise Begaye for that matter. I wish I could have said good-bye, but what good would that do? I maybe would have cried and felt so sad, and I'd still be just as gone. People move in and out of your life, that's all. One day you have friends, a routine, a place in the world. Then poof, you're sitting in the back of a Chevy Vega with your underwear in a plastic bag, and your place in the world is getting smaller and smaller in the rearview mirror.

How are you, Q.T.? Have you been eating all right?" Ma was sitting across a long folding table, watching me pull a paper clip along the table's edge like it was a car on a highway. "You need a haircut again," she said. She didn't have any makeup on and her hair was a little messy. "I didn't want to go. I knew you'd be all right with the sisters. I had to go, they said they were going to..."

A man in a tie and a long, white coat stepped in and wrote something on a yellow pad. He took the chair next to her. Ma folded her arms over her chest. "Hello, Mary. I'm Doctor Rodriguez. I understand you've been having some problems."

"I don't know what you're talking about," she snapped, gazing at the wall.

"You haven't been hearing voices?" he said, softly.

She turned her eyes on him. "Of course not. What kind of question is that?"

I felt my mouth fall open. I had never heard her lie before. I pictured Father Connell in his cramped confessional. When I looked at the doctor, he was studying me. I closed my mouth.

"All right, Mary. I'm sure we can do something to help you." My mother breathed an exasperated sigh as he got up.

"Deborah, may I see you outside?" I followed him out the door and he closed it behind us. I spotted my brother at the reception desk down the hallway.

"You seemed a little surprised by your mother's answers in there. Do you think she's been hearing voices?"

I nodded.

"How do you know that? What does she do?"

"She doesn't hear me. She screams sometimes, laughs a lot. She always asks me if they're hurting me."

"Um-hmm. Has she ever tried to hurt herself? Has she ever tried to hurt you?" he continued in that soft voice.

"No way! She would never do that." I didn't like where this was going, and I was beginning to think I should have kept my yap shut.

"Well, she's going to be okay, but she'll have to stay with us for awhile. Okay? You can live with your brother for the time being, how'd that be?" He patted my shoulder.

I had been having these little talks with doctors since I learned how to string words together. They all said the same thing in different ways. One of them explained it like this: Let's say Ma's brain is like a TV, and that TV is on the fritz. The doctors know that the television isn't working–the picture is all wrong and fuzzy–but they don't know exactly why, so they try different drugs and treatments until they find something that clears up the reception. It's kind of like banging on the side of the set. Sometimes it works, and the picture clears up, but they don't know why. Not really.

I knew Mom hated the hospital. Hated the drugs that made her feel all empty and groggy, that made her shake all the time, so when she was let out she always stopped taking the pills. Who could blame her? So no matter what this doctor was saying, I knew it was only a matter of time until Ma's picture went all snowy again.

My brother's place was not so bad. It was a whitewashed rental house squatting under a cottonwood tree at the end of a long dirt road. A ditch ran along that road for a ways, the water splashing and gurgling up a racket. Walking home from school was my favorite part of the day. When I got home, tired and hot, I'd sit down under that tree–its branches spread over the hard, baked ground–and I'd listen to the insects buzz and breathe in the paper bag smell of the brown grass.

My sister-in-law tried very hard to be nice to me, talking to me as if I were a baby at times. I got the impression that she hadn't really been around kids much. My brother worked long days, coming home long after the sun had set, covered in black and smelling of grease. Elandra was forever trying to wash that muck out of his clothes. I thought it'd cut down on all that laundry if his mechanic uniforms were made of plastic. You could just soap him up and hose him down in the driveway.

There was a skinny brown dog that would wander the yard, searching for a shady spot in which to lie, and chickens laying in a weathered coop in the back. On dark mornings, a rooster would stand on that coop and crow his fool head off. Orlando. He was glossy black and small for a rooster. Mean as lightning, he chased after me every chance he got, spurring and pecking at my legs and back, and I was plenty scared of that devil.

Life in this new place was very lonely at first. I was surrounded by strangers at home and strangers at yet another new school, and it was hard not to blame my brother and his wife for my homesick sorrow. I may as well have moved to a distant star, all ties to my old life having burnt to ashes. It was what I had feared the most. Still, it was nice having a yard and trees again. I was able to explore the farmland around our house, being careful to watch out for Orlando and his sharp claws.

On weekends, my brother would put on a clean, white shirt and we'd all visit Ma in the hospital. Dr. Rodriguez would stand off to the side and whisper with my brother while he held an elbow in one hand and his chin in the other.

It's always so good when Ma becomes herself again. She pulls me onto her lap and she looks me in the eye and she hears me when I talk to her. It's always so very good.

B en slowly circled the hospital parking lot. "There's one!" I chirped, but when we got closer, I saw the rear wheel of a motorcycle jutting behind the bumper of the sedan in front of it. He cruised two more rows before finally sliding into an empty slot. I ran to the glass doors and they shushed closed behind me. I threw myself into a seat near the reception desk and rocked back and forth before running back to the door to wave my brother and his wife in. Ben talked to the nurse behind the counter, and I tried out chair after chair. Finally, a door opened up and Ma stepped out, carrying an orange suitcase. I threw my arms around her waist. She leaned down and hugged me tight.

"Hello Q.T., how's my baby?" she said. "Your bangs still need cutting, I see."

"There's really nothing like freshly baked bread, is there Mom?" Elandra said, nudging her glasses up her nose with the back of a floured hand.

"Oh yes, my mother used to bake bread, but I was never very good at it. I make good sopapillas, though." Ma was rolling out a circle of elastic dough with a floured rolling pin. She and Elandra were chopping and frying and going through all the elaborate motions of dinner as they chatted and laughed cautiously together, feeling their way through conversations. Ma moves stiffly now, her hands always trembling and her voice flat and even because of the little vial of pills on the table by our bed. She walks from one end of the house to the other, with no particular expression on her face, her hands swiveling at the ends of her sleeves. Still, she's present and involved, awake during the day, and sleeping all night through.

"Yes, she's growing up, isn't she? Pretty soon, there'll be boys sniffing around." I snapped back to the conversation at the counter. Elandra was grinning at me.

"Oh, no," my mother said. "She's too young for that."

I sat at the table with a cup of Kool-Aid, reading a book about dinosaurs and trying very hard to look unconcerned.

"I don't know. They have little dances at that school of hers."

"Well, that's all we need," my mother said.

I sat in the suffocating heat of the old plywood doghouse, wondering how I was ever going to get to the safety of the back door. The sound of my own blood rushed in my ears and sweat popped out on my upper lip. I had come out into the yard to put food and water in the scratched up plastic bowls for that ancient dog. I'd crawled in through the rough cut doghouse doorway to straighten out the dirty towel that was all wadded up in the back. Then I'd remembered Orlando.

I thought, "Maybe he's on the other side of the yard." At that, Orlando's pointy profile appeared as a silhouette, blocking out the sun and the kitchen door beyond, and then he was gone. It got very, very quiet, with only the sound of my pounding heart in my poor ears. Suddenly, an explosion of feathers and clawed feet ripped the stillness. He beat at the door of the doghouse with furious wings, his craggy, clawed feet stabbing and trying for blood.

I kicked at him, crawling forward out of the darkness, and then I was free. I got to my feet and I ran. I could feel that demon chicken at my back, spurs hitting my arms and legs, stiff feathers beating at my shoulders. I reached for a two-by-four lying in a pile. I turned on the run and brought home the board squarely onto Orlando's back. He wobbled a step or two and then fell to the ground. I stood, panting and sweaty with the board in my hand, dirt in my mouth and blood oozing from scratches on my arms and legs. I stared at the pile of shiny, black feathers and looked down at the board in my hand. A bent nail pointed from the end of it, a bit of down still clinging to it. I threw the wretched piece of lumber away and dropped to my knees. I reached out and grabbed the crumpled bird. I tried propping him up, but his legs wouldn't work. His head lolled to one side and his eyes rolled around like a doll's. His long, yellow toes were curled up, the claws still wicked and needle-sharp.

I began to sob. When my brother got home, I was going to be deader than old Orlando. I let the chicken drop and I ran. At first, I zig-zagged crazily around the yard, just running back and forth, and then I made a beeline for the old storage shed. I slammed the door behind me and hunkered down behind the fat sacks of feed. I cried until the sobs dissolved into hiccups, finally nodding off to sleep.

I started awake when my brother opened the door to the shed and called my name. He took a seat on the bags of grain and folded his arms across his chest.

"You gonna stay in there all night?" he said. I ran a hand under my nose. "You want to tell me what happened?"

"I...was...feeding..." Between sobs I told him about the towel and the two-by-four and the end of poor Orlando.

"Well, sounds like self-defense to me," he said. "Come on out. It's okay, come on out." He put out a hand and helped me to my feet. He took a look at my legs and whistled. "Ouch. No jury would convict you. We should get inside and get those cleaned up."

Stiff and dirty, I limped back to the house, keeping my gaze away from the black fluff fluttering in the breeze.

After a bath and a change of clothes, I told the whole story again. There was a lot of "What?" and, "My goodness," but nobody was mad and my brother winked at me a couple of times. Later, the two of us sat on the couch watching TV, waiting to get called to supper. We had fried chicken and it was awfully tough, as I recall.

I t's about time we got you a training bra, huh?" Elandra plucked a wispy bit of pink clipped to a plastic hanger from a rack and held it up to my chest.

"Yow, hey, cut it out."

"You can't hide them much longer, you know. There's no reason to be embarrassed. Every woman has them." The lady one rack over glanced at me. I felt my face color.

"Oh my god."

"Okay, I'm just going to get it for you and you can wear it when you're comfortable. How's that?"

"Where's my mother?"

"I think she's up front by the door. You're going to thank me for this later!" she shouted after me.

Mother was pacing up by the automatic doors. As they shushed open with every customer that came and went, I got in stride with her.

"Had your fill of shopping?" she said.

"You could say that. What do you think of Elandra?"

"Oh, she's a sweet girl."

"I think she's pushy."

"Do you?"

"Sure I do. Like she calls you "Mom." You don't think that's kind of weird?"

"Not really. I'm her mother-in-law. She can call me "Mom" if she wants too."

"Bob called you "Mary.""

"Oh, Bob. He was just a little boy."

"Still, I liked Bob better."

Oh, man!" My favorite jeans had been in the dryer over an hour and they were still damp. Different shades of denim had been stitched together to make an artistic mosaic, the pants fit in all the right places, and more importantly, they made me feel cool. I would be going to my first school dance today, and I needed all the help that I could get. I bumped into Elandra as she sauntered down the hallway, fastening an earring.

"What's the problem?"

"The dryer isn't working." I held up the jeans with a pout.

"Oh right, your brother said he was going to look at it, but he hasn't had a chance. How wet are they?" She picked up one leg and felt the length. "Yeah, still pretty damp. I think you're just going to have to wear something else," she said, with a sympathetic look. I moped to our room and balled up the jeans, throwing them into a corner. I emptied my drawer, but nothing else would do. Everything else rode up too high, or sagged in the seat, or looked dowdy and dated. I pictured myself at the dance, looking cool and confident in my perfect pair of pants, chatting and laughing with my peers, the life of the party. I sat on the bed and eyed the garment in a heap on the floor.

"Q.T., are you going to school?"

"Yeah, Ma. Class starts late because there's a dance this afternoon. I'm trying to figure out what to wear."

"Ooo, a dance. I used to love to dance." She shuffled her feet and swiveled her hips with her hands balled up into fists. She danced over to me and pulled me off the bed, shuffling and bouncing in front of me. "Mom, please! I gotta find something to wear." She let go of my hand laughing and breathless. "All right, all right, sourpuss. Why don't you wear the red ones? Those are cute."

"Yeah, if there's a flood, I'm all set."

"What? I think they're very stylish."

"Yeah, yeah."

"Have some breakfast. You're going to need your strength if you're going to be this unpleasant." She chuckled and danced out of the room. Her off-key humming trailed after her.

A brilliant idea floated into my head and I snatched the jeans up off the floor and hurried to the kitchen. Folding the pants over once, I laid them on the top rack of the oven and turned the knob. Smiling, I went back to my closet to pick out a top and accessories to go with my perfect pair of pants. I decided on a scoop neck t-shirt emblazoned with a rhinestone butterfly. I stood in the mirror, wearing the shirt with my pajama bottoms. My mother came from behind and put her hands on my shoulders. "Very nice," she said.

"I wish I wasn't so skinny."

"You are not skinny. You are slender. You've always been very willowy, and there's nothing wrong with you." She gathered my long hair behind my neck and held my chin in her hand, turning my face this way and that. I could feel the warm, electric current of her trembling fingers. "See there? You are a beautiful girl." She smiled, her eyes locked to mine in the mirror. "Do you smell something burning?"

"My jeans!" When the door to the kitchen opened, it parted a thick cloud of smoke. I made my way to the stove and opened the oven door. Through the haze, I could see flames licking merrily from my perfect pair of pants.

"Look out!" Elandra nudged me aside and coaxed the flames from the oven with a broom handle and a dustpan. She rushed the pile of smoking pants through the kitchen and out the back door, dropping it in the dirt. We all stood there, watching what was left of my favorite perfect pair of pants burn to ash.

"Well, I guess you won't be wearing those." Elandra turned to me and stifled a giggle, one hand on her mouth. Mother was laughing too. I watched the last of the flames puff out on the miserable smoking heap.

"Perfect," I said.

"Oh, it's not that bad. At least you didn't burn down the house. Why don't we go buy you another pair? I've put a little money aside for a rainy day, and I'd say this was a category thunderstorm. You'll be a little late, but you'll make it. Just don't do anything like this again, okay? And don't tell your brother."

The new jeans were okay, and I certainly was grateful to my sister-in-law for her kindness, but these new jeans could not replace the perfect pair of pants. Still, they fit all right and they had a snappy bit of embroidery on the pockets. As I stood off to one side in the dark gym in my cool new clothes, with the music thumping and the lights whirling, I felt completely naked and alone. Kids stood in clumps, laughing and talking. Once in a while, someone would glance over at me and whisper. I tried to stand with an air of sophistication as I concentrated on the record, but my feet were cold and numb and I couldn't quite breathe right.

I was old enough now to know that I was not an alien experiment from another planet, but when I commingled with my fellow classmates, I still felt it. The differentness, the total otherness that was me. I kept the inkling deep down inside that maybe, just maybe, one of these days, that big, shiny space ship would still show up and take me away.

"Would you like to dance?" A boy with dark hair and a slight overbite stood before me. I considered my options. I could continue to play the wallflower and feed this self-conscious beast, or I could give the new jeans a workout. It was a dance, after all.

I nodded and followed him through the sea of fifth graders. He settled into an awkward bouncing motion, arms swinging before him. At first, my feet would barely move, icy and numb as they were, but soon, I was swaying and bumping to the beat, borrowing steps from the Jacksons, the Osmonds, and the groovy dancers from *Laugh-In*. I noticed kids watching me. Some smiled. I smiled back. When the song was done, the boy escorted me back to my spot by the wall. I was good and warm now, feeling loose and well-oiled.

"I like the way you dance," he shouted over the music before shuffling away. I watched him walk back to his friends, feeling more human than I ever had before.

Eight

MRS. SHUSSLER'S PLACE

I lay in a patch of grass in the tiny front yard, warming my bones to the first real days of spring. Clouds overhead drifted past in puppy dog and dragon shapes. The blooming lilac bushes wrapped me in a thick, sweet aroma, causing my eyes to grow drowsy and heavy with sleep.

"Deborah? Deborah!" Mrs. Shussler's voice scratched at the breeze. I stretched and sat up. The sun on the mesh screen made her look wispy and ghostlike. She motioned me over with a stiff hand.

"Hi, Mrs. Shussler!" I shouted, one foot resting on the first red step outside her door.

Mrs. Shussler was an old woman when Jesus was a child, and she was just about deaf as a post. She liked her support hose rolled halfway down her bony, veined shins. She peered at me through thick cat eye glasses, her skin gray and paper-thin. A wild shock of wispy, snow white hair moved around her head with the breeze.

"Can you come in and give Jimi some water?" she asked. "My arthritis is so bad today."

"You bet." I started up the stairs, stopping next to her so she could grip my arm, her knuckles big as marbles. I tried to imagine Mrs. Shussler as a young woman. Surely some of the smiles in the fading sepia pictures that crowded her house were hers, but it was impossible to pluck out familiar features from the road map that had become her face.

Mrs. Shussler also chewed tobacco. She would spit the juice into a Royal Crown Cola can that generally rested under a doily on the small oak table near her padded rocker. She would stare out the window through the lace curtains into the yard, rocking just slightly, the shush of her slippers whispering against the wood floors.

Then the birdlike arm would slowly, so slowly, tremble its way toward that R.C. can. She'd grip it with her swollen knuckles and the can would journey back to her mouth where–ptoo!–a jet of tar-colored spit would shoot expertly into the narrow opening at the top. She never missed, but she often had the brown juice left on her chin or lips. She always smelled like mint because of the chaw.

I guided her over to her chair and helped her ease into it. She was light as a bird when she put her weight on me.

"Okay then, I'll go get Jimi squared away!" She smiled and nodded at me. I headed for the kitchen in the back of the house. Mrs. Shussler had a lot of heavy, dark furniture, most of it covered with white lace of one type or another. Her kitchen was old, though well cared for, and clean and cheerful.

I retrieved the chipped cereal bowl that served as Jimi's water dish and carried it to the sink. There were wiry white hairs cemented to the sides with dried dog spit. I heard the click, click of claws as Jimi appeared in the doorway. The long hair around his eyes blinked at me.

"Hiya, Jimi. How's life in the slow lane?" Jimi was a miniature poodle, once upon a time white, I think. Now he was kind of a washed out maroon color. His hair was so thin that his pinkish-brown skin showed through, making him look like he had gone through the dryer one too many times. Now and then you could see the odd flea spring into action and then disappear inside his thin pelt.

He had leaky eyes that still served him well, though they were milky and bluish, dripping a steady flow of tears that stained lines the color of dried blood down his face.

I washed his bowl in hot water and ran the tap until it was so cold that the faucet started to sweat. Carefully, I filled the bowl and carried it back to its home against the wall, willing it not to slosh out onto the floor.

I guess you would say that Mrs. Shussler was our landlady, though technically, her son handled the money. We moved out of my brother's small house and rented the furnished one room cottage across the driveway from Mrs. Shussler. The couch had a sag to it and the carpet, cut in uneven sections, rolled up in places, exposing the hard packed dirt floor beneath, but I did not care. There were two actual beds, and for the first time in my life, I got to sleep by myself.

Thick adobe walls and iron radiators kept the place cozy in the winter, though the one tiny bathroom in the front alcove was unheated and icy cold. It was a race to get out of my pajamas and under the warm shower water on snowy mornings before school. The kitchen/front room/bedroom had a wide sink, and I sometimes used it as a bathtub when I just couldn't face the frigid shower stall.

Mrs. Shussler's place is not thirty miles from the very spot where I cracked my head on the pavement under that memorial cannon all those years ago, where the world drained away with the unpaid light bills and the dry water faucets, where Ma and I had meals over a campfire in our starry little back yard. I wonder if that house is still standing, if the little store that I walked to for Moon Pies is open and doing business right this minute. Thirty miles. It might as well be on the moon.

My brother had bought a house of his own. A nice little two bedroom ranch-style on the opposite side of town across the river, and lately, at least when we saw him, he was in a much better mood.

Mrs. Shussler had a lot of property. Her son lived in a large house in the back and he farmed the acres of alfalfa that grew sweet and emerald green in the fields around our house. In the summer, I'd walk out into the middle of it and lie in the soft beds, feeling happy and light as air. I'd make a show of trying to find a four leaf clover, but as soon as I sat down to search, the pull of the springy stuff would win out and I'd end up doing nothing but staring at the sky for hours.

Jimi ticked his way over to his water bowl. His tiny velvet tongue tapped out a sloppy tune as he lapped it up. When I walked back to the sitting room, Mrs. Shussler's R.C. can was on its final approach back to the doily.

"Sit down and join me for a bit," she croaked.

I sat on the ottoman diagonally from her. "The weather's been nice, huh?" I yelled across the divide.

"I'll swan," she said, shaking her head. When she didn't hear something, she'd either say "I'll swan," or just go "mmh, mmh, mmh."

She asked me how school was and I nodded, saying that it was all right. She said that was good, and she continued to rock. We sat in silence for a time, just listening to the old grandfather clock tick. I gave Jimi a scratch behind the ear. Outside, I heard Ma calling me back for lunch. She was framed in the window beyond Mrs. Shussler's chair, hand over her eyes, scanning the yard for me.

I shouted that I better be getting back. Mrs. Shussler nodded, saying her thank you's. I looked back with a last little wave as I moved from the cool dark of her doorway to join my mother in the full sun of the yard.

Ma loved the singer Engelbert Humperdinck. She would hum *Release Me* while she did the dishes. She'd mumble a word or two and look all dreamy, with a dopey little smile curling her mouth. Englebert was the only man in my mother's life. She was married twice, but that was long before my time, and there had never been any kind of boyfriend sniffing around.

Mr. Murray was a handyman that did work around Mrs. Shussler's place, and he'd visit now and then, bringing fried chicken for lunch or taking us for a drive, but you couldn't call him a boyfriend. He was a lot older than Ma, and a lot shorter. Ma would call him "that little man." He wore Farmer John overalls and drove a great old truck from nineteen-fifty-odd-something.

"Ma, Mr. Murray's here!" I watched as he checked what was left of his hair and climbed out of his car. Today he was in the gray sedan, his "sporting around" car, as he called it.

"Well, aren't you Johnny-On-The-Spot?" he said, when I opened the door before he had a chance to knock.

"Hi, Mr. Murray. Ma'll be ready in a minute."

"You up for some exploring?" He hovered near the front door, rocking on the balls of his feet and glancing around the room.

"Oh yeah. I checked out a book on Chaco Canyon and the ruins. Can't wait."

"Good, good. Oh hey, I brought you something." He fished in his pocket and handed me a fat chunk of shiny rock. "It's called iron pyrite. Fool's gold."

"Wow, cool! Dang, it's heavy."

"Yeah, many a prospector cussed a blue streak over them nuggets, which is why they named it that. Really, it's a kind of lead."

"Thanks, Mr. Murray." My mother emerged from the powder room, rubbing lotion into her hands. "Mom, look what I got."

"Wow, we're rich," she said. "Hello, Mr. Murray, how are you?"

"Fine, Mary. Just fine, thanks. Nice day for it, huh?"

"It's called Fool's Gold, Ma. It's really lead though. Isn't it pretty?" I held it up so that it caught the light.

"Yes, it certainly is lovely." I wasn't sure if the answer was meant for me.

"Ma..." She gathered up her sweater and sunglasses.

"Yes, yes, the rock is very nice. Get your coat."

A flock of birds burst from the scrub brush and careened across the sky as we followed the two-lane highway that cut through the New Mexico territory known as Chaco Canyon. Wind and water had carved jagged features in the sandstone, sculpting the banded cliffs and mesas that sprung up out of the desert. Looking at the remote landscape through the glass, it was hard to believe it had been such a cultural and economic hub a thousand years ago.

"For my money, Audie Murphy did it better than anybody," Mr. Murray was saying. "*That Red Badge of Courage?* One of the greatest movies ever made." He held onto the wheel with both hands, leaning in my mother's direction now and then for emphasis.

"Oh yes, that was a good one. They don't make them like that anymore, do they? Pictures now, they have to show everything. No finesse. No more Tracy and Hepburn, no Gary Cooper. Now it's all bad language and worse."

We turned off the main highway and crunched onto a rugged dirt road. I sat up and clung to the passenger seat head rest.

"Deborah, you're on my hair." The back of her hand swiped at me in slow motion.

"Sorry, Ma. How much longer, Mr. Murray?" I said.

"We've got about twenty miles of this, I'm afraid."

The bumps and the ruts dislodged my mother's sunglasses, sending them slipping down her nose. Finally, she sat with a bouncing hand pinned to one lens. Her nails dug into the armrest. Her lipstick had started to bleed tiny lines around her mouth.

"Beautiful country, isn't it?" Mr. Murray breathed deeply.

Mother attempted to wipe the sides of her mouth, but the jarring ride sent a finger up one nostril. Back in the rear of the car, I was beginning to feel a little green around the gills.

Finally, the road opened into a wide field, a series of crumbling walls beyond like broken teeth. Mr. Murray killed the engine and the quiet after the violence of the ride was startling. I stepped out of the car. A hot wind pulled at my hair. Mr. Murray was helping Ma out of her seatbelt.

The word "ruins" didn't do it justice. It seemed that the very earth was reaching up and slowly pulling the whole place into the sand. I had expected to find a lot of people milling around, a gift shop, souvenirs. Instead, there was nothing but the quiet desolation of a dead culture. The engine ticked. I raised dust as I walked toward the crumbling structure.

"Be careful, Q.T.," Ma said, pushing her glasses up her nose. I shot her a look. "I mean...Deborah. Just be careful."

I'd told her that I didn't like her calling me Q.T. around other people, but she never could seem to remember.

I followed the wall around and stepped through a low doorway. The place was a maze of piled rock and eroded adobe bricks. Some of the rooms were perfectly round and descended deep into the ground. Others were narrow and compact, with smooth walls and small windows cut in for light and air. The structures looked like the letter D from above, which Mr. Murry had made a fuss about. The whole of it was much larger than it looked in the books, and it was impossible to see the D shape from the ground, but the fuzzy aerial photos in my books had shown the distinct figure.

It was called Pueblo Bonito, Pretty Village, and I'll bet it was, too. The people who lived there were farmers. The rain visited their pretty little town, making the corn grow tall and sweet. Mothers wiped away tears because of skinned knees. Men gathered together to smoke and tell bad jokes. The people lived there. They survived. Until they didn't.

I sat down on a stone ledge in a neat little room that was shaded and cool, in spite of the late midday heat. I looked around and imagined this family at home. Women weaving baskets. Napping children.

Over the years, the rain deserted the people, and they came to know that they couldn't survive in their pretty little village anymore. They set a cleansing fire to the only home they had ever known. They watched it burn, and then they set out to walk through the desert and on to a new life.

I had dug a trench in the dirt floor with the heel of my shoe and it blurred as my eyes brimmed and stung with emotion.

"Deborah!" I heard Ma's voice sift through the rocks. I wiped my eyes and climbed the steps to the main trail.

"There you are." She caught up to me, out of breath.

"It's incredible, isn't it Ma?" I said, looking at the puzzle of structures as far as the eye could see.

Ma squinted across the ruined landscape. "Looks like a big mess to me."

Have you heard the news about your cousin?" I was getting myself settled for my third period class when the girl sitting in the desk ahead turned in her seat to face me.

"Which one?" I asked. I was very close to my cousins when I was younger. Girls near my own age, we were best friends, talking into the night, laughing and dreaming of lives outside of New Mexico. Had I stayed, we very likely would have been more like sisters, but I grew up far away and when I got back to this neck of the woods, my cousins were strangers. At family functions, we would glance at each other, nodding heads and half smiling. At school, we avoided eye contact all together. We had nothing in common and nothing to say to each other. I often wondered if we'd still be close had I stuck around.

"I think her name is Laura," the girl said, coloring tiny flowers in ballpoint pen on the back of her seat. "She got thrown out of gym class. Suspended for being drunk. I heard that she fell off the balance beam. Mary Torres said she was rolling around the mat laughing while the whole class stood around watching her."

I pictured the circle of stunned seventh grade girls, all in frumpy gym uniforms, looking on as my cousin toppled from the beam and giggled sloppily on the blue rubber mat. I started laughing. "I wonder who was spotting her."

There's not a lot that's better than riding your bike in a summer rain. On a hot day, it smells so fresh and brand new. Ma would say it washed everything clean. She'd open up all the doors and windows and we'd stand in the shelter of the doorway, watching the drops and listening to the sound of falling water.

I was riding my bike in the rain down the ditch bank, past fields of hay and chili, chewing on a Big Hunk candy bar. I was on my way home from The Store. The Store didn't have a sign, or any kind of markings, and it really wasn't a store at all anymore. It closed down a long time ago. The lady that lived in the house behind The Store would still sell me a Big Hunk if I knocked on her door, though. The place was dark and musty and silent, but the shelves were still stocked and the merchandise was still arranged in careful rows. I would walk over, get my dusty candy bar, and hand her the change. She'd give me a little smile and then she'd close the place up again. I heard that her husband used to own The Store, and when he died, she just locked it up on the spot because that's all she could do.

I finished off the sticky taffy and licked my fingers as I turned off the ditch bank and onto the main road home. A car horn nearly sent me into the roadside gully. I stopped my bike, heart pounding. A long silver car pulled up alongside me.

"Hey, Lil Deborah, better watch yourself. Traffic around here can be deadly." My cousin Paul smiled mischievously from the steering wheel.

"Paul, you jerk, you nearly gave me a heart attack!" He threw his head back and laughed.

"Poor Lil Deborah. Still high strung, I see." His windshield wipers threw a stream of water at me with every pass. "Are you on your way home? Great, I'll see you there." And with that he spun his wheels, throwing up a cloud of spattering mud and exhaust.

So, do you like living in that place?" The glow from the dashboard cast a green tinge to Paul's face as he drove. In the black of the backseat, my cousins Laura and Cindy were fighting over a lipstick.

"It's okay," I answered. "There's a lot of land around there. I like that."

"I mean the house. You like that house?" He was glancing between me and the road.

"Yeah, I like it." He continued his glances. "What?"

"Nothing. I was just wondering." He punched in the lighter in the car ashtray and held it to the end of a cigarette. He breathed deeply and looked at me again. "How's school?"

"Boring. You?"

"Awesome. High school is just one big business opportunity. Houston is the only place to be. You can make serious coin there. You should move."

"Eh, it's so hot."

"Exactly," he said.

He steered the car onto the shoulder, threw it into park, and turned to talk to Laura and Cindy in the back. "Okay, we don't have enough cash for everybody, so you two are going to have to get in the trunk."

"What the fuck? I ain't getting in the fucking trunk." My cousin Cindy crossed her arms across her chest.

Paul giggled. "It's just for a few seconds. We'll pay, go through, and pull far enough away so they don't see us let you out. That way, we can all watch the movie. There's plenty of room back there. C'mon, don't screw it up for all of us." Cindy pursed her lips and, to my amazement, she got out of the car. He pulled the keys from the ignition and raced around the back.

The two climbed in. "Ow, you're on my hair."

"Sorry," Laura sniffed. They struggled into the roomy trunk and eventually, after they folded themselves into fetal positions, the lid was lowered.

"You better let us out quick, asshole." The darkness closed around Cindy's face, and then she was gone.

Paul looked at me. "Come on."

We crawled forward, inching our way through the line of cars to the plywood Zuni Drive-In box office.

"Six dollars, please," the tall boy in the window said.

"Six dollars! That's an outrage! You people oughta be arrested." The boy blinked. Paul counted out six bucks and handed it to the kid.

"Enjoy the movie," the boy said, without so much as glancing at us.

Paul pulled slowly away from the little shack and around to one side of the gravel yard. Cars were lining up in rows, all facing a huge screen on the other side of the lot. Paul hit the gas.

The car shot forward and shrieks issued from the trunk. He fishtailed the car and threw it into a donut.

"Paul, you motherfucker! I'm going to kill you when I get out of here!" Cindy screamed from beyond the padded back seats. Paul was nearly crying he was laughing so hard. He slammed on the brakes and threw the car into reverse. Gravel flew.

"Ahhhh! Oh my god! Paul! Pauuuuuuul!" Finally, he started the up and down trip through the rutted lot, driving past lines of speaker boxes on steel poles. He selected an isolated spot and threw the car into park.

"You asshole!" Cindy's hair was everywhere when the trunk was opened. They both climbed out and Laura fell in the dirt. Paul offered her a hand and she slapped it away.

"What the fuck?" she said, smoothing her hair from her face.

"C'mon, it was really fun," he teased, and she hit him hard on the arm.

"I think I'm gonna be sick."

"I'll get you a Coke. You'll feel better." Paul grinned his Cheshire grin and rubbed his arm.

We carried drinks and popcorn back to the car and settled on the hood and roof to watch the movie. Paul pulled a joint from his pocket. "Hey girls, care to partake?"

"Fuck yeah."

"Awesome."

"Lil Debs?" The paper tip blazed under a match flame in the dark. He inhaled deeply and offered it to me.

"No, thanks," I said. He shrugged and handed it to Laura.

"So Lil Debbie, how's Auntie Mary?"

"Why do you have to call me that? Why?"

"Because you're little, ssst, sssst, and you're Debbie," he hissed, holding smoke in his lungs. He passed the butt down to the waiting fingers of the girls on the hood. "Now, Auntie Mary?"

I sighed. "She's fine. Fine, I guess."

He nodded. "Right, right." He looked at the screen. "What's with all the shaking?"

"She takes pills that make her shake like that so she doesn't hear the voices."

"Oh my god! She hears voices! Oh my god!" He grabbed my shoulders and shook me.

"Cut it out. God, you're annoying." He laughed.

"Poor Auntie Mary, huh? She's like, gone. She used to be so much fun, remember? She'd sing and we'd dance around. Now she's...like a zombie or something."

I stared at the screen. "As long as she stays around. As long as she stays put," I said. He turned and looked at me.

"How was it when you left? I heard you were living with the Indians."

"Actually, I was living with the Catholics. Much more barbaric," I said.

"Seriously, what the fuck happened to you?"

I shrugged. "We spent four years in one room in a Catholic boarding house for Indian women," I said. "With a bunch of nuns."

He stared at me for a moment, his lids heavy, and then he burst out laughing. He laid back on the roof of the car and he laughed until he was doubled over and tears streamed from his eyes.

D id you have fun with Paul?" My mother bounced from foot to foot as I ate my breakfast.

"Yeah, I guess. We went to a movie."

"That poor little boy. His mother was never easy on him. I mean, Charlene is a good person. She was always so good to us, you know, but she was hard on him. He certainly has grown up now, hasn't he?" she said, heading off on her ritual walk around the room.

"Well, not ALL grown up," I muttered. "You done with the milk, Ma?" She continued to pace. "Ma? Earth to Mother." Finally I sighed, put the milk and my dishes away, and kissed her goodbye as I headed out to catch the bus.

I looked at the clock. Two-fifteen. I was wondering if time had stopped in the outside world. I felt like I was never going to get out of math class. The school secretary appeared at the door. She said something to the teacher and then called me over.

"Bring your things," she said. I closed my book, a bad feeling creeping into my gut.

"What's going on?" I asked on the quiet walk through the hall. She just turned and smiled at me. When I got to the office, Elandra was leaning on the counter, talking to my aunt Betty. They both looked at me and smiled the same weird little smile the secretary had used. Elandra signed something and ushered me out. My cousin, Cindy, hovered beyond the glass windows of the office. In the parking lot, Elandra put a hand on my shoulder, turning me to face her.

"Mom is in the hospital, Deb. I found her passed out with an empty pill bottle next to her," she said. "She's going to be okay, but they're keeping her there in case she tried to kill herself. They just want to talk to her. We're going to the hospital to see her right now. She's going to be okay, though. All right?"

I stared into her face at her big teeth. I noticed she had smudges on her glasses. A strand of hair was stuck to her lip. I nodded. My aunt and my cousin looked uncomfortable. We got into the car as Elandra got behind the wheel and my aunt climbed into the passenger seat. In the back, Cindy looked over at me and gave me a weak smile. I made my mouth smile back at her. The world rolled by the fishbowl car windows. Cardboard sets of the Piggly Wiggly and the Exxon station whizzed past, none of it real. I heard a high-pitched wail, like a siren. My aunt jerked her head toward me and I realized that the sound was coming from me. My mouth was open and I was sucking in air, producing a teakettle scream that filled the confines of the car. A thin strand of drool had escaped my lips and it clung to my chin. I closed my mouth and wiped my face. My cousin concentrated on the scenery. My eyes brimmed and my nose had started to run.

The hospital in Belen is a small, single-level building, and it looks more like a grade school than a hospital. The double glass doors have PULL written on the handles, and you actually have to pull them open yourself. I thought how tough that would be in a wheelchair. The place smells kind of musty with all that antiseptic.

My brother was in the hall and he came up and hugged Elandra. Her brown purse dangled from her hand down his back. He turned and smiled at me under his mustache.

"Hi, sis. It's okay, Mom's okay," he said, nodding nonchalantly. "She just got a little confused and took too much medicine, that's all. She's gonna be fine." He smiled wider and winked.

"Of course she's going to be fine," my aunt added.

"Let's go see if she's awake." Ben started down the hallway and we all followed after him in a loose clump.

Ma was propped up in the bed, pillows stacked under her. She was asleep, tubes snaking in all directions. I had never seen her look like that, so vulnerable and small. Mortal. My brother held her hand, but she didn't stir. He looked at me. "She's just resting. She's had a tough time."

I nodded and said I'd be outside. I walked out of the room and down the hall, away from my family. I sat in the waiting room alone. How could anyone in their right mind think she would actually try to kill herself? Did they know her at all? If she were going to do something like that, she would have done it a long time ago, when things were really crummy. Not now. Things were going pretty good now. No, if Mom was good at anything, it was keeping on. She just wouldn't quit. One foot in front of the other, no matter what. And of course, nothing is more important to her than being Catholic. That means any kind of early checkout is out of the question, especially with all that endangered mortal soul stuff.

Still, I was scared. Really scared. If it were true and someone as tough as my mom could try and kill herself, what chance did the rest of us have? I whispered something to God, something about promises, something about regrets. I had always said the same prayer for as long as I could remember. Anytime I saw that first star or found an eyelash or mumbled before slipping off to sleep, I'd ask for the same thing, for Mom to voluntarily take those stupid pills, to want to not be sick anymore. Now, I thought, maybe God had a strange sense of humor. Be careful what you wish for, huh?

And when they found her in Gallup, remember? Thank God the nuns called me. I was worried sick..." They were talking in hushed tones in my brother's kitchen. I heard him shush Isabelle.

"Well, look who's up. Morning, sleepy head," she said. I poured myself a glass of juice. Isabelle had come in on the red-eye. Judith drove in from Albuquerque, where she now lived with her boyfriend. I joined them at the table. Isabelle had the newspaper open to the classifieds. The only sound was the turning pages.

"Well, this is a perky bunch." Judith pulled a beer from the fridge and twisted the cap.

"Isn't it a little early?" my brother asked.

"Maybe for you." She took a delicate swig, pinky out. "Always four o'clock somewhere. Sure you don't want one? Put hair on your chest. Suit yourself boy-ah." She did a little dance back to the table.

She ran her fingers through my hair. "How is my little chili pequeña? Huh?" She kissed me on the cheek and sat back down with a smile and a wink.

I looked around the table at each of them. My brother looked tired and gray. Judith had a booted foot resting on her knee and was peeling the label from her bottle. Isabelle looked pressed and fresh, her thick blonde hair falling around her shoulders.

I wondered how she always managed to look like that. I hadn't slept well and I couldn't get my hair to lay down on one side. I smoothed it self-consciously.

I never could get much rest in a strange bed. Lately, I wasn't sleeping well at home either. Ma had taken to staying up all night again, keeping the lights burning and the radio and TV on, filling every square inch with noise. At least now I had my own bed, so I couldn't feel her thrash around.

I had begun to wonder if she was going to leave again. I'd sit in class and imagine what I would do if she showed up at the door. I wasn't a kid now, I could say no. But would I? Or worse, would she even come for me this time? Had I joined the ranks of the left behind, left to wait and wonder?

It never came to that, of course. Ben took her to the hospital and the doctor had sent her home with a bottle of pills. A little plastic bottle, with a white cap and a paper label. Such an innocent looking thing.

Pretty soon, breakfast got eaten and dishes got washed. Everyone dressed and put on socks and shoes and we went to the hospital again. I rode in the shiny rental car with Isabelle. We chatted about school and friends. She wanted to know if I had a boyfriend. The ride was a hundred times better than the one the day before.

This time, Mom was sitting up in bed, and there were no tubes. She smiled and she was shaking again. The rail on the side of the bed was lowered and we all hugged her.

"Hi Mom, how you feeling?" I held her hand.

"Oh, I'm all right. I wish everyone would stop making such a fuss."

"That'll be the day, when we don't fuss over our mother. Uh-huh, that's for sure." Ben winked at her.

"You didn't bring me a burger or a fish sandwich by chance? The food here is terrible."

"Well, you won't have to be in here much longer," Isabelle declared.

"Good. I'm about to go out of my mind."

After awhile, we said our goodbyes and Isabelle took me back to school, just like nothing had happened.

The girl in third period asked where I'd been. I said my sister was in town from Texas and I had to go out with my family. I got the homework from my teachers and I went home on the bus like I always did. There were moments where I would forget that it ever happened. I read my books and talked to classmates, laughing and blinking in the sun. Then I'd remember everything and the tightening in my chest would return.

I held my books in crossed arms and walked home with a slow shuffle. The bus closed its doors with a hiss and belched a black cloud before lurching back onto the rural highway. When I opened the front door, there were boxes everywhere. Isabelle was sealing a big one up with packing tape.

"Happy moving day!" she chimed out. She'd rented an apartment for us in a complex not far from my brother's house. I guess she wasn't thrilled with Mrs. Shussler's place.

The apartment complex was laid out like a motel, with a single row of continuous apartment units throughout. Across the yard, past the pool, half the property still operated as a traditional motel.

The school bus would drop me off right in front of the neon VACANCY sign. Our building was brick, with dark brown paint around the windows and doors. The grounds had whitewashed, concrete walls, which were built at crazy angles here and there, around the lot. There were four doors to the left and six doors to the right of our place. It had wall-to-wall carpet and heat in every room, along with a little weedy back yard. We had access to the pool and to the game room, and the apartment had two bedrooms.

Two bedrooms. I went into my own room and closed the door. Alone, at last.

It didn't take long to settle in to the new place. We didn't have much to unpack. Clothes, dishes. I put up a couple of posters, some drawings. I laid back on one of the twin beds in the room and surveyed my surroundings. Pretty swank.

Ma is very careful with that pill bottle now. Elandra comes by just about every day and casually checks on her. Personally, I think that waking up in that hospital scared the bejeezus out of my mother. I think she did some soul searching. Now if she starts hearing those voices, she tells my brother and she goes to the doctor and she takes her medicine. Now she's a prisoner of that medicine. She feels the drowning and the teeth-chattering tremors. Being so happy makes me feel guilty, but I'm grateful to her anyway.

She paces back and forth across the living room, bouncing on the balls of her feet, hands shaking. She walks all day long, back and forth, taking breaks to sit for a few minutes until she can't stand it anymore, and then she walks again. Well, at least she has more room now.

Is this Debbie McCarroll?" The voice on the other end of the line was soft and cheerful.

"Yes?"

"This is Julie Harris. I used to ride your bus."

"Uh...oh, really?"

"Yeah. I hear that you live off of Highway 304 now," she said. "Hello?"

"Uh, yes. Sorry, who is this again?"

"Julie Harris. I'm at my grandparent's house and they live on Fulton, not far from you. I was wondering if you'd like to come over."

"Come over?"

"Yeah, come over here."

"Sure." She gave me the address and detailed instructions and I hung up.

Now, why did I say that? I didn't even know this person. I had no idea how she knew where I lived or how she got my phone number. I didn't even know all that yet.

I put my coat on and walked the few blocks to Fulton Avenue, kicking a rock the whole way and puzzling over the situation. I rang the bell and she opened the door behind the white gravel drive. She let me in to the big house and offered me a soda. I met her grandmother, and then Julie and I went into a bedroom that I supposed was her home away from home.

"I remember you from the bus," she said. "You were real quiet, but I remember." We sat on the bed, drinks in hand.

"Huh, really?"

"Yep. You ever see me before?"

"Uh, yeah, I guess so."

"I used to ride the bus with my brother. We did a lot of yelling and fighting. He was a year older?"

"Oh yeah, I remember you now. You threw things at Melissa Chavez."

"Not anymore. I don't ride the bus anymore." She took a swig off her soda. "My brother died in a car accident," she said, matter-of-factly.

It all flashed in my memory then. Her dad owned the Sale Barn north of town, which was a livestock auction house a half mile or so from Mrs. Shussler's place. Her family was prominent in town. A photo of the large funeral crowd, along with a yearbook picture of her brother, was in the paper.

"Oh, I'm sorry," I said.

"His friend was in the car with him. He was with him when he died. He knows what his last words were, but he won't tell anyone. He won't tell me." Her face was very still. "I wish I knew what he said. I never even got to say goodbye. It's weird without him."

"I'm sorry," I offered again. She shrugged.

Then she just talked. She talked about her life, before and after him. Her parents. How she grew up. How she lived.

I stayed for a couple of hours, and then I said I had to get home. She thanked me for coming and made me promise to visit again. I said I would and I stepped out onto the brown bristled mat, which let me know I was WELCOME.

I made my way down the drive and out onto the street. When I looked back, she was still in the doorway.

Nine

LEARNING TO NAVIGATE

"What am I going to do? What the fuck am I going to do? Can you tell me? Huh?" Julie paced back and forth across her parents living room. She was wrapped in a plush purple robe, the collar turned up to her cheeks. When things got bad, it was all about the robe. Purple catharsis.

"Calm down. Whatever happens, it's not the end of the world."

She stopped and looked at me with bloodshot eyes. "Not the end of the world? Not the end of the world? You think my life wouldn't be over, I mean OVER, if I had to tell my father that I was pregnant? Is that what you think?"

"Look, all I'm saying is that anything can happen. We don't even know for sure that you're pregnant. You never know, your dad might be cool. You could maybe get married."

She came over and knelt down in front of the recliner where I was sitting. She grabbed me behind my knees and yanked me closer. "I'm sixteen years old, Debbie. Sixteen. Do you think my dad would let me get married? Do you think I WANT to get married? Huh?"

"I'm just saying." She got up and began to pace again.

"Julie, it's going to work out, one way or another. Hell, for all you know, your mom was in the same boat way back when."

"Hah! Are you kidding? She schedules her periods. "Nope, can't fit you in right now. Try me next week." The television was whispering in the background and throwing a blue strobe light around the darkened room.

"For Pete's sake, would you stop wearing a hole in the rug? You're making me tense. Come over here." She continued to walk, biting her thumbnail. "Come here!" I wriggled to one side of the chair and she slumped down into the other half.

I took her hand. "Look, you and I have been friends a long time, and I know you better than just about anyone. You're generous and kindhearted and a royal pain in the butt. Hell, your love is so big that it runs right over most people. It's bigger than life, man. So you're gonna be okay, and if you're destined to bring up a kid right now, well that's the luckiest fucking kid there is. That kid will know what it is to really be alive. To see all the good things in the world and to laugh at least two hundred times a day, and I should know, because that's what you give to me. Look, I know you're scared, but there isn't anything that you can't do, because you're Julie Harris. And you know I'm here for you, whatever you decide."

She wiped her nose and hugged me tight. "I love you, ya skinny twerp."

I saw it as soon as I opened my locker. The neatly folded square of notebook paper had been slipped through the gills of my locker door. *Debbie McCarroll* was scrawled in loopy blue felt tip. Only my family called me Debbie. And Julie, of course, but only to be annoying. The name smacks of buttoned up sweaters and flavored lip gloss.

I had been finding these notes in my locker for the past couple of weeks. They were always short and cryptic. This one said:

I think you're cute. Hint she not he. – RP

Another of the notes had said *Are you a boy or are you a girl?* and it was also signed RP.

"Guess what?" Julie skipped up behind me and muttered behind her hand. "I got my period."

"Oh, thank god. Have you told Nick?"

"I know, whew. I've never been so happy to have cramps in my life. Go cramps. Yeah, I told him. I told him to keep his hands to himself. I'm not going through that again."

"Yeah, right."

"Ho-ly shit, you got another one." She snatched the sheet of paper out of my hand. "Aren't you curious? Who is writing these damn things? It's driving me nuts."

"I don't care who's writing them," I said. "I just wish they'd leave me alone." I exchanged my history books for science and headed for biology class. Julie walked alongside, studying the note.

"Oh come on, you have to be a little flattered. You have a secret admirer. You are sooo popular."

"Creepy is what it is. You know what kind of person leaves anonymous notes? Outcasts, serial killers, the socially inept. Oh, or D, all of the above."

"Maybe this person's just shy. Besides, they're not anonymous. The notes are from RP. See?" The chipped nail polish of her index finger tapped at the chunky initials.

"I'm just saying, it's freaky. I'm shy too, you know. You don't see me dropping clandestine bullshit messages into peoples' lockers. Creep show, man."

"They're so weird though. "She not he..." What the hell does that mean? There should really be a comma after "hint." There has to be a way to find out who's doing this," she said, biting her thumbnail. Her fingers had smeared the upside down *Debbie* on the back of the note.

"Uh, don't you have English this period, and isn't that the other way?"

"Oh crap, I'll see you in Mrs. Corrigan's class." She turned and ran back down the hall, dodging loitering teenagers like a drunken linebacker.

"Hi, Mrs. McCarroll." Julie waited in the living room while I collected towels and sunscreen.

"Hello, Julie. I made some cupcakes, would you care for one?" Ma held out a plate of cupcake shaped rocks.

"Oh no, thanks, I just ate. They look great, though."

"You sure? How about some Jell-O? Would you like some Jell-O?"

"No ma'am. Thank you."

"I think I have some pudding in here. It wouldn't take a minute."

"You know what I could use is some water. I'm pretty parched."

Ma handed her a glass of water over ice. "Here you are. Feel free to take the cup to the pool. It's hot out there."

My mother's New Mexican cuisine could make you weep. It was so delicious and completely satisfying. Recipes handed down from my grandmother, tried-and-true, in her blood. Second nature. When she strayed beyond those confines, however, disaster often struck. She simply did not have the patience, nor the desire, to follow recipes or instructions on a box, feeling that cooking should be an intuitive and natural experience. It should be personal. Julie was aware of this.

"Your mom is so freaking sweet," she said, as we lounged poolside.

"She's all right, when she's not trying to poison me."

"Now that's just not nice."

"She believes that medium-rare chicken is a delicacy. "Oh, it's just a little pink, it's good food, eat it," and yet she burns every hamburger patty she makes and then plops it between two slices of white bread slathered in mayo. I don't know how many times I've told her that I don't like mayonnaise on my hamburgers, and she always says the same thing. "You don't? Since when?"

"You don't like mayo on your burger? I do."

"Not on bread. It melts because of the hot patty and soaks a neat, greasy ring into the bread. Ugh."

"Still, she's just...nice. Like when you used to hang out with that slutty girl Rhonda?"

"Hey!"

"It's true. Your mom was all "Can I get you a cookie, Rhonda?" and Rhonda's all decked out in a tube top with a pack of Camels stuffed into her hot pants. My mom would not have let that chick into our house."

"Yeah well, Rhonda never had anything but the nicest of things to say about you."

"Oh, you didn't even know me then."

"God, you have skin like the belly of a fish."

Julie shot me an evil eye as she rubbed sun block on her pale legs. "I prefer to think of myself as porcelain, thank you very much. Not all of us have that swarthy thing going, so shut up." She replaced her sunglasses and leaned back in her lounge chair. "How's Mike?"

"Good. I'll see him again next weekend."

"Who'da thunk a skinny twerp like you would be going out with a college man?"

"Didn't you know? Mature guys prefer a more slender physique as opposed to the, shall we say, full-figured gals like yourself."

"Oh-ho, touché!"

The glare on the white concrete around the pool was blinding. I laid back and covered my eyes with the corner of a towel. "What's the story with Melissa? I heard you were on her lawn screaming at her house." Julie shifted in my direction.

"Who told you that?"

"I just heard somebody talking in the hall. I don't know who it was."

"Can you believe it? That bitch was talking about me behind my back. I told her that if she had something to say, she should say it to my face. I told her I was going to have a talk with her after school so she went home early. I marched right down to her house. Chicken shit, I saw her peek out of her front window, so I yelled at her to come out and face me. She just cowered inside."

"Where were her parents?"

"I don't know."

"Mmm, you probably scared them too. You are so mean."

"What? That chick had it coming."

"It was a little extreme, don't you think? Screaming at the house from the front lawn? And what about Alicia Strong? You absolutely torture her."

"She's an idiot. That ugly pig comes on to Nick right in front of me."

"Well, I feel sorry for her. She's probably lonely."

"Yeah well, she brings it on herself."

"What about Diane? You bloodied her mouth in gym."

"It was a wrestling exercise!"

"Yeah, I saw it. It was more like assault. Nobody else would get on the mat with you after that."

"What can I tell you? I'm a strong competitor."

"When you talk, do you hear what comes out of your mouth?"

The gate at the end of the pool clanged shut and my sister Judith strolled toward us wearing a terry shortie and a pair of daisy flip-flops.

"Oh boy." Julie opened a magazine and pretended to read.

"Ohhhh, yessss." Judith removed her robe and sank into the recliner next to me. She was wearing a bikini basically made out of dental floss. "Can you help me here?" She handed me the tanning oil. I greased up her back and handed the bottle back. The smell of coconut and chlorine perfumed the air.

"Hello, Judith. How are you?" Julie said sweetly, flipping through her magazine.

My sister was reclined with one shiny knee delicately crooked. Her sunglasses were large and opaque on her face. She slowly turned them on Julie and lined her up in the lenses. "Just...fine," she said, finally. Then she turned her face back to the sun.

"How's school, pequeña?" My sister's knee had started to sway slightly.

"Good, I guess, I..."

"Oh damn. I forgot my beer."

"I don't think you can have alcohol around the pool," Julie offered.

"I don't think I was talking to you." The knee stopped moving.

"What is your problem with me, exactly? You've never liked me." Julie slapped the magazine onto the concrete. "What did I ever do to you to make you hate me so much?"

My sister swung her legs over the side of the lounger and sat up. "I don't care about you enough to hate you," she said, and she dropped her glasses onto her outstretched towel and dove into the pool.

Julie shook her head with a smirk and picked up her magazine.

I was in art class at Belen High. I was parked at one of the long folding tables with a handful of other displaced students. The class was mostly a clearing house for kids that were failing everything else. The stoners, the Special Ed kids, the jocks that needed to maintain their average with an easy class. We all sat in creaky folding chairs, our canvas boards and palettes gooped up with blooms of smeared paint. Julie only took it so that we'd have a class together. She didn't need it, Honor Society Type A that she was.

"Arrghhh!" Her board was mostly brown with streaks of green and blue. "How the hell are you supposed to do this? It all goes to mud."

"What's it supposed to be?"

"A meadow."

"Oh, wow."

Guy Hernandez leaned in, his ear inches from my face. "Looks more like a swamp." He was wearing a faded army shirt with the arms torn off. He reeked of pot smoke.

"Shut up, idiot. It's not like you're any Picasso." He was painting a dragon playing an electric guitar with fire shooting from the strings.

"No, YOU are more like Picasso. You can't tell what the fuck it is," he countered.

Julie sat stewing, arms at her sides. Then she wound up and frogged me hard on my left arm.

"Ow, what the hell!" I rubbed my arm, feeling the bruise already forming. "I didn't say anything!"

"I couldn't reach him."

"Girls! What is going on?" Mrs. Corrigan was sitting at her desk in her usual magenta tie-dyed lab coat. "Am I going to have to ask you girls to leave?"

Footsteps echoed on the stairs beyond the open door and Gloria Fidel strolled into the classroom. Short, slouchy Gloria Fidel. She was a year behind us, and I'd never exchanged so much as a single word with her. She walked over to me and offered up a neatly folded note with the same "Debbie Mc-Carroll" from the other notes scrawled in blue felt tip.

"Someone told me to give this to you," she mumbled. I looked around the room. All eyes were on me.

I stared down at the blue-lined paper clutched in her hand. Finally, she put it down in front of me and walked out.

"What is it?" Guy asked. I reached across the table and picked up the folded piece of paper.

I glanced at Julie. Her eyes were big, pinned to the note as I unfolded it.

Go to the 7:00 p.m. movie at the Oñate Theater tonight. There will be a ticket waiting for you at the box office. Go to the seventh row from the back and sit in the aisle chair on the left. – RP

"Holy shit!" Julie had been reading it with me. "Who is doing this? Are you going to go? Holy shit!" I looked up at Mrs. Corrigan. She had forgotten all about us and was engrossed in a paperback novel.

"What does it say?" Guy said, craning his neck. I folded the note back up.

"Nothing. It doesn't say anything. It doesn't matter anyway." I put the note in my pocket and picked up my paint brush.

"Are you gonna go?" Julie whispered in my ear.

"No," I answered.

You about ready to go, Ma?" I was so excited I was about to jump out of my skin. It was a beautiful day, all sunshine and soft breezes, and I was going to drive my mother to my grandmother's house. In my very own car. Isabelle had arranged to have the compact delivered to my brother. He'd shown up asking if I could go to the store for him, and then he'd dropped the keys in my hand.

"Deborah, are you sure you can do this? Maybe you should practice some more."

"Mother, I have my driver's license. I can do it, I promise. Come on, it'll be great. You want to see Gramma, don't you?"

"All right then. Let me get my purse."

We cruised the two-lane highway that led to my grandmother's house, fields and orchards in bloom, tender and green. The best of spring, unfolding and splendid. I adjusted the air conditioning and set the radio. Mother sat staring straight ahead, fingers moving in her lap.

"It's beautiful isn't it, Ma? Isn't it beautiful?"

She stopped then and looked out the window. "What?"

"Everything!"

"You know, Mother, I think I've definitely settled on art. I want to go to art school, I think."

"Art school? That's all we need."

"What? I've always been good at art."

"Well sure, but how do you make a living? Just take typing, whatever you do. Just please take typing."

I drove by the house we lived in next to the water tower and parked the car at the curb. The cannon still sat across the street, but now it just looked silly. Forged steel and heavy artillery, guarding the school lawn. The house sagged, looking small and decayed.

"Jeeze, it's tiny. Does it look tiny to you, Ma?" She sat still, staring out the windshield.

"Ma!"

"What?" I crooked my head in the direction of the house.

"Oh, what are we doing here?"

"I wanted to see it. It's been a long time."

"That's all in the past. Why would you want to dig that up?"

"I don't know. It's nice to go back sometimes. Remember where you came from. I have such strong memories of this house. Remember the back yard? When you'd cook back there? Remember Kalina?"

"I remember. I thought we were going to Gramma's."

"Okay, okay. Sheesh, what a grouch." I took one last look at the sad little house and put the car in gear.

"You're sure not big on memory lane, are you Ma? You never talk about your past, how you grew up. You never talk about anything, really."

"What's the point?"

"There doesn't have to be a point. People usually talk about things. Like I'd say something like "Oh Mom, remember that old house and how you'd read to me?" and then you'd say something like, "Yes, Q.T. Those were hard times, but we all had each other, and it made us stronger." Something like that."

"Oh brother," she said.

I took the long way to round to my grandmother's house, savoring the freedom and sheer slipperiness of the steering wheel. Finally, we pulled off the blacktop and onto the dirt road that led to her property. I could see the squat structure in the distance, a canopy of trees shading the front yard.

"Look Ma, we're almost..." That was when ground disappeared from under the car and I saw my mother literally hit the roof. I bit down hard, my teeth clacking together. I had driven completely off of the road that bridged the railroad tracks and we'd fallen a good eight inches or so into the space between the steel rails.

"It's okay, it's okay," I panted. "How you doin, Ma?"

"What happened?"

"We fell off the road."

"Oh, for heaven's sake!"

"It's okay, we're almost there. No big deal."

"My head hurts."

"I just have to get back up on the road. It might be a little bumpy."

"A little bumpy?"

"It's okay!"

I tried to drive forward but the back wheels spun. I put the car in reverse until the front tire hit the back rail, then I put the car in drive and gunned it. We shot forward and bounded over the rail, my mother bouncing out of her seat twice, once when the front wheels cleared the steel and again when the back wheels bumped up and over. Gravel flew as I forced the car back up onto the road.

The short, rutted drive to the front steps was comparatively smooth. I pulled up to the house and killed the engine. "There, see? No problem."

"Let me out of this car." She fumbled with the belt and bolted to my grandmother's porch.

"You're going to have to drive home with me, ya know!" She disappeared into the house and slammed the door behind her.

The phone rang during *The Carol Burnett Show*. Ma was in the kitchen cleaning up dinner dishes. "You're missing it, Ma!" I padded over to the phone as Carol was fielding a question from the studio audience. "Mmyello," I chirped.

"How come you didn't go to the theater?"

"Who is this?"

After a bit of scuffling, she said, "Gloria."

"Why are you doing this to me? Why can't you just leave me alone?"

"What do you mean? We're not doing anything." There was a pause as she covered the mouthpiece. I heard faint murmuring and a commotion before she came back on the line. "Besides, we like you. We think you're cool."

"What are you talking about?" I said. "You don't even know me." More murmuring.

"Well, you know, you're a senior and that's cool. Besides, we've seen you around. We know you. We know you and...we think you're cool."

"Look," I said, "Don't call me again. And stop leaving notes in my locker. Forget about me. Forget that you think I'm cool or whatever it is you think and leave me alone. Okay? Please. Please, can you do that for me? Now good night." I set the phone back in the cradle. My ears were hot and my mouth felt like an old sock. When I plopped back on the couch, Carol and Julie Andrews were singing *Anything You Can Do, I Can Do Better.*

"Who was that?" Ma was wiping her hands on a dish towel as she sat down next to me.

"Nobody. Wrong number."

My mother smiled at the television. "Ooo, Julie Andrews. I just love her."

"Hand me that chisel there, would you?" Mr. Murray had taken the back door off its hinges and it leaned against a pair of weathered saw horses. The door had been sticky with the mild weather. He tapped the chisel with a ball peen hammer that looked like it came over on the Mayflower.

"Gotcha." He picked away the splintered remnants of a knot with a thick thumbnail. "Ever use one of these?" He held up a beautiful old plane. The handle was the color of blood and worn shiny where the meat of the palm made contact.

"Not like that one," I said. "I took some woodshop, but all those tools were brand new. That one's a beaut."

"Give 'er a try." He turned the handle my way.

"You don't think I'll mess it up?"

"Naw, you got shop experience, don't you? Good enough for me," he winked.

I braced myself and ran the plane down the edge of the door. It moved, smooth as glass, blonde curls of fresh pine corkscrewed behind it.

"Wow. It cuts like butter."

"Take care of a tool and it'll take care of you. I like the way you work it. You let the blade do its job without forcing. I've seen experienced carpenters don't use a plane that good." He pulled out a blue handkerchief from the pocket of his overalls and wiped his face down. "What'd you build in shop?"

"Well, we started with simple stuff–bird house, paper towel holder, that kind of thing. But we got to pick our final project and I made a coffee table and end table for my brother."

"Don't say? How'd you do?"

"Looked pretty good, I thought. I used dovetail joints and I routered the edges and everything."

He whistled through his teeth. "Nice. Lot of girls in that class?"

"Me and one other. I have to fix stuff around here, you know. Drawers don't work right or shelves need putting up. Thought I should know how to work things."

He neatly folded his handkerchief and burrowed it back in his pocket. "You and your mom, you been alone for a long time, huh?"

"Long time," I said.

He nodded. "I've never met anyone like her, your mother."

"Me neither."

"She's tough as nails, but a kinder soul never walked this Earth." I nodded. "You take care of her, huh?"

"I'll try, Mr. Murray."

"Oh hey, I almost forgot. I don't know if you even want this sort anymore." He reached in his pocket and handed me a fine clear crystal, fiery and sparkling in the sun.

"Wow, that's a nice hunk of quartz. Are you sure you want to give that up?"

"If you're willing to take it. You still collect?"

"Absolutely. I don't have anything as nice as this, though. It's beautiful. Thank you so much."

"Well, it's good to have somebody to share them with. This old Earth, she cooks up some gorgeous dishes, don't she?"

"Oh, here's where the party is." Judith leaned out the screen door. "Hi, Mr. Murray. I'm going to steal her away for a little bit, if that's okay. Debbie, I have something for you." I followed her back into the house and left Mr. Murray to his work.

My sister had her arm around my shoulder and she leaned in to my ear. "Think he's trying to get in Mom's undies?"

"No way! God!"

"I'll bet," she leered.

She plopped down on my bed and nudged a box toward me. I flipped the top off of a buttery pair of dingo boots the color of caramel candy. "Oh, yes! Thank you, thank you. I love them. Just like yours, huh? How did you know?" I gave her a squeeze and sat on the opposite bed to kick off my shoes.

"Oh please, like you haven't been hinting." She leaned back on her elbows and crossed her ankles, studying the drawings and posters on my walls. "Why do you think musicians dress so weird?"

I followed her gaze as I pulled the cuffs of my jeans out of the boots. A group of five musicians were posed in satin and feathered finery with plush hats and platform shoes. "I don't know. I guess when all you do is pull feelings out of the air and spin them into stories, maybe it does something to you. Like Alice and the looking glass."

"Oh, how deep. Don't get weird on me, little girl. You're still the same scrounge with the tangled hair, marching down the sidewalk and eating the PB&J that you pulled out of the garbage can."

"Do you have to bring that up every time you see me? God, you love that story."

"I do. I really do."

She laid back and stretched. "I like your drawings. Is that what you're going to do? I mean, you know, for a living?"

"I hope so. I'm looking at schools now. I get pictures in my head and it's so frustrating when I can't get them down on the paper." I sat down next to her. "Sometimes I get so mad that I throw the pen across the room and tear up the paper." I breathed a little laugh. "It's getting easier, though. I hope school will help."

"Man, I hated school. I had the same classes Isabelle had a year earlier and all the teachers were like "You're Isabelle's sister? Really?" Shit, I couldn't wait to get the hell out of Dodge. What's the story with that hole in the hallway wall there?"

"Oh uh, Ma has her good days and her bad days. That was a bad day."

"What happened?"

"She threw the scissors."

"I thought the meds were supposed to control that."

I shrugged. "It happens, but just every once in awhile."

"Must be nice to have your own room, huh?"

"You have no idea."

"Do you ever think about it? About becoming sick like that?"

"I used to. I used to monitor myself all the time. But I read somewhere that it skips a generation. And one time I heard one of the aunts whispering about Grandma's aunt or something like that. Anyway, I decided there were better things to worry about."

She stared up at the ceiling. "I think about it. I do. Sometimes, when I think I'm going crazy, I think I'm really going crazy. Know what I mean?"

I closed my locker door to find Julie standing behind it. "Jesus Christ, could you maybe give me an actual heart attack next time?"

"I know who wrote the notes." She was the picture of the cat that swallowed the canary.

"Not this again," I said, as I closed the door.

"Yes, this again. Maybe you didn't hear me. I know who wrote the notes."

"How?"

"Well, I figured since RP was friends with Gloria Fidel, RP was most likely a junior, so I asked my aunt Ginnie–school secretary–if I could help out in the office. During lunch, I peeked in the files for all the eleventh grade students with the initials RP. There were only a handful, so I then went to each person's math class and asked to help grade papers."

"My, but you're helpful."

"I know it. As I was saying, I went to their classes and compared the handwriting on the tests to all the RPs from the files until I found one that matched. I know who RP is."

I braked and a boy in thick glasses bumped me from behind. He muttered a "sorry" before moving around.

"There's really something wrong with you, you know that? Get help. I say it as a friend."

"What? Are you telling me you aren't the least bit curious?"

"Okay, fine. I'm curious. Who is it?"

"Say "Pretty please.""

I gritted my teeth. "Pretty please."

"With sugar on top."

"Julie!"

"It's Betty Preston. Her full name is Roberta. Roberta Preston. RP is a girrrrl!" Her voice rose to a squeal and she hopped, just a little. "Plus, Gloria Fidel hangs around with her, so that clinches it."

"What? No, that can't be right. You made a mistake."

"No mistake, missy."

"B-but why? I don't even know that girl."

"Well, I don't know, but she's the one that's been sending you all those little messages. She loooves you."

"Huh," I said, and I started for my next class.

"Huh. That's all you have to say? Huh? I put a lot of time and effort into this. You could show a little enthusiasm. What are you going to do?"

"Well, there's nothing to do, really. I mean the notes have stopped, right? And you know...it's really sad when you think about it."

"What are you talking about?"

"Well, I mean that must be so hard. A hard way to live, I mean. Always having to hide. Sneaking around. Can you imagine? Must be so lonely."

"God, you ruin everything."

Ten

ARE WE THERE YET?

"Come on, let me come over. It can't be that bad. Besides, I have pictures. You gotta see some of these bozos in their caps and gowns." One day after graduation, advancing armies of chicken pox marched across the visible skin peeking from the end of my pajama sleeves. I strained to hear Jules as I held the phone away from my ear while trying to keep Calamine lotion from clogging up the little holes.

"Tempting, but no. I haven't bathed in days and I have open weeping sores on every inch of me–including on my scalp and in my ears–not to mention the pink goo caked in every crevice. Are you seriously saying that is something you want to experience?"

"Doesn't bother me, I've had the chickenpox. Besides, we don't have much time left together."

"God, don't bring that up," I sighed. "Tell you what. I'll get myself cleaned up and we'll spend all day tomorrow to-gether, okay?"

"Oh, all right, you big baby. I'll be over there at nine in the morning and you better be up. I'll bring breakfast."

"Your sympathy during my time of need is underwhelming. See you tomorrow."

"*She's my sweetie, yes she is, she's my sweetie that I looooove.*" My mother sang her way into my room carrying a tray. "Don't scratch, Q.T., they'll scar."

"Easy for you to say."

"You poor thing. I brought you a snack."

"Thanks, Ma."

She put the dishes on the bedside table and touched my forehead, sweeping my bangs back from my face. "Well, your fever seems to be all gone. You must be feeling better."

I smoothed my hair back over my forehead to hide as many of the pox as possible. "I guess. It's just all so gross though."

"Well, it'll get better now. Do you feel bad about missing your graduation?"

"Naw. I was afraid of falling on my face, anyway. It's probably all for the best."

She sat down on the bed next to me. "You know, I had the chickenpox when I was a girl. I remember having to wear mittens on my hands so I wouldn't scratch."

"You were actually a little girl? I don't believe it."

She looked indignant. "Well, of course I was."

"I'll bet you carried a purse, even then, and wore your pearls to school."

"Oh, we were far too poor for any of that. It was all Mother could do to keep us all clothed."

My mother rarely talked about her past and almost never went to a time that she didn't have children of her own. I tried to conjure a picture of her as a child, but could get no further than a black and white image of bare feet and a gingham dress.

I shook my head. "I just can't imagine it. What were you like?"

"Well, I don't know. I was the oldest and there were so many of us, so I suppose I was always feeling like I needed to take care of something. We lived in the mountains, you know, and my dad was a logger. He had an old truck and we'd bounce around in the back on those rutted roads. There weren't any cars back in those days, so those roads were all pitted from the wagon wheels. Oh, how I loved the smell of all that green. My sisters and I would pick flowers and piñion. I miss it sometimes. It was a hard life though."

I realized I was holding my breath. This was more than my mother had ever talked about herself. "I could take you, Ma. I could take you up to the mountains. We could go if you want to."

"What? Are you kidding? Could you just see me hobbling around a mountain? That was a long time ago, Q.T. I wouldn't know what to do up there now." She shook her head. "Why don't you have a bath? You'll feel better. I think it'd be all right now that your fever's down."

She smoothed my hair away from my face and gave me a smile on her way out. I watched the empty doorway, wanting to call out for her to come back. Come back and tell me more about another time. A time before her demons engulfed her and the slender thread of medication kept her tethered to us. I bit my lip and finger combed my bangs back down over my forehead.

I answered the door the next morning to find Julie standing on the stoop, a paper bag in her hand. "Yeah, you like like crap," she said.

"Whatcha got? I'm starving."

We had our breakfast alongside the duck pond that was cut into the golf course bordering our Del Rio Apartment property. The morning was still cool and heavy with that smell of possibility that every new morning brings. We laughed and talked easily, savoring each other's company and feeling the thick history between us.

"...and when I went up there and picked up that damn piece of paper, I looked out there, knowing you weren't..." Her voice caught and tears began to spill down her cheeks. She pulled a paper napkin from the bag and dabbed at her eyes. "Just watch me get knocked in the head with a golf ball. That would be the cherry on top," she sniffed.

"Naw, there's usually no one out this early on a weekday."

She nodded, rearranging the soggy bit of white in her hands. "I can't believe it. I can't believe you're really leaving."

"I know. Me neither. But hey, I'll be back for your wedding this summer, right? You'll be so busy planning it that the time will fly."

"It doesn't matter. You know it doesn't. Nothing will ever be the same again. We'll keep in touch at first, but eventually, we won't even talk anymore. You know, you helped me get through the lowest point of my life. I was more screwed up than I even realized, just so angry. I mean, I felt this rage all the time. I don't know what I would have done without you."

"First of all, of course we'll talk. You're the best friend I've ever had, dumbass. And you know, it won't be the same, but it'll be okay. You'll go to school and have a family and great things will happen to you. And this thing here won't be the same, but it will just grow into something else. Something just as strong. You have great things to do. And your big mouth will reach to Houston to tell me all about it." I concentrated on the handfuls of grass I was pulling. "I'm going to miss you. And I'm scared about that, so I really don't want to think about it right now. I just want to concentrate on the fact that we'll talk on the phone all the time and I'll be back in a few months. Okay? Can we do that?"

She sniffed and nodded. She breathed in deep and shuddered out a sigh. One of the ducks in the water made a ruckus chasing off a rival.

"Here's something, though."

"Yeah?"

"What made you call me that first day? You know, when you were at your grandmother's? I mean, you didn't even know me."

"I have no idea. I just remember feeling like I had to talk to you. I looked up your number and dialed without even thinking about it. I HAD to talk to you." She turned her bloodshot eyes on me. "I guess you and me were just meant to be."

The air was musty and stifling in the darkened room. I blinked, trying to think where I was. Ma was snoring lightly in the bed next to mine.

The hotel room smelled of smoke and disinfectant and the sheet chafed. I got up with a rustle and moved through the stale air of past occupants. I relieved myself and looked in the bathroom mirror. The ticking white light overhead made me look like something on a slab in a morgue. I pulled my lower lids down and made a corpse face at myself. The faucet dripped in the quiet. I wet my hands and ran them through my hair, trying to smooth the shelf on the left side of my head.

Mom and I were following a line drawn on a map in yellow highlighter pen. The line ran from the lonesome little dot of Belen, New Mexico to the elaborate webbing that surrounded the big capital letters of HOUSTON, TEXAS. We had driven all the previous day, stopping at a truck stop for beefy burgers and fries, a pathetic little museum where I had bought a phony Indian headdress, and finally at a cheap motel outside of El Paso.

We took our time, pausing often to look through souvenir shops and roadside attractions (Toilet Seat Rock, World's Largest Navajo Trading Post–See Fry Bread Being Made!). In Truth or Consequences, I'd parked near the weathered door of a deserted shop where I'd found a very good chunk of smoky quartz, heavy and sharp as black ice. The place was dim and quiet, smelling of cobwebs. I wondered about the woman that sold me dusty candy bars all those years ago. I wondered if her wounds ever scarred over. If she ever cleared those shelves.

Through the following days, Ma sat in the seat beside me, quiet and unfocused as we followed the asphalt through juniper, stretching as far as the eye could see. At rest stops and gas stations along the way, she'd pace and stretch and flutter her hands out in the open like birds escaping a cage.

It was an odd feeling to be at the wheel, speeding through the same parched landscape that had passed so slowly, so painfully, when I was a child. As every hill rose before us, I'd picture the two dotted figures at the top of the rise growing larger until finally, we'd fly past them, whipping at their clothing and sending a hot trail of wind to water their eyes and remind them of their misery.

This pile of steel and glass had put me in league with the desert. Friends after all, it seemed. When the school day was done, I would pack a couple of chicken legs and a bottle of orange soda and I'd drive out into the loneliness until there was nothing but the whistling wind. I would sit on the roof of the car, chewing my dinner to the bone as the sun melted into the mesas. Then I'd drive home in the dark, feeling every bit the tempest, blowing fast and free. The ride could be peaceful or savage, windows flung open and the gale bullying me, as I screamed and howled until I was breathless.

To fill the tank, Julie and I took a part-time job at the flower shop on River Road, Jean's Flowers. Mainly we made deliveries in the shop's old, white van. "Don't break the mums, they'll milk," Jean would rasp at us. She appeared to be in her late fifties, dry humored and craggy. She was slim, her face deeply lined. Her hair was white and pinned with rows of bronze bobby pins. She chain smoked and her voice was coarse as dark sandpaper. She was never without the long cigarette dangling from her lips. It bounced crazily when she spoke, causing her to sometimes close one eye to shelter the tender surface against a tendril of smoke. She frequently had ash scattered across the work table and the front of her blouse. She was stern and fair, and she always paid us in cash.

I pulled what remained of the money I'd squirreled away from the delivery job out of my pants pocket. Fifty six dollars and fifty two cents.

I finished brushing my teeth, took one more pass at gluing my hair into place, and flicked off the light. My mother was up and digging in her suitcase.

"Morning, Ma," I said.

"Good morning, Q.T. What time is it?"

"Almost nine. How'd you sleep?"

"Like the dead. I feel a little groggy still. I need some water on my face."

While she prepared for the day in the dismal bathroom, I mapped out the route ahead. I traced my finger along the yellow line, reciting the turns to myself, trying to commit them to memory. Ma was a useless navigator. Every question sent her into a panic. It was easy enough to pull over and consult the map anyway. Best to let her rest, to soak up the day at her pace.

We packed up our toothbrushes and rumpled clothes from the previous day and got back on the road. The landscape flattened out and green crept into the moving picture out the windows. Fields of emerald corn and beans spread out like giant quilts for miles. We passed the time talking or singing with the radio, laughing when we didn't know the words. She sang ahead of the lyrics, hurrying the melody and trilling ahead, as if she just couldn't wait to get it out. She'd sing the hymns in Mass like that too, her voice cutting right through the dull chorus of congregational voices. It used to embarrass me when I was younger, but now I think it's a scream.

She was sitting in the passenger seat, chatting easily as the radio played softly. "I'm going to miss my mother," she said. "Who knows how many years she has left? God bless her." Ma was nineteen when she developed her illness. My grandmother was a traditional and grand Spanish lady. She had no idea what to make of my mother's behavior. Talk of demons and possession flew through the family. Ultimately, Ma left my grandmother's house. Whether to save her mother the embarrassment or because she was forced to go, Ma would never say.

"And my sisters. Oh, I'm going to miss my sisters."

"Well, you didn't see them much anyway."

"Still, I knew they were there. Bugles came over once in a while."

"Yeah, a little lunch, a little voodoo."

"Oh, Deborah."

My Aunt Helen developed the nickname Bugles because she used to go crazy for Bugles corn snacks when she was a kid. After Ma's overdose, she took my mother to a Santeria priest. When Isabelle found out about it she went ballistic, saying that was the last thing Mother needed. I thought it was sweet of my aunt to try and help, however unconventionally.

"What happened in that little session?" I said.

"What session?"

"You know, the Santeria thing."

"Oh." She rolled her eyes. "We went to someone's house and I sat in a man's kitchen while he burned candles and something smoked in a bowl. He chanted something or other. He shook a dead chicken around me and put some blood on my forehead."

"Holy cow, I can't believe you put up with all of that."

She shrugged. "I didn't want to disappoint Bugles. She seemed so excited about it."

We finally laid eyes on the lights of Houston after a long day in the car, the city glittering under a hazy orange-tinted sky. The buildings towered over the freeway and I could see the car reflected in mirrored windows as we zoomed past. My face flashed in the shiny panels like individual frames in a strip of film.

We stopped at a McDonald's, stretching and unfolding stiff legs. I called Isabelle and got directions to her house. I took a wrong turn and had to trace my way back through the suburbs, where every street looked identical to the last. By the time we pulled into the long driveway past the manicured lawn, Mom and I were both exhausted and relieved.

Isabelle materialized from the back gate, beaming and embracing my mother tightly. Her husband, Mark, carried our bags into the house and they all disappeared in the doorway, leaving a yellow wedge of light spilling out onto the back step.

I looked up at the hazy orange sky and listened to the drone of strange insects. The air was thick and damp, a slight breeze moving through the palm trees. I took a deep breath and followed my family inside.

My mother had always been a quiet force in my life, an undercurrent that hummed and pulsed behind each and every moment. A protector and compass, constant as the morning star and as taken for granted as the ground I walked.

Even as she was taken away, it was her absence I had grieved, not the prospect that she would not return, because I knew she always would.

Now, as I sat on the funny little bumper pool table in my sister's house, I studied my mother. I watched her wear a brand new path into Isabelle's living room rug. She stared ahead, her eyes so much like my own, fixed and serious. Each step was careful and deliberate, as if counted, and when she turned at the end of the course, she always turned with the same number of steps and the same amount of effort. Each time she completed a stride, I would send the red billiard ball in my hand spinning across the green felt. It would hit the far bumper and return to my waiting hand. She would walk and I would roll the ball, catch it, send it again, all the while committing each movement and inflection of her to memory. For the first time, I noticed the lines around her eyes and soft flesh at her jawline. For the first time, I noticed my mother's aging. I was so lost in my discovery of her that when she spoke I started.

"You know what we ought to do?" she said.

"What? What, Ma?"

"We should take a walk. Look around a little. We've been here two days and I don't even know where the grocery store is."

"All right." I caught the ball and sent it for a final spin. "Let me get my shoes."

All the houses looked alike, cookie-cutter and unexceptional. Different colored bricks occasionally cropped up in one house or another. Perhaps a driveway curved in a different direction, but on the whole, the lots were interchangeable. "A good place to raise kids," everyone would say.

"What you think, Ma?"

"About what?"

I spread out my hand. "The neighborhood, the weather...I don't know. What do you think about things?"

"Pretty nice. These people seem to have good lives."

"You don't think it's all a little "Stepford?" All the houses

look the same and all the lawns are clipped the same and
all the driveways sweep around to the same two-car garage.
Nothing terribly unique. No identity."

"Well, there are a lot worse things than that, Q.T. I think
it's a lovely neighborhood."

"What is that, Ma? What does that mean, that Q.T.?
How'd you come up with that?"

"Well, it's just short for Cutie."

"Mom, Cutie is short for Cutie. Q.T. isn't any shorter."

"Seems shorter to me."

"Oookay."

We walked past the groomed lawns and the rows of tennis
courts, past the park with gleaming jungle gyms and vacant
swings, until there were no more finished houses. Fields of
turned earth stood dark and fresh, waiting for men in hard
hats to pour cement into foundations that would sprout into
more trim brick houses, safe from any wolves looking to huff
and puff. The new concrete road turned right and threaded
eventually to the freeway beyond.

"Guess we should head back, huh?" I said.

She stood gazing at the slender horizon, as if reading smoke
signals on the slip of a freeway beyond, tiny cars speeding the
length of it. She took a step forward.

"Mom?" She swallowed. "Mom!"

She turned and focused on me. "Yes, I guess we should go
back," she said.

Laughter bubbled out of me and I bent to rest my hands on
my knees. "Okay. Great. Great. Maybe tomorrow we'll go the
other direction. See if the grocery store's that way, right?"

Eleven

B . F . F .

The smell of coffee and bacon permeated the cotton in my head as I opened my eyes to the early morning Texas sunshine in my window. I groaned and buried my head back under the covers. There was a soft knock on the door.

"Q.T., you're going to be late."

"I'm up," I said, in pain at the thought of leaving the warmth of the bed. I sat up and rubbed my eyes. Another day, another dollar unearned. I stretched, scratched, and headed for the shower.

Half an hour later, I emerged from the steamy bathroom smelling–according to the shampoo bottle–like a meadow after a spring rain. I searched for clean matching socks, made myself relatively presentable, and grabbed my portfolio from the hall closet.

"Gotta go Ma, I'm late." I grabbed a slice of bacon and a soda.

"Deborah, let me make you a proper breakfast. It's bad for your digestion to go racing around like that. At least have some juice." I hitched the strap of my thirty pound bag further up my shoulder and gave her a drive-by peck on the cheek.

I popped the top on the can and took a swig, passing the sparsely decorated Christmas tree, which was favoring its left side. "It's the breakfast of champs, Mom," I said. "Love."

"Love," she answered, following me into the living room.

"Q.T., at least...where is the glass to my coffee table?" She looked at the gaping hole in the middle of the table squatting in front of the sofa.

"Oh. Yeah, I need it for a school project. Photography."

"Deborah June, you put that back right this minute."

"I need it, Ma. Please?" I clasped my hands together. "I'll bring it back safe and sound this afternoon, I promise. Oh man, I'm late. Kiss, kiss."

"You couldn't go into banking," she muttered as the door closed.

The sun warmed my bare arms as I negotiated my way out of the small patio, kicking the gate shut with a pirouette. It was hard to get into the Christmas spirit with the sunshine and palm trees looking like a travel postcard. Wish You Were Here. Back in New Mexico, there'd be a layer of snow to scrape off the windshield. I climbed in the car and hit the air conditioning.

My hatchback bumped onto the school parking lot, tires screeching on asphalt. I grabbed my portfolio, locked up the car, and raced for the door.

As I slipped in through the back door of the drab upstairs classroom, Mr. Grayson was writing on the board, his back to the class.

"Ah, I take it Ms. McCarroll has finally made it in according to her own personal schedule," he said, turning slightly to glance at me. "Please do me the honor of seeing me after class, Ms. McCarroll." Tittering bounced around the room and I slumped into my seat.

After the last bell I got a thorough chewing out for being late. Again. Blah, blah, blah, potential. Blah, blah, blah, won't be tolerated. I'd gotten it all before and I felt bad about it. I really did. And every time I got this little speech, I put the proverbial nose to the grindstone, only to slide back into my lax ways in a week or two. Somewhere in the back of my mind, I always heard my mother say, "You look tired. Are you getting enough sleep? My poor baby."

And of course, hanging out with my friend Beth didn't help. She was reclined on the floor in the hallway outside. The Design students generally reclined along the walls of the corridor, working on homework or just wasting time in torn jeans and rumpled t-shirts. The Fashion students stared at us in disgust as they clattered by in high heels and sculpted hair-don'ts. The Industrial Design students usually stayed downstairs, and their pants tended to ride at a length that exposed their ankles.

Beth was the exception, of course. Beth was a work of art unto herself, and she didn't fit a student profile. Today's ensemble consisted of a black miniskirt, white tights, a pink half-shirt with suspenders, and high-top Chuck Taylor Converse tennis shoes, one pink and one red. She had a cigarette behind each ear and she offered one up to me in a "Ta-Da" gesture.

"Ah, you know, Ms. McCarroll, if you are going to continue to be tardy, you're going to have to buy your own goddamn cigarettes," she offered in a nasal tone. Her gangly legs stretched halfway across the floor. She pursed her lips, gripping the filter. It bobbed from the right side of her mouth.

I held my sides in mock laughter. "Oh God, please stop." I dabbed the corners of my eyes with the heel of my palm. "You really should take that on the road. Don't quit your day job though. Oh wait, you don't have a day job. You mooch off your parents." I grabbed her outstretched hand and pulled her to her feet.

"No, but I give a pretty good BLOW job, though," she said, eyes wide with a kind of "get it?" look on her face.

Beth Rathstetter was a good six inches taller than me, and she was a good looking girl. She had silky, dark brown hair that spiked softly all over her head. She had legs that went on forever and she had big boobs. She would have been too pretty for me to hang around with if it weren't for her goofy sense of style and an inherent gawkiness that filtered into her walk. She had a long, bouncy stride and she'd go up on her toes at the end of it like a stork in a Loony Tunes cartoon.

"Leppy, I'm starving. Can't you get to class on time? I've been growing old out here waiting for your little lecture to conclude."

I first encountered Beth in my Life Drawing class, a class where painfully ugly people get paid a pittance to take off their clothes and sit still while a bunch of jerky students struggle not to draw the genitalia in too much detail.

As I myself was struggling with the genitalia problem, an oddly dressed stork-girl with purple and orange eye shadow and a cigarette stuck to her lip leaned over and asked me if I had a light. Right there in the middle of class, like she was going to have a leisurely smoke while sketching the naked hippie on the stage in front of us. Without missing a beat, I whipped out my snazzy leopard print Bic lighter and struck a flame. We'd been inseparable ever since.

We made quite a pair, really. Where she was tall and lanky, I was small and unbelievably skinny, despite a diet made up largely of fat, salt, and sugar. I had the loveliest shade of Miss Clairol Auburn Sunset in my cropped wavy hair. Very fetching. One day, Beth took a drag off of her cigarette, took a long, hard look at me and my hair and said, "You know, you remind me of a Leprechaun. A Leppy, LEPPY Leprechaun." As if to say most Leppy Leprechauns don't have the same middle name as their first name. But you? You're special.

So at any given moment, I could be merrily making my way to class and I'd hear, "Leppy, Leppy Leprechaun!" echo down the hallway in that grating sing-song of hers. It reaped me loads of shit from teachers to classmates to cleaning staff, as I'm sure you can imagine.

We charged down the stairs and left the building, wrestling with the bulky vinyl art supply bags that left my legs dotted with bruises at the end of each day.

We crossed the parking lot and clambered into her car. The Bethmobile. It was big and what wasn't rust on it was a royal metallic blue. It had rib-stitched, roomy bench seats and we sat real low in it, all shades and smokes.

After pulling out of the parking lot, we headed east on Richmond in the direction of the Montrose district. Beth steered the car through a drive-thru, where I filled my tank with a hearty helping of fast food.

Happily munching and dipping into white paper bags, we cruised down Westheimer to do a little second hand shopping alongside the junkies and the bad drag queens.

Beth was playing air drums on the steering wheel, one eye squinting against the smoldering cigarette dangling dangerously from the left side of her pretty pouty lips. I sucked on my straw as we made our way past the rows of cluttered shops along the avenue, which were decorated with fading tinsel and Christmas lights. Shops with names like *Minnie's Closet* and *The Gypsy Trader*.

"Art student" is just another term for "poor," so to stretch our pennies, we'd comb the rows and rows of mismatched hangers for thrift store chic or the perfectly faded t-shirt. It was getting tougher to find affordable couture as the girls and boys of the Houston club scene raided the racks. I'd struck gold in a particular little store called *Jimini's* on a number of occasions, so we agreed to try there first. I was hoping to find something snazzy and festive, in keeping with the holiday season. On our last treasure hunt, I'd dug up a fetching black half-shirt with zippers running up the front to the shoulders. I had to retire it however, after the zippers branded my left breast in the relentless Houston sun. I scratched at the scab as the car sailed past *Jimini's*. Beth took a left, keeping an eye peeled for a parking spot.

I had my arm hanging out the window, enjoying the unseasonably warm weather, even for Houston. The air whipping through my fingers was thick enough to float on. I ran a hand through my hair, pushing it out of my eyes as I spotted a space up ahead.

I opened my mouth to direct Beth's attention to the vacancy, but the words gathered steam and grew into a shrill tea kettle scream. I pulled my hand out of my hair to find a bee pinned to the webbing between the pinky and ring finger of my right hand, his behind furiously pumping venom into my swelling flesh. I screamed again.

"What! What! What the hell is it!" Beth had swerved the boat of a car, narrowly missing an oncoming Volkswagen Beetle.

"A fucking bee bit me!" I shouted, bouncing in my seat and scraping the offending insect and stinger from my twitching hand to pitch it out the window. I examined the wound. My fingers were beginning to resemble breakfast sausages.

"Bees don't bite, Leppy, they sting," Beth said with a superior air, glancing from me to the road.

"Oh god, thank you. Thank you for the lesson on bee behavior. The fact that my hand is on fire doesn't really seem all that important now."

"Hey, I like that. Bee-havior? Eh? Eh?"

"Are you actually retarded?"

She stuck out her lower lip. "Poor Leppy. Who's a little grumpy, hmm? We'll get you some ice, my little friend. That's pretty fucking hilarious, though." She slipped her sunglasses down her nose and gazed over the rims at my misery. "Wow, it really got you, huh? That looks so gross."

"Why do I hang around with you? Why?" I leaned back in my seat for the excruciating ride home.

An hour later, I was lying against her white and gold veneer headboard on an ancient pink twin bedspread. On the stereo, Dexi's Midnight Runners were trying in vain to convince Eileen to c'mon.

I hated that song. My hand hurt and I was in a very foul mood. The ice in the Ziploc baggie Beth had given me was starting to weep onto the lap of my jeans. By the time I noticed, the wet spot had spread across my crotch, looking for all the world like I had wet myself.

Beth was reclined on the worn rug and studying an album cover, her bare foot resting on an upturned knee. Her skirt had fallen around her waist, allowing a generous view of her red striped panties, and in turn, one round, bulging butt cheek. This did not seem to bother her in the least.

Beth's room was an odd hodgepodge of high school memorabilia, adolescent furniture and, well, junk. She had a tendency to glue, pin, or tape anything that struck her fancy to the wall, which she had painted a sloppy grass green. Newspaper clippings, photos, jewelry, beer tabs, ribbons, fortune cookie slips, money. There was even an old sock up there. Art supplies littered the floor and everything reeked of cigarette smoke and incense.

"How's the hand, Lep?"

I was examining the baggie for leaks. "Well, except for the drippy bag, it's better, I guess. The swelling seems to be going down."

"Have you talked to Jason anymore?"

"Nope. He's still treating me like I got the plague. Can't blame him, I guess. Breaking up is hard to do."

She nodded and sat up. Her skirt slid down her thigh, but red stripes still peeked out here and there. "I got a letter from Bobby," she said.

Her boyfriend Bob had gone off and joined the Army. He was tall and blonde and gorgeous, but Bobby really wasn't the brightest Crayola in the box.

"He won't be back for Christmas." Beth picked up a blue Sharpie and began to draw careful curly hearts all over the album cover and onto her thigh.

I tossed the baggie onto her side table. "Oh man, that sucks."

"Yeah, he's going to Fort Lauderdale with some of the other guys from boot camp." She held the record cover out to examine her work.

"What? What the hell is that?"

"He asked me to go too, but I don't have any money, you know, and my parents would shit."

"Well, why the hell doesn't he come home then? What an idiot."

She shrugged. "I'll see him in January, I think."

"Oh, that reminds me. My sister has offered to take me skiing in New Mexico for my birthday, and she said she'd pay for you, too." Beth dropped the record sleeve.

"What? Don't play with me, Leppy. Are you serious?" She sat up and rolled onto her knees.

"I'm not playing with you. You wanna come with?" My hand had started to sting again and I plucked the baggie from the puddle on the bedside table.

Beth sprang to her feet. "Holy shit, why didn't you tell me before? Of course I wanna come with."

"I've been meaning to. You know I'd rather go to a beach somewhere, really. I hate the cold but she loves to ski, so..."

"Oh man, this is so cool, Leppy." She jumped up on the bed and started bouncing me across the pink bedspread. "You know, I've never really seen snow. Awesome!"

"All right, all right, you're making me nauseous." I slapped her knee with the incontinent plastic bag. She bounced onto her behind and put me in a bear hug.

"Yee-ouch! Get off me."

"Oh, sorry." She patted my sore hand, sending shock waves of pain coursing through my lumpy fingers.

"Okay, okay. Just stop touching me."

"When is it?"

"End of January," I groused, as she giggled and skipped off to ask her mother.

I negotiated the door and practically fell through our front door. I dropped my bag and slumped. My hand was still swollen and red. The sight of it depressed me. "Ma?" She was in her room, sitting with her back to me. The bed bounced slightly as she worked her feet. I knew she'd get up and pace any second. She never could sit for long. "What a day, man. You can't believe...What's wrong?" Her face was slack, one eye squinted.

She seemed startled to see me. "Oh, Deborah. How was school?"

"What's wrong, Ma?" I sat next to her.

"Nothing. I feel so cooped up, I guess. I wish I could see my mother. My sisters."

"Aw, I'm sorry, Ma. Why don't you call them? Phone's right there."

She got up and started to walk. "Oh, it's so expensive. I wish I could work. I wish I could do something. I feel like an old dishrag." She shook her hands in front of her.

"Good thing you don't look like a dish rag. Good thing you're such a looker. I'd say you're more in the pashmina category." She stopped and laughed at me. "Look, you have a sister that lives here, you know. Why don't you call Charlene? That doesn't cost anything."

"Yeah, that's true. What happened to your hand?"

"Oh yeah. I got stung." I held up the ugly thing.

"You should put some ice on that."

"So I've heard."

In the living room, she stopped and turned toward me. "Did you bring the top to my coffee table back?"

I was doing homework when I heard the front door slam. Muffled voices pulled me to the front room. My aunt Charlene was helping my mother remove her coat. Ma was weaving ever so slightly.

"Hey, you girls are home early," I said, basking in the glow of the Christmas tree lights.

"Your mother can't handle her liquor," My aunt Charlene pronounced, draping Ma's coat across the back of the chair. "Those margaritas." She winked at me while carefully patting at her tower of sprayed blonde hair. "I'll see you later, kid. You take care of her, huh?" She pulled a lipstick and a compact out of her purse for a freshening.

My mother took a wobbly seat on the sofa. "Whoo," she breathed. Her face had a nice, shiny blush to it.

"You going back out?" I sat down next to my mother. She was patting her cheeks.

"You bet I am," Charlene replied. "Plenty of music and men left out there. Can't leave 'em alone for too long, or they'll both go cold." She gave me another wink. "Okay, Mary. I'll call you." My mother lifted a hand at her sister. My aunt caught my mother's eye and something passed between them. Decades of fights, reconciliations, and devotion in a single look. My mother offered up a crooked smile and Charlene was gone.

I put a hand across Ma's back. "How you doin' there, Ms. Pashmina?"

"Oh, boy," she said, running a hand across her forehead. "That Charlene sure can drink. I finally said I had to come home. She was always either at the bar or on the dance floor."

"My poor mother," I soothed. "Too much excitement, huh? Did you at least get to dance?"

"Oh yes, there was a little man that wouldn't leave me alone," she said, leaning back.

"Well, there you go. At least you had a good time, huh?"

She rolled her eyes and threw her hands up. "I couldn't see over the top of his head."

"You seem very popular with the more diminutive male. I wonder why that is? Well, I'll get you some water and a couple of Aspirin."

"Oh, thank you, Q.T. I'm going to put on my gown and go to bed. I don't think I'll ever drink again. How was your evening?"

I ran cool water into a glass and padded into her bedroom. "Oh, thrilling. Homework is every bit as fun as drinking and dancing with short men." I kissed her on the cheek. "Goodnight, Ma. Holler if you need anything."

"Goodnight, sugar. See you in my cheams," she said.

"See you in mine."

"Whoo," I heard her say.

Christmas morning had been a doozy, a far cry from a simple meal cooked over a hot plate and a basket of gifts from the nuns. Presents had been stacked high under the tree and the day started with plenty of joy and good cheer as gifts were exchanged with smiles and embraces.

Remnants of tattered holiday wrapping and bits of ribbon were strewn across our living room. Isabelle and I gathered the trash, filling a large garbage bag and stepping over my brother, who sat stretched on the sofa, reading a newspaper.

"How much longer, Mother? I'm starving." Isabelle stowed the bags in the corner and put an arm around her.

My mother had insisted on cooking this Christmas. She'd gotten up early to spread ingredients over the kitchen counter, chopping and stirring in a flurry of activity.

She cracked the oven door, revealing a golden brown turkey. My mouth watered. "I believe it's done," she puffed. "Deborah, help me get it out of there, would you?" I pulled on the old oven mitts and moved the golden bird to the stove top. Mashed potatoes, beans, and all the fixings were laid on the table. The turkey graced the center and my brother sharpened a knife, preparing to carve.

"Brother, would you say grace?" Isabelle said. We all sat around the table and took each other's hands with bowed heads.

"Dear Lord, we thank you for family and for the bounty before us. We pray that those we love may stay healthy and happy, and we remember those that couldn't be with us today. In Jesus' name we pray, amen." My family made the sign of the cross and Ben grabbed the knife and fork.

He went at it tentatively at first, but the knife hardly sank below the surface. He smirked and we all tittered, joking about adding a few more weights to the bar when he went to the gym. He dug in with more determination. Soon the bird was wobbling dangerously, the pan dancing around the table as the knife hacked and stabbed at the poor, naked fowl.

"What in the heck?" He stopped and examined the wounds. "What is this? Ice? Mother, this thing is frozen solid. How long did you cook it?"

"Well, it's been in the oven since six this morning. It should be done. I don't understand."

Isabelle got up and went to the stove. "Did you defrost it at all? Mother, this thing is only set to like, two hundred degrees. And it's on broil!"

Ma's resolve was beginning to waver. She looked around the table. "Yes, that's right. Broil. Isn't that right?"

"Mother, broil means that it just cooks from above. You have to bake a turkey. Also, it shouldn't be frozen solid when it goes in."

Ma crossed her arms. "Oh, for heaven's sake."

Luby's Cafeteria had plenty of turkey and all the fixings. We crowded around the table, a stack of trays waiting for the wait staff to clear away. My brother was just sopping up the last of the gravy on his plate. "Good thing it was frozen. We all could have gotten Salmonella," he said.

"Mother, what did you do with that cookbook I got you?" Isabelle put a hand on Ma's arm. Ma rolled her eyes.

"And what's up with the pumpkin pie? It's kinda gray." I gnawed at my turkey leg.

"There's nothing wrong with that pie, it's good food." We all groaned. She crossed her arms.

"Just wait until next year."

Twelve

THE BLACK SHEEP, THE FOX, AND THE FRAIDY CAT

Plosh! The loose snowball plastered my cheek with slush. "Oh man, you are so dead," I said, hurrying to gather up a good chunk of powder from the nearby bank. Beth had sunk to her knees and was packing a snowball the size of a compact car.

Judith pointed a manicured finger in my direction. "Keep away from me!" She didn't ski, but she was dressed in a hot pink ski bib and matching pink fur head wrap to keep the chill from her tender ears. Her dark ponytail jutted from the back.

As I wound up a missile for Beth, a projectile plowed into the back of my head, filling my collar with snow.

I gasped and turned to find Isabelle already cupping hands around another snowball, ready for a full assault. "Oh, a sneak attack, huh?"

Judith screamed and held her palms up as snow and slush whistled past her on the front walk of the Alpine-style lodge. Isabelle picked up a perfect white ball and smiled wickedly at Judith. Everyone froze.

"Don't you dare," Judith hissed. "I mean it."

Isabelle shrugged and dropped the snowball. "Okay, Miss Priss. Sheesh!" She walked toward Judith, clapping ice from her wet hands. "I like the pink," she said, smiling. "You look like a marshmallow cake."

"Look who's talking."

Isabelle was dressed all in white. Even the gloves that jutted from her coat pocket were a spotless white. Her blonde hair spilled over her shoulders. Next to my sisters, I looked like a skinny thirteen year old boy.

"Yeah, we're a couple of desserts, all right." Isabelle looked her sister up and down. "You look like you've gained weight. Have you gained weight?"

Judith looked mildly irritated and inhaled deeply. "I don't think...whoa!" Isabelle had wrapped her arms around Judith and hoisted her off the ground.

"Let's see...yeah, you feel a little chunky," she managed. Back on her feet, Judith struggled to lift Isabelle through layers of fleece and down. A couple of demented meringues wrestling each other up off of the snowy sidewalk through fits of grunts and giggles.

My mother took a tentative step out onto the front porch. She was ruddy-cheeked and smiling, though she walked stiffly down the three steps, arms out, cautious of the ice.

"Here's the snow bunny now," Isabelle called.

My mother struck a swollen Betty Grable pose in her quilted coat and then inched her careful way along the walk. The two brothers-in-law joined the party and we all piled into cars for the short drive to a cozy spot for dinner.

The waiter pulled tables together and seated the seven of us, with a place left for my brother, who was still on the road. Judith's husband, Matt, pulled a chair out for her and rested a hand on her shoulder. She slapped it away and gave him an icy look. I searched the happy table for another witness, but everyone was busy taking off coats and opening menus.

My brother joined the din, shaking off the cold and talking to Isabelle's husband, Jack, about traffic and the route he took up the mountain. Judith and Ben still lived in New Mexico, just a couple of hours south.

Matt put an arm around his wife and again she knocked it off, glaring at him. Beth caught my eye and raised her eyebrows.

Isabelle leaned in. "We had a good time today, didn't we Beth? You missed it, Debbie."

"Oh Leppy, you just wouldn't believe what it's like up there. It's amazing," Beth said.

After being fitted with rented skis and boots and deposited with a scruffy instructor to demonstrate the finer points of snow plowing, we'd wobbled and teetered across the bunny slopes, just hoping to stay vertical and in one piece.

That was yesterday. This morning, Beth headed up to the Black Diamond with Isabelle, Matt, and Jack. Those slopes were reserved for experienced to expert skiers.

"I mean, it's almost vertical! I didn't think I was going to make it, but it's so...just white and shimmering." She paused, her hands hovering before her. "Soft snow up to your knees in places. Beautiful," she said, with reverence.

"Yeah, she went down the mountain on her butt most of the time," Isabelle added.

Beth nodded, grinning. "I know. I'm going to be so-o-o sorry tomorrow. My poor booty." She shifted in her chair and winced. "It was totally worth it, though. And Matt, he rolls his own cigarettes? Right, Matt? Isn't that a trip? He let me try one. You gotta keep the papers real tight and make sure you lick all the way up the edge, or it'll fall apart," she said, gingerly rolling an imaginary cigarette between curled fingers.

"You think you're so fucking cool, don't you?" Judith was staring at Beth with no particular expression on her face. Beth blinked, her fingers still frozen in the pantomime of rolling papers and pouch tobacco. Her hands melted to her sides and her eyes grew wide as they fixed on me. Matt laid a hand on Judith's shoulder, but this time she actually shoved him backward in his chair.

Isabelle leaned in and in a quiet voice said, "What's the matter here?"

"What's the matter? You want to know what's the matter? This little girl has no respect." Judith's face was tight and hard as a fist. "Talking about licking cigarettes and "make sure you wrap it tight." You think I'm stupid?"

My throat closed up. Beth had the eyes of a trapped animal and conversation around the table evaporated to uncomfortable silence. Out of the corner of my eye I saw the waiter approach, assess the situation, and turn on his heel back to the kitchen.

"I, I..." Beth's mouth was working furiously, but she couldn't manage much beyond a squeak.

"Oh Judith, can't we all just be nice and get along?" My mother was shaking her hands and bouncing in her seat with a pained expression on her face.

"Oh, could there ever be a time that you didn't take Isabelle's side, Mom? She was always your favorite, you never failed to make that clear."

"Well, I love all my children just the same. That is just not true." My mother's voice had gone up an octave and the bouncing had intensified.

"Don't talk to Mother like that. My god, she's your mother..." My brother had picked up the baton and he was running with it as Isabelle turned to me.

"Debbie, why don't you and Beth take another table for just a minute, hmm?" Isabelle winked and purred in a low voice. "It's fine, just take another table."

I pulled my chair back and gestured at Beth to follow me. "What's your problem?" I said to Judith, my bravado paper thin and pathetic.

"What's MY problem? MY problem? Are you kidding?" She turned her body so that she followed us as we rounded the table. "I'm your SISTER. Your SISTER. You got that? What's she to you? Huh? Nothing, that's what." She was shouting as we traveled across the room. Diners were glancing over their shoulders and whispering.

I pulled a chair out and took a seat. Beth sailed right past me and headed for the ladies room. I kicked the chair back and puffed along behind her. By the time I got to the bathroom door, she had locked it and I could hear her crying.

"Beth." Silence. "Come on Beth, let me in, huh?"

The lock on the door clicked back. Tears had smeared her makeup; her nose was red and shiny and it was running profusely. The humiliation and confusion was magnified in her drippy eyes. This was the first time I'd ever seen Beth cry. I'd known her to be surly and morose, and we'd certainly had our share of serious moments, but never had I seen her so emotionally stripped down.

"I didn't do anything. I swear," she sniffed.

"I know that." I walked into one of the stalls and pulled at an enormous roll of flimsy paper. It ripped after one sheet. I swore and clawed at the narrow opening in the dispenser.

"Why would she say those things, Leppy? I would never do that. I never would." She had started crying again in a fit of stifled hiccups. I offered her a handful of shredded tissue. She took the bits, dabbing at her eyes and blowing her nose.

"I don't know. She doesn't trust anybody, that's all. It doesn't mean anything. Don't let it spoil our trip, okay?" We leaned on the sinks and she sighed, dropping her hands. I gave her a nudge. "I mean look, we're at a ski resort, right? We can't let this ruin it. I think we should march over to that bar and have a delicious frosty beverage. Or maybe something hot with piles of whipped cream. It's my birthday, for Pete's sake, we have to have a toast. Can't have a decent birthday of any kind without a toast, right? What do you say?"

She nodded and looked in the mirror. "Oh, yikes."

As we made our way to the bar, Isabelle caught my eye and motioned us back over. There was no sign of Judith and Matt, only empty chairs where they had been. The mood had lightened considerably and the buzzing chatter had resumed. We took our seats and Isabelle apologized to Beth, joking that wait staff run when they see our family coming. Beth smiled weakly and blew her nose.

I sank into the sofa next to my sister, putting my feet up on the table. The place was quiet, everyone else in bed. "Some night, huh?" I yawned.

"Exciting." She smiled.

"What happened?"

"Jack asked them to leave. He said she was upsetting everyone and if she couldn't get along, she'd better just go home. I thought fire was going to shoot from her eyes."

"What was her problem, exactly?"

"She thought Beth had made a pass at Matt, or Matt had made a pass at Beth, I guess. Something along those lines."

"Something like this seems to happen every time we all get together. Remember the Red Lobster incident?"

Isabelle shook her head. "Yes, we're quite a pack, alright. Poor Beth. She'll never go anywhere with us again. Happy birthday, right? Twenty. My baby sister is twenty. Hard to believe. You know, I remember the day you were born. I heard Mom call my name and I went into the back bedroom and there you were, all squirmy and wet. She just went and laid out some sheets on the bed and had a baby. Not many women can say that. When they made our mother, they broke the mold. I got to name you after my best friend down the block, Debbie Henderson. I had to cut your umbilical cord with a pair of scissors."

"Gross."

Isabelle chuckled and gave my knee a squeeze. "Well, it's been a long day." She yawned and stretched. "Happy birthday, Q.T." Her satin pajamas whispered as she crossed the room. "Sleep well."

O
h no, absolutely not."

"Mother, come on!" She ignored me and opened the dishwasher to drop a glass into the rack. "It's ridiculous to hang on to that thing. It's ancient technology."

"It's a perfectly good phone and I'm not replacing it." The flesh-tone rotary dinosaur had traveled with us, along with various odds and ends, from the Catholic Indian Center. It weighed a good two pounds and time ground to a virtual standstill as the chick, chick, chick of the rotary dial ran the numbers round. It was especially maddening if you were trying to win concert tickets from a local radio station.

"Oh, we're replacing it," I said.

"No, we're not." She stood up straight and glared defiantly. Something settled in me then. Something cold and small.

A slight smile crept across my lips and I quietly went to my room.

The next day, I rose before my alarm, showered, dressed, and picked up my school bag on my way out the door.

"I made hotcakes," she sang as I passed. I headed straight for the door and left without saying goodbye. I pouted all day about that damn phone, hardly paying attention to my art history lecture. Why was she so stubborn? It would be for her benefit, really. A cordless phone would mean that she could trot around the place to her heart's content, no longer chained to that tangled cord on the kitchen counter. Why couldn't she see that?

When I got home, she emerged from the hallway. I went to the kitchen and pulled fixings for a sandwich from the fridge.

"How was school?" she asked. "Oh I see, you're not speaking to me, is that it?" I carried my snack into my bedroom and closed the door.

It just so happened that Isabelle had scheduled a portrait the following day, right in the middle of our Big Fight. "What is going on?" Isabelle said, as she signaled and exited off the freeway.

"She isn't speaking to me," Mother sniffed.

"What?" Isabelle put the car in gear and turned around to face me. I smiled.

"She doesn't like my phone."

"This is over that ugly telephone of yours? Mother...you could use a new one."

"There is nothing wrong with that phone. I don't want to hear another word about it."

The photographer positioned us in various poses, instructing, "Turn your head a bit to the left. Put your hand on her shoulder. That's it, very nice."

"She's not speaking to me," Ma said, through smiling teeth, when we were all posed like a family of happy mannequins. "She doesn't like my phone."

The photographer nodded and snapped the photo.

It went on like that for six days. Six days of the silent treatment. She had resorted to following me around the apartment, just having her side of the conversation as if everything were normal, ignoring the fact that I hadn't uttered a word in almost a week.

One morning, I plodded to the kitchen, yawning and stretching as usual. There, on the Formica, in place of the rotary phone, was a brand spanking new push-button cordless. I picked up the handset, punched a few numbers, and set the phone back in its cradle. It looked cold and out of place. I wondered if the dinosaur was stashed in the back of her closet.

"Good morning, Q.T. Would you like some eggs?" she asked.

"Morning, Ma. I'd love some."

There was a lot of commotion, exclamations, and excited chatter. "What's going on?" I had read the same sentence in my cheesy detective novel no less than three times, never once comprehending it.

"Your cousin Paul is coming to visit," Isabelle beamed.

"Oh Paul, little boy, little boy," my mother sang, clapping her hands as if he were still the golden toddler.

"Tell him not to come," I said.

"What? No, what's wrong with you?" Isabelle wedged her briefcase between a chair back and the kitchen table.

"Deborah," my mother chided.

"Don't look at me like that. You know he's trouble. He's always been a major pain in the butt. Have you forgotten all the stuff he used to pull? He burned down his own house, for Pete's sake."

"Oh my god, he was eight years old." Isabelle reached in the fridge and popped the top on a soft drink.

"Remember that?" my mother said in a hushed tone. "That was terrible."

Isabelle pulled out a chair and sat with a sigh. "How could I forget? I was on a date with Bobby Parks and I saw the flames. I ran in the trailer and pulled the two of them out. When Charlene got home, the place was ashes." I had heard this story a thousand times. Paul playing with matches, setting the drapes alight just to watch them burn. He and his sister probably owed their lives to Isabelle. The trailer had occupied a bald slice of my grandmother's property before burning to the ground.

"There you go," I said. "I've got a bad feeling about this, I'm telling you. He used to make my life hell."

"Debbie, he was a kid. A little boy. He has a business now. He travels. He's grown up."

"I'll bet."

He arrived the following day. The door flew open and there he was, blonde and shaggy and grinning that big, goofy grin of his.

He grabbed my mother and hung on to her. She was laughing and flushed. "My beautiful Auntie Mary. Don't you ever age? You look exactly the same as you did when I was ten years old. It's incredible!" He looked around the room and green eyes came to rest on me.

"Lil Debbie? Really?" He marched over and pulled me into a bear hug, cutting off my air supply. "I can't believe it. I haven't seen you since high school."

He released me and held me by my shoulders at arms length. "Skinny as ever, I see." He winked and turned back to my mother.

"How is Charlene?" Ma asked, hopping from foot to foot. "How is your sister? Are you hungry? Can I make you something?" She was jiggling and her hands were shaking furiously.

"All fine, Auntie Mary," he said. "I don't want to put you out. I'll grab some fast food or something."

My mother's eyes got wide and indignant. She began banging cabinets and pulling out pots and pans.

Paul took a seat at the dining table and looked over his
shoulder at me, patting the chair next to him. He smiled and
turned to face my mother again. "You know, I'd be at my
mom's right now, but she's out of town so I gotta find a hotel.
You know of any around here?"

Oh no. No, no. Don't do it, Ma. Please don't do it.

"Don't be silly. You'll stay here," she offered. "I can't have
you in a hotel when we have a perfectly comfortable sofa."

"Really? You sure? That would be great. It would give us
a chance to get to know each other again." He turned and
smiled at me.

The next morning, he was sitting on the couch, in his boxers and a t-shirt, as I poured myself a glass of juice.

"Hey Debbie Q, what you got going today?"

I leaned against the counter while sipping my juice. "I'm
helping my friend Beth with a project," I fibbed.

"Oh naw, why don't you come with me? I have some stuff
to do at the U. It won't take long, and I was hoping we could
hang out." He was half submerged in a nest of rumpled linens.

"Paul has a concert business," my mother crowed.

"Really?" I downed the last of my juice.

"Concert security," he said. "Would you mind pouring me
a glass of that?" He gestured at my empty glass. "As long as
you're already up."

My lip twitched. "Of course." I went back to the kitchen
and washed out my glass, laying it in the drain board. I
poured a fresh glass and handed it to him. He grabbed my
hand and pulled me down next to him.

"Listen, I know I did a lot of crummy things to you when
we were kids, and I just want you to know that I'm sorry
about that. Even though it was a long time ago, I'd hate to
think there was any bad blood." He smelled like unwashed
towels.

"Well, it was a long time ago."

"Remember when we all took Grandpa's tractor?" he
laughed. "Here we are, chugging down the road, and my mom
drives by."

"Yeah, and you said it was my idea, even though you had to beg and threaten all of us into going along with you," I said. He sank back into the sofa, giggling maniacally.

"Hey, I knew that Auntie Mary was too nice to do anything to you. My mom would have beat the hell out of me. As it was, I got a couple of swats."

My mother was laughing nervously, looking confused. I could tell she remembered my aunt Charlene bellowing and pointing at me as I cowered in my grandmother's kitchen. My aunt had followed that ancient, belching tractor onto the shoulder of the farm road, charging out of her Chrysler La Baron, screaming and yanking Paul out of the driver's seat. I think I was six. My other two cousins and I had huddled behind the seat. We were little girls, wide-eyed and terrified.

I never had told my mother the truth about that day, and I never told her about the time he stole her diamond ring and raced out the door in the middle of the night in his pajamas screaming "Oh, I LOVE my new ring!" I never told her about the time he pushed me off the roof of my brother's car, knocking the wind out of me and leaving me gasping like a beached trout while he laughed his stupid head off. Or the time he hit me in the temple with a rock, causing stars to explode in flashes of red and white. Or how he would always try pulling off his underwear when he had to sleep with us girls on the wide porch of my grandmother's house. I especially never told her about how he liked to pretend he was a girl, slipping his feet into her high heels, a towel draped over his head. Stroking the length of the towel, he'd say, "Isn't my long, golden hair beautiful? Isn't it just beautiful?"

I felt oddly sorry and protective of Paul, as if he were a sweet little bird that cooed and preened and pecked me bloody. But to be honest, it went beyond feeling sorry for him. The truth was that it was intoxicating being in his confidence. That sweet, hot draw of power bad boys give off like perfume. He made me want to impress him. Made me want to please him. I could feel the pull of it again, and it made me hate him all the more.

He put his arm around me and yanked me under his armpit. "Why don't you come with me?" he said, kissing me on the forehead. "I'll buy you lunch. I could use a hand anyway."

I sighed. "Okay. What time do you want to go?"

"Concert security is good money." Paul was speeding my car down the freeway through a gleaming canyon of office buildings.

"College campuses are teeming with big bruiser guys wanting to get into shows for free," he bragged. "The chance to get a security t-shirt and a backstage pass has 'em lining up around the block."

He took the exit at warp speed and screeched to a halt at a red light. He turned and looked at me, reaching out to muss my hair.

"Lil Suze," he said. "You went red, huh? It looks better than the brunette. You should go blonde, though. Blonde is beautiful. I'm so glad I got the blonde hair. I feel so sorry for Ilene, getting the dark coloring." He looked wistful, feeling genuinely sad for his sister's tragic brown hair disability.

"What?" I said.

"Did you see the sign for the U of H? I wasn't paying attention." He brought the car back up to nail biting speed, weaving and dodging around cars, though he didn't have a clue where he was going.

"Turn left on Elgin," I said, gritting my teeth.

We made it to the university in one piece and I followed him through the campus and into several cookie-cutter buildings as he taped fluorescent flyers to cluttered bulletin boards and posts.

The flyers had a bold, black headline that said **Men, Have You Got What it Takes?** It promised front row access to the hottest shows for guys willing to work the concerts, and it had our phone number at the bottom.

"Uh Paul, did you ask my mom if you could put our phone on that thing?" I asked him.

"Of course." He looked at me with an appalled look. "I wouldn't do anything without asking my sweet Auntie Mary first."

The following week, sweet Auntie Mary did his laundry and cooked all his meals, waiting on him hand and foot. Every day I'd get home from school and there he'd be, slouched on the sofa in the same rumpled bedclothes.

"Hey, Leppy's mom." Beth closed the front door after her and followed me into the living room.

"Oh, hello Beth. How was school?"

"Delightful and educational as ever, Mrs. M."

"Would you care for a buttered biscuit?"

Beth glanced at me and I grimaced. "No thanks, Mrs. M. I'm sure they are unbelievably delicious, but I'm on a no bread diet right now. You got any Cokes?"

"Oh yes, I'm trying to lose a little weight myself," she said. "I run up and down this hallway all day long." My mother burst into a run in place, smiled at Beth. "Pepsi okay?"

"This is my cousin Paul," I said, crooking my head at the couch.

He had the phone smashed between his ear and his shoulder, even though one hand rested on his lap. "Uh-huh. And how tall are you? Uh-huh." He had a yellow legal pad balanced on his knee as he twiddled a pen between his fingers. He looked at Beth and tipped the pen in her direction and then wrote something down. "Well, I'll be selecting staff for an upcoming show on Saturday. Uh-huh. In front of the Wortham Theater. Right, two o'clock."

Beth looked at me and rolled her eyes. "I gotta be taking off, Leppy."

"Oh man, really?" I gave her a pleading look.

"Sorry Lep, I promised I'd help my mom clean out the garage. Never thought I'd look forward to that. Odd sensation."

"Don't forget your soda." Mother pulled the tab back on the can and handed it to Beth. "For the road." Beth took the drink and was out the door.

Paul hung up the phone and jumped up to take my portfolio. "Here, let me take that thing." He yanked the bag out of my hand. "Jesus, what do you have in here? It weighs a ton." He was already in the hall, heading for my room.

"Paul, I'd rather you didn't go..."

"How about helping me out and letting me borrow your car on Saturday?" he urged, dropping the bag in the corner.

"Oh man," I whined.

"Last time, I promise. I'm getting wheels next week. It's just taken me awhile to arrange financing. My money's tied up and it took some time to liquidate."

"I don't know, Paul. I'm supposed to take Beth to soccer on Saturday."

"Please, please, please?" He came over and got on his knees in front of me, his fingers clasped together.

"Paul, c'mon." He lifted my shirt and gave me a sloppy raspberry, spitting all over my stomach. "Hey, okay, okay." I yanked my shirt away from him and he lurched up at me, burying my face in his neck.

"Thank you, Lil Debbie, Deb," he said. "Last time, I promise. And I'll take good care of it."

I spent Saturday with Beth trying not to picture my car wrapped around a tree. I was helping myself to a piece of Kentucky Fried Chicken when he walked through the door that evening.

"Hey, Litto Deb-o-rino." He grabbed the chicken out of my hand and sat down to take a bite. "Here are your keys."

"Do you have to call me that?" I said irritably. "You're not even a full year older than me."

He laughed and mussed my hair. "I can't help it. You'll always be my Lil Debbie." I glared at him. "Okay, Lil Deborah. How's that? Where is Auntie Mary?" "She went to Mass."

"Now? Isn't it kind of late for that?"

"Never too late for Mass. It's a Day of Obligation. Ma doesn't miss those." I wiped my fingers and mouth with a dishtowel and shoved the box of chicken in front of him. "I'm going to have a shower. Try not to burn anything down before I get out." He giggled and helped himself to another piece of my dinner.

When I emerged, Paul was still at the kitchen table, but fried chicken had been replaced by stacks of five dollar bills and scattered piles of photo contact sheets. Row after row of black and white faces stared up at me. Beefy boys, thin boys, pimply-faced boys with glasses, and fresh-faced frat boys with close shaves and cropped hair. Black, White, Asian—every variety of college-aged male animal. Paul was licking his thumb periodically and counting the fives in each stack. He laid the last on its pile and swept the photos into the garbage can.

"Uh, don't you need those?" I asked.

"I told them they were for the security badges," he said. "They won't be needing no stinking badges." He had started on the next pile of fives.

"What does that mean?" He continued to count. When he had ticked through the last bill, he swept another bunch of photos into the trash.

"I charged them a five dollar application fee. It doesn't mean they're going to be chosen."

My mouth gaped. "Paul, that's fraud. Do you even have the authority to do any of this security? Is any of this even real?"

He laughed and stood up. "Oh, Lil Debbie. You're so naive. This is how business works. You have to have a little seed money to get anything off the ground." He mussed my hair.

The front door opened and my mother and Isabelle walked in, chatting and laughing. Paul swept the cash and the photos into a large manila envelope.

"Hey, here're my girls now," he crowed. For just an instant, there was the faintest look of distaste on my mother's face. She smiled at him and went to her room to remove her pearls and put her good purse away.

He was sitting on the sofa in his ever-present boxers, though it was nearly noon. He was eating a bowl of cereal while the television blared. My mother was doing her usual pacing back and forth from her bedroom to the living room. She had become unusually quiet as the weeks had dragged on, Paul remaining in his underwear on our couch.

"Auntie Mary, can I have some more juice?" he hollered, as I grabbed my keys on my way out to Beth's house.

My mother stopped and turned. She danced in place, her hands working furiously. Her eyes were wide and shiny and there was a wild look just at the edges.

"Paul, you have to go!" she screeched. It was a desperate cry, primal and explosive.

Paul's spoon froze in midair. The keys fell from my slack fingers.

"You have been here too long and it's time for you to go!" she repeated, her face coloring. He dropped the spoon in the bowl, sat back, and grinned.

"Okay, okay, Auntie. You're right. You should have said something sooner." He got up out of the impression his butt had left on the sofa and kissed her on the cheek. She looked flustered and unsteady.

"Well, I'm sorry, but, well..." She continued to bounce in place, looking as if she wished she could disappear in a puff of smoke.

"It's okay, Auntie. I'll pack up and move out today. No problem." He sat back down on the couch and continued to eat his cereal. My mother went to her room and closed the door.

We're looking for a Paul Gordon." Two humorless police officers stood outside our door in the shade of the patio.

"Uh, he left last week," I informed them. "You're welcome to come in though." I stepped aside and they strode heavily in, all shiny metal and creaking leather. The big one smelled like Old Spice. My mother froze at the sight of them. When I was a kid, she frequently called the cops, complaining of conspiracies or the fact that the TV anchorman was watching her undress from the glow of the television. This was the first time I'd ever seen her surprised to see them.

"What's this all about?" she asked.

"Do you know the whereabouts of a Paul Gordon?" As my mother bounced in place, her right eye squinted nearly shut.

"No. He was staying here for a while, but he left last week. He's my nephew. His mother might know where he is. Did something happen to him? Is he all right?"

"Are you aware that he defrauded hundreds of students on the University of Houston campus? The dean is wanting to press charges." The big one was doing the talking while his smaller partner stood back with his arms crossed. I could see the white all around Ma's eyeballs.

"Oh my goodness. Oh my goodness," was all she could say. I looked at the smashed sofa cushions where Paul had parked his keister the previous month. A giggle threatened to spill out of me. I cleared my throat.

"Look," I said, "we don't know where he went. He mooched off of us for about a month and then he left. You should really talk to his mother. Ma, give them Aunt Charlene's number, huh?" She looked stunned for an instant and then hurried to the address book, crammed with scraps of paper and Post-its whose numbers had long since lost any connection to their owners. She thumbed through the book as the officers and I stared dumbly at each other.

"Here," she said, triumphantly. "Here it is." She picked up a pen, but she was shaking so badly that she dropped it. I took it from her, jotted down the name and number, and handed it over.

"Sorry we couldn't be of more help," I said. "We hadn't seen him in years. He just sort of showed up and then he was gone. As it was, he put our phone number on that damn flyer and everybody and their uncle was calling here."

"Oh, yes. I couldn't get him off of that telephone," my mother interjected, her hands flying in the general direction of the phone.

"Please call us if you hear from him," Old Spice said, handing me his business card. Officer Hector Alasandro, Houston Police Department. Officer Alasandro tipped his imaginary hat and he and his partner filed out. I closed the door behind them.

"Oh, my dear Lord!" Mother held her flushed cheeks in both hands.

"Are you all right, Mom?"

"It's not funny, Deborah. The police are looking for your cousin."

"It's a little funny." I pulled her hands from her face and held them.

"It's not," she said, cracking a smile.

"Hey Mom, I'm awful sorry I made you get rid of your phone. I know the nuns gave that to you, and it probably had memories for you, and you should be able to have whatever phone you want," I offered.

"Are you kidding? This one's so much better."

I had a hard time getting to sleep that night. Every time I closed my eyes, I saw Paul's grinning face and my mother's anger and desperation. Eventually, I plunged and I found myself back on that empty desert highway again, the ardent sun making each step every bit as heavy and laborious as I remembered. But this time, I was grown and I held the satchel. My mother lagged behind and I struggled to keep her fingers in mine. "Keep up," I kept saying. "You have to keep up." Finally, she stopped altogether and stood looking at me on the shoulder. "Mother, we have to keep going."

"I'm tired, Q.T. I've walked enough. You go on ahead."

I could feel the sun baking the top of my head and I longed to run. "Are you kidding? I'm not leaving you."

She smiled and turned. "But you will, Q.T., I know you will."

Thirteen

A BRAND NEW LEFT EAR

Oh Deborah, I'm so scared." My mother walked into my room, arms outstretched. I embraced her and felt her tremble against me.

"Why, Mom? Why are you scared?" She released me and stared blankly, as if suddenly waking from a dream. She turned to leave.

"Mom?" Her hands were working as always, but her eyes were glassy and wide.

She had been taking the medication continually for so many years. The doctor here in Houston had put her on a medication that required injections. Lately, near the end of the month, before her next shot, she would go into severe withdrawals. Her skin would flush and the tremors would intensify, causing her to perspire and puff, pulling at her hair and clothing. She'd come to me saying she was afraid, but never saying why or what it was just beyond the darkness, or beneath her flesh, that made her cringe and fret. Whether it was the fear of being locked up again or what the voices said that terrified her, I couldn't say.

I sat in the living room and watched her pace. She let out a shudder and fluttered her hands, as if she could shake them free of her like the shedding of gloves after coming in from the cold.

"Mom, can I get you something? A water or something to eat? I could go out and get something. Anything you want." I felt pathetic, sitting there with nothing to offer, no poultice for her misery.

"Nooo," she squeaked. The phone rang.

"Hi, sis," Isabelle said, brightly.

"Hi, Isabelle. Mom is feeling bad."

"Let me talk to her."

"Oh Isabelle, I'm so sick." The phone shook against Ma's ear. She listened for a moment and then handed it back.

"I'm about fifteen minutes away. I'll give her a shot then."

"Isn't it too soon?"

"I think it'll be all right. I hate to see her suffer like this."

We said our goodbyes and I hung up, my hand still on the phone. Where would we be without Isabelle? She took Mother to the doctors and filled out countless forms. She housed us, clothed us, and she faithfully administered that shot to my mother every month to keep her as sane and healthy as possible. Even the sight of the needle made me queasy.

Mother was just turning to make another round across the room when Isabelle breezed through the door. She embraced her and gave me a smile and a wink over Ma's shoulder.

"Hi Shayba," she said.

Shayba is my mother's word. It can mean different things depending on how it's used. It can mean voluptuous or shapely, like "That dress makes you look shayba," or sexy, like "Shayba! Shayba!" But mainly it just means beautiful.

"Oh Isabelle, I'm so sick. I'm about to jump out of my skin," my mother wailed, pumping her hands up and down.

"I know, Mother." My sister put her hand on Ma's cheek. "Let's get you feeling better." She pulled a white pharmacy bag and a hypodermic out of her slim briefcase. She inserted the needle into the vial and pulled the plunger back. Clear fluid bubbled into the syringe. She pulled the needle from the bottle and pushed the plunger up until a drop or two dribbled out, clearing air from the chamber. The room smelled fantastic with her perfume wafting all over the place.

My mother stood in place, raising one foot and then the other. Isabelle dabbed Mom's arm with alcohol and I shut my eyes.

I sat cross-legged, buried in Isabelle's living room shag carpet, a stuffed photo album balanced on my lap. As I turned the page, a picture fluttered from the book. I picked it up and studied it. Graduation day. A picture was snapped through the reception crowd. Ma and I were surrounded by figures, soft and out of focus. A beehive of activity, people bustling in and out of the viewfinder while she and I, in the eye of the storm, share a quiet moment. The two of us stare at my diploma. She's in mid-sentence, her mouth in the shape of an A, her face proud.

"Hey Mom, remember this?" I handed the photo to her on her pass back to the hallway.

"Oh, yes. That's a lovely suit on you. Did Isabelle give that to you, or did you just borrow it? Lord, I look so fat."

"What? You do not. Give it here." I snapped the picture at her before slipping the picture back into the photo album. I returned the book to its cluttered place in the cabinet and sighed as I picked up the paper. Back to the want ads.

The white noise of the weed whacker outside quieted, leaving me alone with the air conditioner and the sound of Mother padding down the hall. My stomach rumbled. I folded up the paper and put it aside to step out into the oppressive heat of the back garden. Halfway across the humid walkway, my jeans were stuck to me. Beads of sweat prickled my forehead.

Isabelle was leaning the garden tool against the garage wall. She wiped her green-stained hands on the seat of her shorts. Her hair was pulled back under a white garden hat and she was covered in grass clippings.

She was brushing at her shirt and face, only succeeding in moving grass from one side of her to the other. She smiled when she spotted me.

"Hey Isabelle, I'm going to go pick up some lunch, you wan..." As I got within range, she reached out and gave me a good, firm shove, sending me pin wheeling backwards into the pool. I surfaced, sputtering and spitting.

"Isabelle!" I panted as I dog paddled to the edge.

"You looked hot," she said, hands on hips.

"I looked hot? I looked hot? You think this is funny, do you? You think this is going to be a comfortable ride home?" I pulled myself, and my now ten pound suit of clothes, out of the water and sat dripping on the edge.

She laughed and jumped fully clothed into the water feet first, disappearing under the surface, her hat floating off with the wake.

"Whew, that is better," she panted. As she swam over to join me, a flotilla of grass clippings trailed after her.

I looked at my rippling tennis shoes and felt them float around my feet. "I cannot believe you just did that."

"Don't be a dud," she said, wringing out her ponytail.

As I squeegeed rivulets of water from my eyes, I heard the back door close.

"Mother, Debbie pushed me into the pool," Isabelle pouted.

"Oh, come on! Does it look like I'm the one that did the pushing?"

Ma took one look and went back into the house.

My ear was throbbing. The dull ache had spread up my skull and down my jaw line, making it impossible for me to chew or even sleep.

"Ear infection," Isabelle had said. "Probably from the pool. You better get that cleared up before next week. Can't fly like that. It'll burst your eardrum."

I sat cooling my heels in the half empty waiting room at the University of Texas Medical Center's Ear, Nose, and Throat ward.

Eventually, my name was called, and I followed a stern looking woman in a stiff, white uniform to a drab little testing room. The nurse directed me to take a seat at a long folding table. As I sat down, she handed me a pair of bulky headphones that were connected to a gray box. It was decked out with a row of buttons and switches.

As she settled into the chair across from me, I noticed the etched nameplate pinned to her uniform. It said "Lorraine." Lorraine had very white teeth and her hair was pulled back in a tight, smooth bun. I wondered if her scalp was sore every night when she let it run loose.

She started in a bored monotone. "Now you're going to hear a beep in your right or left ear. When you hear the tone, press on the corresponding button in front of you." She ticked off the information as she snatched up the clipboard in front of her. "If you hear the tone in the left ear, push the left button. If it's the right ear, push the right button. The light on top will glow, letting me know which you have selected. Is this clear?"

Nurse Lorraine had clearly made this little speech hundreds of times.

"A sheep? I'm going to hear a sheep in this thing?" I said, looking at the box.

"What?" She looked directly at me for the first time.

"You said I would hear a sheep and to push the button when I heard it. Why a sheep? Are they a particularly good pitch for this kind of test or something?"

She hesitated, her brow furrowed. "What? I did not say sheep. I said tone."

"I know you said tone later on, but at first you said sheep. I thought it was a sheep-like tone. Like a bahhhh."

She started to mumble the little speech to herself. "Now, you're going to hear a...beep. I said beep. Obviously."

"Oh. Uh-huh. I thought you said sheep." I concentrated on the box. "So I won't be hearing farm animals of any kind, then?" She flipped the switch on the back and I heard a smooth "beeeep" in my right ear. I pushed the right button and smiled up at her with satisfaction. She wrote something down.

It went on like that. Some of the beeps were louder and some were softer. The ones on my left sounded like they were beeping through a thick door.

When the test was done, I was escorted to a regular old examining room and Lorraine pointed to a padded table with a membrane of white paper on it. "The doctor will be in shortly," she said, and she was gone.

"Thanks for the warmth, Lorraine," I muttered and I hopped up onto the table. The paper crackled under my behind.

By the time the doctor arrived, I had counted the tiles in the floor and memorized everything on the counter. I'd perfected my own system. I'd look once, taking a mental snapshot, and then I'd close my eyes, whispering the name of each item. Cotton ball dispenser, twirly-instrument-holder-thingy, Lucite pamphlet display with pamphlets on proper ear care...

"Hello, Deborah. I'm Doctor Norris." I jumped at the sound of his voice and opened my eyes. He had short, sandy hair and a baby face. He picked up the clipboard that Nurse Lorraine had left. I hoped she hadn't made any side notes about me. "I understand you've had some discomfort in your left ear. How long has that been going on?"

"About a week," I replied. "I'm hoping to catch a plane on Thursday, so I'd like to get it cleared up by then if possible."

"Uh-huh. The results of your test show a fairly diminished sensitivity in that ear, more so than you would expect from a simple infection." He pulled out a scope and a pen light from his pocket. "Let's have a look."

He peered in, squinting one eye closed. "Wow, it's really blocked." His lips were curled back, giving him a horse mouth in my peripheral vision. "I'm going to get a more powerful scope," he said, extinguishing the penlight. "I'll be right back."

I hate going to the doctor. Actually, I've never spent a single night in the hospital. I've only ever actually HAD to go to the doctor twice. The time I sprained my wrist getting clocked at dodgeball, and that time I put the BBs in my ears, of course.

Looking back, it all must have cost a fortune. No insurance, minimum wage job, and then after all the waiting and money spent, the damn doctor had the nerve to tell my mother that he was confident the BBs would fall out on their own.

190

Which they did, in time. One morning, I woke up and there was one lone BB resting on my pillow. The other fell out in the shower. I was sure of it. I remembered the soft "tik" of the thing hitting the shower floor. I was maybe twelve.

Dr. Norris returned, brandishing a large economy-sized scope with its own built-in light.

"Uh, this is probably, heh, heh, nothing," I tittered as he squinted, looking for all the world like Mr. Ed. "But when I was in grade school, I put a couple of BBs in my ears because the boy that sat behind me in second grade was bugging me. But, I gotta tell ya, I'm sure they fell out a long time ago." He then clicked off the scope and took a step back.

"Yep. That's what it is all right," he said. "You have a BB stuck way up in your ear canal. A thirteen year old BB." He shook his head and snorted.

"Oh," I said.

He pulled a small, shallow tray and an evil looking pick from a drawer along the far wall.

He laid the tray against my neck, under my jaw line, and went for the ear. "I'm going to try to be as gentle as I can, but it may be uncomfortable."

He started digging gingerly. I could hear the scratching of metal on metal. After a bit, he withdrew and leaned against the examining table.

"It's moved really far up there," he said. "Difficult to even get to it. If we can't get that out of there, you may have to have surgery."

"Oh man, really? Isn't there anything you can do? Can't you flush it out or something?" I whined.

"I don't think we can do that with the infection behind it," he said. "We could damage the ear drum. Let me check on something. I'll be right back." I thought about the doctor who examined me when I was eight, imagining various exotic torture devices clamped to random body parts.

After a bit, Doctor Norris returned with an older gentleman. This doctor had gray, thinning hair and a pair of spectacles on the end of a sharp nose. He looked like Vincent Price.

I didn't think this boded well for me. Doctor Norris explained the circumstances as his colleague grabbed the pick and tray.

He then proceeded to dig a tunnel straight into the soft tissues of my brain. I could feel myself slumping lower and lower on the table, and he followed me down every inch by painful inch.

I was seeing flash bulbs burst around the room and the left side of my head was on fire. Finally, I heard a "clink," and the BB hit the tray. Dr. Phibes set the tray on the table, handed Doctor Norris the pick, and left the room. Doctor Norris yelled "Thank you!" after him, which exploded in my left ear. He pulled a pair of tweezers from his pocket and plucked up the BB. It was black and covered with an unappetizing crust. He scratched at it.

"Wow, lead. They don't make 'em like this anymore. They're all made of copper now. Probably for just this reason, huh?"

When I left his office, I had a bottle of drops and a brand new left ear. I could hear my own hair grow, and the simple sound of the wind through the trees was deafening. As I watched palm fronds at their noisy play overhead, an airplane scratched a line across the wide, blue sky.

The hot tarmac lit up the windows of the 747 cabin like a row of light bulbs.

"Where's Mother?" I looked up from my book as Isabelle settled into the seat across the aisle. I scanned the rows of seats, all lined up like blue dominoes. People were chatting and slowly making their way back to stowed carry-ons and rumpled sweaters.

We'd been parked at the Cancun airport for nearly half an hour, which was a brief stop to load and unload passengers before going on to Cozumel, Mexico. Isabelle stood and craned her neck, scanning the crowd. Jack was moving up the aisle toward us, dodging stragglers with a sunny yellow gift shop bag in hand.

"Have you seen Mother?" Isabelle whispered to him.

"I think she was in the gift shop," he said. "I didn't see her when I left, though. I thought she'd gone back to the plane."

"I'd better go find her." Isabelle tried to squeeze around him.

"They're not letting anyone else out there. I think we're taking off pretty soon here." He tossed the bag he was carrying onto one of the seats.

"Well, we have to do something. She's going to miss the plane." They started back up the aisle. A flight attendant gestured for them to take their seats. There was some discussion and then she shrugged and let them pass. I had a bad feeling.

The last of the passengers had been seated and the flight attendants were closing the overhead bins. I considered trying to get off the plane myself. The thought of going on without Ma made me queasy and short of breath. I pasted my nose against the window, trying to see what was happening. Jack was running across the asphalt, my mother hanging on to him, doing all she could to keep up.

When they appeared between the blue curtains up front, they were both red-faced and out of breath. One man joked that we nearly left them as they passed his seat. Jack's hair was sticking up in back and there was a sheen on his forehead. My mother looked like she might keel over. When she dropped into the seat next to mine, she smelled of heat and unfamiliar places. I helped her with her lap belt and kissed her on the cheek.

"Ma, where have you been?" I asked. She was blinking and her twitching hands hovered in front of her.

"I, I don't know. I got lost." Her voice was a husky whisper.

"She was wandering around the airport," I heard Jack say to my sister as we taxied down the runway.

"I went to the gift shop and then I don't know, I guess I took a wrong turn." My mother turned and looked at me. "What would I have done out there? What would I have done?" Isabelle leaned across the aisle and took Ma's hand.

"Mom was trying to start the vacation a little early, huh?" She laughed and gave her hand a squeeze. The wild look in my mother's eyes evaporated and she laughed too.

"That's right," she sighed. "That's what it was."

The days passed, languorous and easy. Hours exploring the clear waters that skirted the beach turned me nut brown. Colorful fish, urchin, and sea snakes dressed up in stripes and spots teemed in shallows warm as bath water. Mother sat stretched on a bright beach towel, sipping on bottles of orange soda under a large straw hat. I watched her as she stared out at the line where the sea kissed the sky, blue on blue. She'd sit for hours surveying the horizon, calm and still, except for her hands. I wondered what pictures she saw, if there were still secret conversations, now muffled and discreet through layers of antipsychotics, or if it was quiet in there.

"How ya doin', Ma?" I unrolled a companion towel and sat beside her.

"Hot," she replied.

"Hey, Ma? Uh, I didn't tell you, but that ear infection? It turns out that I still had that BB in my ear from when I was, like eight."

She turned to face me. "What? You're kidding!"

I nodded. "The doctor dug it out. It looked huuuuge, and it was all black." I discreetly omitted the bit about the lead.

She shook her head. "You kids. You know, when Ben was little, I had to take him to the doctor because he got a lima bean stuck up his nose," she mused. "Here he comes, his nose swollen to the size of a golf ball, and his dirty face streaked with tears." She held her hand to her nose, demonstrating the swelling. "I'll never forget the look on his face."

"How did they get it out?"

"The doctor stuck a thin scalpel up his nostril and cut it out, piece by piece. Must have softened with all of the mucous."

"Ewwww!" My mother laughed and gripped her hands together. "At least they got it out." She sighed and we listened to the water lap up the shore. "It sure is nice here," she said.

I nodded and followed her gaze, squinting against the glare of the sun. "What happened at the airport, Ma?" I asked, watching as a pair of snorkels surfaced just offshore like tiny submarines.

She was quiet and I wondered if she'd heard me. "I got confused," she said, finally. "Sometimes I think I'm losing my mind."

She took another sip from her bottled soda and laid back, pulling the hat over her face.

Fourteen

STORM WATCH

Combing the classifieds paid off. Three interviews and my very own apartment later, I was working at the University of Texas Medical Branch on Galveston Island, which was forty minutes south of Ma's front door down the Gulf Freeway if you didn't spare the gas pedal. My official title at UTMB was Medical Illustrator, but really I was a glorified graphic designer–research pamphlets, campus magazines, that kind of thing.

My apartment was dreamy. It looked out over a vacant lot and the wide Atlantic across a two-lane street. Isabelle basically moved her living room into mine and completely remodeled her own house. I loved my job. Steady hours, challenging assignments, and great people. But outside of work, my life was somewhat lonely. Bobby had returned back to Houston after basic training, and he and Beth were living together, so I rarely saw her anymore. My mother was the most social interaction I had these days, and I was feeling mighty pathetic.

"Hey, weirdo."

"Well, if it isn't the twerp." Julie's voice on the other end of the line made me long for those leisurely days by the pool. "Still skinny as ever?"

"Funny you should ask. With all this heavy Texas chow, I've put on a good hundred and fifty pounds."

There was a pause. "You have not!"

"Naw, but I wanted to throw you a bone."

She sighed. "You'll probably always be skinny, but I'll always be younger."

"Gonna beat that dead horse again, huh?"

"Until the day I die. How's everything?"

I shrugged on my end. "Eh."

"What's the problem, honey?"

"Nothing, really. Everything is grand, I just don't know anybody here. I'm kind of boring and pathetic when I'm not working."

"I got news; you've always been kind of boring and pathetic. But if you want to meet people, you should get out there. Besides, you just moved. Give it time." There was a thump and some rustling behind her. "Janie Marie! You get down from there right now or I'll pop your little head right off your shoulders, I mean it."

I heard a tiny little voice say "I'll pop YOUR head off YOUR shoulders," and then peals of giggling and running footsteps.

"You're pretty mouthy for someone three feet tall!" Julie sighed. "I am cursed with myself for a daughter. Would you think poorly of me if you discovered that I had auctioned her off to the highest bidder?"

"Jack would never allow it. Besides, this is your just deserts. Your mother always said you'd be sorry when you had a kid just like yourself."

"Yeah, payback is hell. Listen, you hang in there. It'll get better. Remember that little speech you gave me when you left? I was a mess for a long time, but you were right, change is good."

"I said that?"

"Sort of. And if it turns out to be a bunch of doo doo, you know I still love you."

Hey, how's it going?" I shared a third floor balcony with the apartment next door and I was getting my first look at the guy who lived there. I'd begun to wonder if it was occupied at all. I'd lived in the building for nearly a month and there was no sign of anyone. My elusive neighbor was paunchy, with bleached blonde, thinning hair and chunky glasses that slipped down his nose. He was carrying groceries up the steps and he nearly jumped out of his skin at the sound of my voice. His magnified eyes rested on me for an instant and then he dug out his keys and disappeared inside, closing his door soundly.

"Mighty neighborly," I muttered, taking a swig from my glass of tea. Next door, the music was cranked up and bass tones thumped, shattering the peace of the waves breaking up the rocks across the way. I downed the rest of my tea and went inside to wash out the glass. My living room pulsed and shook with the music next door.

"You gotta be kidding me." I looked at the pictures on the wall. The frames were bumping and dancing to the musical stylings of Van Morrison's *Brown Eyed Girl*. A solid month and this guy's persona non grata, suddenly it's Studio 54? I walked across the balcony and banged on his door to no avail. I waited until the song was over and knocked again. The song started over but he opened up. The music doubled and the din all but blew my hair back.

"Would you mind turning it down?!" I shouted. He never actually looked at me, studying the hinge on the door the entire time, but he nodded the second time I yelled my question. Back in my own cozy place, the music had reduced, though it still leaked steadily through the wall. The same song was starting for the fifth time when I left. I carried a plastic basket and a box of detergent across the complex to the laundry room, grateful for the quiet. I counted out quarters and began feeding separated socks and dainties into the machine. Down the way, a handsome guy in a beard and a gray fedora hat was pulling his clothes from a dryer.

"Hi, there," he said.

"Hi, yourself." I smiled.

"I saw you moving in. You're up on the third floor, right? I'm the next row over on two. Apartment two fourteen. My name is George Tinopolis. Good to meet you." He came over and shook hands with me. He was stocky and well proportioned with a short, black beard, weathered Bermuda shorts, and bare feet.

"Deb McCarroll," I replied. "Tinopolis. Greek?"

He smiled. "By way of Akron, Ohio. Me and Klinger from M*A*S*H, Akron's greatest claims to fame. Listen, I'm just on my way back up and I make a killer guacamole. Why don't you stop by?"

"I'd love that, George. Thanks."

He was right. His guacamole was excellent. So were the icy Margaritas, which came straight from the blender on the weather-beaten table between us.

"Thanks for the invitation, George. I must admit, it's been kind of difficult meeting anybody on this island."

"When the weather lets up, you won't have a problem. People are more holed up right now. But when in doubt, you can't beat the laundry for socializing." We clinked glasses.

"Actually, I was hiding out in the laundry," I said.

"Hmm, I'm intrigued."

"No, no, nothing like that. My neighbor appeared today for the first time in weeks, actually since I moved in, and he proceeded to blow me away with his super cool stereo system."

"Ah, I see. All quiet for weeks, huh? He probably works on an oilrig offshore. Those guys are out for a month or more and back for a few weeks. Sounds like your boy."

"Does the song *Brown Eyed Girl* have any significance to the average offshore roughneck, because this one sure loves that song."

"Not to my knowledge. Must be personal."

That night, I was sound asleep when *Brown Eyed Girl* came banging through my subconscious. I got up and pulled on some clothes. As I stepped outside, the manager, accompanied by a couple of Galveston's finest, were topping the last step and heading for my neighbor's door. They continued to bang until the song ended, not waiting for the quiet and adding to the general mayhem. The door opened and my neighbor stood shirtless in the light, which was pouring from within. He was weaving just slightly and he gripped the knob to steady himself.

"Jerry, now you've been warned. You either gotta turn that music down or you gotta wear headphones. People are trying to sleep. I don't want to have to toss you out of here, Jerry."

"That's right, sir. Get yourself a pair of headphones. Then you can enjoy your music as loud as you like without disturbing your neighbors." The officer had a kind tone, trying to reason with old Jer.

Jerry pushed his glasses up his nose and nodded.

It was all quiet on the western front for weeks, and I had settled comfortably into my little community, meeting more of my neighbors and finding out that island life suited me. I was leaning on the railing on the balcony, watching the rain move in from out at sea, when Jerry stepped outside. I smiled and he avoided eye contact, but he leaned on his adjacent rail and we watched the weather in silence.

"You're a girl, right?" he mumbled finally, digging at the callouses in his thick palms.

"Last I checked," I replied.

"What do girls like?"

"I'm sorry?"

"If someone wanted to do something for a girl, what would be a good thing to do?" Ah, the *Brown Eyed Girl*, I presumed. Our man Jerry was in love. I considered briefly whether he could be referring to me and discarded the notion, believing that he would not be asking if I were, indeed, the object of his affection.

"Well, some girls like flowers or cards, stuff like that. But me? It means a lot to me when someone takes the time to talk to me and find out what interests me. I'll give you an example: I dated this guy that overheard me saying once that I liked a particular artist, and he got me a book about that artist. See, that was thoughtful and it was interesting to me and, unlike flowers, it didn't die, only to be thrown away. I still have that book and I still love it, even though the guy is long gone. That's just an example, of course. It could be anything. And small gestures often mean the most."

His brow was furrowed and he was nodding. He stood up straight and looked at me with very serious eyes. "Thank you very much," he said, and he went back inside.

Please! Please, I have to go to work tomorrow. I'm begging you." I sat up and rubbed my eyes. Jerry was at it again. I looked through the glass and there was a young woman standing at Jerry's door in her robe. She was pounding with balled up fists and she was sobbing.

"She finally snapped," I said to myself. The police and the manager came traipsing up the stairs again and I dressed in a hurry, not wanting to miss it. *Brown Eyed Girl* started over, but Jerry never answered the door. The manager stood front and center with her pass key and the door was flung open. There, on the floor, Jerry was passed out with a pair of new large headphones cupped securely to his ears. He had a bottle of Jack Daniels in one hand and the jack to the headphones in the other.

The following week, Jerry was gone. I took a tour of his empty apartment, mystified that an actual human being lived there. His kitchen floor had a quarter inch layer of dried mud that cracked and crunched under foot. The stove had clearly never been cleaned during his tenancy, and I will forego description of the bathroom.

Poor Jerry, I wonder if he ever got his brown eyed girl, I thought, as I stuffed a change of undies and a toothbrush into my backpack. The island had been issued an official hurricane warning, and I was going to hole up in my old room at Ma's place.

I zipped up the bag and trotted downstairs to my car. George was out on his balcony, gathering potted plants to carry inside. I threw the backpack into the front seat and stepped up to say hi.

"Hey, George. You need a hand?" George was a warm bear of a man, and I had come to love him dearly. He had a generous pelt of hair on his shoulders and back, even having to shave his neck. By the cruelest twist of fate, he was also bald.

"Sure," he chirped. "The ivy has really taken off. I could use some help getting all of it inside." A roll of masking tape rested on the concrete.

"Taping off the windows, huh? I'm not sure if I did mine right. Is it just an X down the length of the glass?"

"That's it," he said. "Some folks go crazy with the stuff, but if the storm hits and you need more than that, your windows are going to be the least of your worries. You going to stay for the fireworks?"

"Not me. I'm a lightweight. So much as a breeze and I'm gone. Gonna spend the night with my mom. You?"

"I'm staying. I don't think it's going to be much. I've been watching the barometer, and I don't think she's got what it takes."

"All the same, I'd rather not be on the island." We transported the dozen or so plants and finished taping up the sliding glass doors.

"Thanks for your help," George called as I jumped in the driver's seat.

I waved and pointed the car for the mainland. The day was bright and sunny, but you could feel it in the air. The wind was pulling at the trees, the clouds piling on the horizon. Ma was just coming out of the gate when I arrived.

"Oh Sugar, what a surprise. What are you doing here?" she asked as I kissed her cheek.

"Hurricane's a comin,' Ma. Gotta head for high ground."

"Well yes, you can't stay on that island, can you? You'll drown," she teased. "I was just on my way to the mailbox."

"Let me drop my stuff and I'll come with ya," I said.

After retrieving the latest issue of the Reader's Digest and several grocery store circulars, we walked to a little sandwich shop in the strip mall next door.

"How is Beth these days?" she asked, unwrapping her tuna on rye. The paper ticked off a cha-cha beat in her shaking hands.

"Well, Beth and I don't really see each other anymore, Ma. I ran into her at the fair and it was kind of weird. We kind of just went our separate ways, I guess. We've become different people."

"Well, that's too bad. You were such good friends."

I shrugged. "It happens. On the other hand, Julie says "hi." I talked to her the other day."

"Oh, Julie. How is she?"

"Great. Her girls are adorable and she's teaching second grade."

"A teacher and a mother, imagine that. It's hard to believe she's all grown up, huh? Where does the time go?"

"Beats me. I'll always be sixteen, you know that, Ma."

"Well, I certainly hope not."

"And what's new with you, Mama San?" I asked, crunching into a potato chip.

"Oh, Deborah. I've been feeling so nervous lately. I have to go back to the doctor next week."

Ma would say she was "feeling nervous" when her medication, or lack thereof, was making her feel particularly jittery and anxious. The anti-hallucinogens were a cocktail of powerful medicines, and finding the delicate balance of how much, and how often, to suit her illness was an ordeal. Each time her prescription was altered, a rough period of intensified tremors, insomnia, and loss of appetite followed as her body adjusted and the dosage was fine-tuned. After so many years of continual medicating, eventually she would develop a resistance to each drug, and the whole thing would have to start all over again.

"Oh Mom, I'm so sorry. Is there anything I can do?"

She gestured with her sandwich. "I wish," she said.

George was right, as usual. Bonnie turned out to be more bark than bite, dumping a lot of rain but causing little wind damage, and by the following weekend, the blue skies were back. George and I were flying kites in the empty field out front, watching the colorful patches of fabric flutter and clap in the ocean breeze.

I was reeling in a line tethered to the struggling kite when Daniella pulled up on her ten speed, looking golden and glorious. She stood leaning on the bike, one hand shading her eyes as she contemplated the swaying patches of color against the cloudless sky.

"Hi, Nan!" I shouted. "We're just about done. The door's open." She waved and parked her bike under the stairs.

"How is Daniella? She found a job yet?" George had already wrestled his kite to the ground and I handed him my spool, rubbing the tightness in my wrist.

"I think so. She's interviewing to be an oceanic observer on foreign fishing vessels," I replied, gathering up the kite and retrieving the spool from George.

"What does that mean?" he asked.

"I haven't a clue. Let's ask her."

We stowed the kites and parked ourselves around a weathered table on the veranda of our favorite watering hole, The Buccaneer. The white noise of the waves crashing on the beach across Seawall Boulevard provided a nice backdrop to the conversation.

"So, where you been? I haven't seen you in a couple of days. I've missed ya," I teased, giving Daniella's arm a cuff. George was at the bar ordering drinks.

"Mailing resumes in case this observer thing falls through," she said in her careful, soft cadence. "Surprisingly, Jacques Cousteau hasn't called. Can you believe how rude?"

George put a beer in front of Nan and handed me a gin and tonic. "What's the joke?"

"Oh, Nan's upset that the Calypso crew isn't beating down her door."

"The nerve," he agreed, taking a swig off his beer. "I understand you have a lead, though."

"Yeah. I'm applying for contract work, but it could turn into something permanent. Fingers crossed. They need biologists to live on foreign fishing boats while they're in U.S. waters, ensuring they don't take anything endangered," she explained. "I'd be out sometimes, weeks at a time, on boats from Spain or Greece or maybe Russia. They all have different schedules out at sea, depending on the catch." George and I glanced at each other.

"Let me get this straight," he said. "You're going to live on a boat, in the middle of the ocean, with a bunch of fishermen from a foreign country, who most likely won't speak English, and there's a good chance that you'll be the only woman aboard? To top it all off, you're going to tell them that they have to throw part of their catch back?"

"That's about right." Daniella was soft spoken, with hair the color of summer straw and gold-rimmed glasses. She had the demeanor of a young English professor, and the image of her surrounded by large, swarthy fishermen was alarming.

"Uh Nan, that sounds awfully dangerous," I offered.

"Well, the crews know they have to comply or they can't fish in our waters, and this is where their catch is, so it's a matter of livelihood. The administrator gave me the onboard statistics on mishaps. The instances of violence are extremely low. The main issue seemed to be that of being washed overboard. That seemed to be, umm, prevalent." She nodded and stared at her beer. "But hey, it's a matter of training, right? I've been on large fishing boats before. I can handle myself."

Fifteen

ARE WE THERE YET?

You're going to live out at sea? With strange fishermen? For weeks?" Daniella had joined my family and me for dinner at one of the historic restaurants along the Galveston Seawall.

"That's the plan." Daniella sat smiling with her hands politely in her lap.

"My goodness, how exciting that sounds," Mother said, behind mounds of cold shrimp and crab claws.

"Sounds stinky to me," Isabelle said.

"Probably a lot of both," Daniella laughed.

A waitress came up behind Daniella and put her in a head-lock, raking knuckles over Nan's skull. "You get a free noogie with the seafood platter," she said.

"Cut it out, Marta." Daniella wriggled free and gave her a playful cuff. "This is my roommate, Marta," she announced. Isabelle looked mildly irritated.

"I'll send some crème brulée over, on me," Marta said. "Hiya, Deb. How about our little sailor, huh? I can't believe you're leaving, Nan. You be careful out on the big, bad sea." Marta embraced her and hurried away to one of her stations.

"Marta went to school with me. She's taken a job with Texaco and she'll be serving on one of their ships."

"My, you girls are adventurous. Dear, aren't you fright-ened, going so far away on your own like that?" Ma put a hand on Nan's arm.

"Well, I'm a little nervous, but it's what I trained for. I'm prepared. I'm looking forward to it, really. When I began the Marine Program at A&M, they didn't even have enough housing for students, so we lived on the ship. I got used to the close quarters, and I loved going out to sea. I think I'll be all right."

"Would you listen to Mother?" Isabelle said. "All she ever did was go off on her own. How many times did I get that phone call that she had disappeared again?"

"Well, that's different. I never went out in the middle of the ocean."

"No, just an ocean of sand," I added.

Here's to freedom," I toasted, clinking glasses with George. The ink on my pink slip bled rings as I replaced my cocktail on the makeshift napkin. I had been let go. "Budgetary cutbacks," the slip said. The recession was hurting everyone, even the number of rigs out in the Gulf had dwindled. Since being laid off from the university, I had papered the East and West Coasts with resumes. I got responses from Seattle and Boston, and since Daniella had gotten her observer position out of Woods Hole, Massachusetts, I'd decided on Boston. When I told George all of this, he'd said "Huh. I've always wanted to go to Boston." Then he'd quit his architect job, gave away all his plants, and started packing.

"I'm going to miss this." He took a deep breath and set his beer down on the ledge. The sky was threatening rain and the clouds were chasing each other along over the water.

"There's nothing like Texas weather. It can be clear on one side of the street and pouring buckets on the other."

"Yeah, I'm going to miss taping my windows every year and fleeing with the tourists."

"Nothing wrong with a little excitement," George said, draining his bottle. "I'm getting another one. You need anything?" He got up and pointed at his empty drink.

"Naw, I'm good." I watched him shuffle barefoot into the living room. This time next week, the three of us would be off to New England. Four if you counted Clouseau, my lop-eared rabbit. His ears hung down either side of his head, threatening to trip him as he tentatively hopped around my feet. I picked him up and scratched his velvety head. George sank back into the groaning wicker chair opposite me.

"Hey George, you ever been in love?"

"Cupid has hit me a time or two, the bastard, though it's been a while. Women are puzzling creatures, don't you find?" He smiled at me and sipped his beer. I regarded the great billowing sky churning down the beach and tickled at Clouseau's chin.

"How did you know you were in love?" I asked.

"Hmm, tricky." He repositioned his fedora higher on his head. "I guess I would have to say the most glaring symptom was lack of sleep. I didn't want to sleep because I didn't want to miss a single thing. I couldn't bare to leave her, even in dreams. I wanted to drink in her voice and her smell and her touch. Sleep seemed a tremendous waste of time. Damn near killed me."

I nodded and lowered the rabbit to the floor. He hopped inside, bewildered.

"I think I might be in love, George."

He leaned back, the ancient chair creaking, and he smiled broadly through his dark beard. "Couldn't happen to a nicer girl."

You should move back in with me. I don't know why you have to go so far away." My mother was picking at her scalloped potatoes as she sat across the walnut veneered table.

We were lunching at Mother's favorite cafeteria, just off the Gulf Freeway. She had the fish, I chose the batter-fried chicken with a side of whipped spuds. I wiped my glistening fingers with a green linen napkin.

"I know, Mom, but you know, I'll probably talk to you more after I leave than I do now. And I'll come home every chance I get. You went to California when you were around my age, didn't you?"

"Oh yes, I spent some years in San Diego when I was a girl. Those were the days. The world has changed, though. I worry about you, so far away. I mean, Boston, it's across the country. And it's so cold. Why don't you just move back in with me? Your room is just sitting there, waiting for you." Her fork fluttered in mid air.

One of the prerequisite ladies of a certain age, in dark brown polyester and rubber-soled SAS shoes, refilled my water glass. Her helmet-shaped hairdo had a purplish tinge to it.

"I wonder why older ladies have blue and purple hair like that," I whispered to my mother when the woman was out of earshot. "Isn't that the strangest thing? Do you know why they do that?" Mom was agitated, her hands raised up, oscillating on either side of her.

"Huh?" She'd zoned out on me, her right eye nearly closed.

"Nothing," I said. "It's not important. How are you feeling, Mom?" She had dressed smartly in dark slacks and a creamy silk blouse with her pearls.

"I'm a little nervous," she managed. Her mouth continued to work after she had finished talking.

"Well, let's get you home. You'll feel better when you get back into your shorts." She had a pair of yellow poly-blend shorts that she dearly loved. When I walked through the door on any given day, odds were she'd be wearing out a path in the carpet, feet bare, shorts on, a trusty tissue wadded up into the shoulder of her white, sleeveless button-down shirt.

I paid the check and left a healthy tip. My mother never really got the concept of tipping. Or maybe it was that she was stuck in another era, but occasionally she insisted on picking up a check, and no matter how much the bill was, she would only leave two quarters on the table. Two lousy quarters. Because of this, I try to tip well. Balance out that family cosmic tip scale.

I pulled into the parking lot and followed her up the walk to the front gate. Everything looked the same. Even the birdcage was still in the corner, though the birds were dead and gone now.

The parakeets had been to keep her company. Mother had complained about the noise, but she would whistle at them and really, I think she loved them. She named them Cheep and Peep. I told her she had come a long way from Kalina.

My cat, Sebastian, would sit on the arm of the couch and stare longingly at that cage for hours. One night, we were awakened by a good deal of cage banging and parakeet screeching.

When the lights came on, Sebastian was swinging from the side of the cage, his claws hooked on the bars. He had planned and plotted and finally risen to the challenge, propelling his fifteen pounds from couch arm to cage. The one hitch was that he hadn't really developed an exit strategy, and the poor thing was completely terrified as he swung in a wide arc, occasionally banging into the wall, his back legs flailing wildly.

I had risked losing an eye to those back claws as I perched precariously on a kitchen chair in my pajamas, grabbing at his considerable bulk on a return swing so that I could lift him high enough to dislodge his front paws.

When he was back on solid ground, he'd made a dash for the safety of the dark recesses under my bed, where he stayed for the remainder of the following day. Eventually, hunger got the better of him and he'd padded into the kitchen to crunch on kitty kibble and enjoy a long bath on the carpet in front of the television.

Peep wasn't as resilient and he died within a week. Cheep persevered another couple of months before we discovered him too, stiff and lifeless at the bottom of the now quiet cage.

"Mom, you want me to take that cage down?" I pointed toward the corner.

"No, I might get another bird. You never know." I considered the empty cage, feeling pangs of guilt.

She changed into her shorts. I sat on the couch and watched her pace for awhile. Back and forth. Step, bounce, shake. Into the bedroom, through the wide double doors, and just past the bed, back into the living room to the couch, repeat.

Finally, I got to my feet. "I'm going to take off, Mom, but I'll see you for dinner on Friday," I said, embracing her. "You gonna be all right?"

"Oh, yeah," she replied. "You know me. Be careful driving and I'll see you on Friday." I closed the gate and blew her a kiss.

The rain lashed the car window, forming streams of water that writhed and danced down the glass. The fading gray countryside painted tiny pictures inside each fat droplet. One by one, cheerful lights in the passing houses winked on as the evening became deep and blue.

From the back seat, I could hear the tempo of the windshield wipers keeping time with the radio's soft music.

George navigated through the downpour. Daniella was asleep in the passenger seat. The rabbit and I sat in the back, taking it all in. He, staring through the gloom, sides rising and falling with rapid breathing.

"What're you looking at?" I said, glumly. His nose twitched.

I turned back to the dim North Carolina scenery fading from view and I wished I were home.

It was late October, and the reality of this little adventure hadn't quite sunk in until the moving van had loaded up all my worldly possessions and driven away. Even when I was packing, it seemed more adventurous. Pretend. Something fun and carefree.

Now I was looking out this dark window with a hole in my gut, feeling every inch the frightened ten year old in the back seat of my brother's Chevy Vega. Was that really even me? It seemed more like an old movie I saw once. Bad color. Faltering sound.

Daniella stirred from the front. Sweet Daniella. "I think I prefer fish to a lot of people I know," she would say. "Fish are more honest."

I told her once that she reminded me of a willow tree, so graceful and soft. But looks are deceiving. The willow is tough, and it bends with the fiercest winds.

Up in the passenger seat, she sat up and stretched. From where I sat, I could see the headlights from the oncoming cars magnified through her glasses.

"Oh man, I drooled all over myself," she said, swiping a hand across her face.

I smiled in the dark and utterly adored her.

Sixteen

CHEESE WITH YOUR WHINE?

Iblew on my hands to warm them against the raw chill of the March morning as I waited in the drizzle of the deserted dock. Ships the size of skyscrapers loomed beyond the smaller fishing vessels that were parked in the harbor just outside the chain link gate where I stood. Tired looking men with thick stubble and heavy coats began to filter down the wet pavement and out the gate. Finally, I spotted her. She was talking to a tall man in a watch cap as she walked, hunched under the weight of her duffle. In the month she'd been out at sea, there had been a vicious storm and one interrupted ship to shore call. Otherwise, no contact.

Daniella said goodbye to the man and slipped through the gate. She dropped her bag and we embraced.

"Hiya honey, it's good to see you," she said in a small, weak voice that moved me deep in my chest. I smelled fish and sweat. There were dark smudges under her eyes and her cheeks were gaunt.

"Nan, where did the rest of you go?" I said, feeling bones under her coat.

"Yeah, nothing like terrible food and fearing for your life to shed a few pounds." She slammed the trunk and dropped into the passenger seat with a sigh.

"Daniella, what happened out there?"

"Just give me a minute. It's good to be off of that damn boat."

When we arrived in Boston last fall, it was cold and gray, the sidewalks piled with dirty drifts. We rented space in a white clapboard house on the south side of Boston, as far as you can get on the subway's Blue Line. It was a converted apartment in the home of a divorcee, Mrs. Landry. "I raised three boys and a husband here," she was fond of saying. Her children and husband had moved on by the time we'd arrived. She lived across a narrow hallway with her deaf, half-blind poodle, Ralphie, and we heard Ralphie's shrill bark day and night.

I threaded through the wet streets while dodging traffic and left Daniella to rest with eyes closed.

"Let's go to Pell's," she said, looking like she was talking in her sleep. "I'm dying for some real food." We picked up cheeseburger grinders from Pell's Delicatessen and sat cross-legged on the living room floor in front of a roaring fire while we had our lunch.

"All I ate the whole time out there was fish head soup and a kind of gruel called kasha," she mumbled between healthy bites. "I'll be very happy if I never see any of that mush again."

"What happened with the storm? It scared the hell out of me when the phone cut out."

As she swallowed and put her sandwich down, she wiped her hands and looked thoughtful. "I've never seen seas like that," she said, quietly. "Out the windows of the wheel house, all you could see was a solid wall of ocean bearing down. Junk's flying all over the place and everyone's shouting in Russian. I can't even tell what the hell's going on. I made my way back to my bunk and I put on my survival suit. I remember I couldn't get the buckle together because my hands were shaking so bad. I don't think I've ever been that scared. All those names on the plaque in the Gloucester, all those boats that went down, I thought, "That's going to be me." She'd modeled the orange neoprene survival suit before shipping off. It came with a signal mirror and dry rations secured in the pockets and, as she stood before the full-length mirror, she bore a striking resemblance to Gumby. She'd laughed, saying what a waste of space the suit was, as it would never be put to the test.

"All this is going on, and they're actually still trying to fish. They fish no matter what. They have families to support back home, and they get paid by the weight of the catch, so if they were going to go down, they were going to do it trying to make some money. Believe me, I was longing for the Italian boats. The Italians get a flat wage, so if it so much as sprinkles, they head back to port. And the food..." She had a wistful look in her eye. She popped the last of her sandwich into her mouth and stretched out, leaning on her elbows.

"Did you get along with everyone?"

"I got along with a couple of the guys, but they really only spoke Russian, and I don't think they were thrilled about a girl telling them what they could and couldn't keep. I heard someone try the door to my cabin in the middle of the night, but whoever it was ran off. I propped a chair against the knob after that. There was a woman on board. A babushka, I guess you'd say. Olga. She knew some English and she took care of me. Oh here, I have a picture." She slid across the wood floor to her duffle and dug around. She handed me a beat up black and white photo. She was standing on deck, the endless horizon behind her. She was in a rain slick oil coat and a watch cap standing next to a closed hanging net, heavy with fish. Beside her, a plump woman in the same coat and apron smiled broadly. She had a long knife in one hand.

"Wow. It looks like something straight out of Melville."

"Yeah, huh? One of the men had a camera and he developed this in the head. It's kind of foggy. I don't think the room was completely dark." She studied her own image. "What a way to make a living."

Three cannoli!" George yelled across the counter at the packed deli. A woman wearing large sunglasses and painted-on jeans shoved past me. Daniella glared at her back.

"Very intimidating," I said.

I had taken a job with an advertising agency downtown. I pasted up movie times in display ads, with a blade and a pair of tweezers, under vitamin-sucking fluorescent lights all day. It was all I could get. As an architect, George had fared better, and he was currently living in a lovely renovated third floor walk-up in Dorchester. The sun had started showing its face more and more as the planet slowly rolled around to summer. We were celebrating with a walk around Quincy Market and some window shopping down Newbury Street.

We claimed our pastries and squeezed our way out of the teeming Faneuil Hall Market Place into the sunshine of the courtyard. The air smelled of ocean brine and pretzels and the market was a madhouse as tourists poured in to snap pictures and gawk at street performers. A crowd was gathering around a guy in black tights juggling clubs. We made our way around the ruckus and meandered toward Haymarket Square.

"...and she kicked that poor blind dog down the stairs." I just caught the end of what Daniella was saying as I pulled away from a strange little boy that was twirling in circles until he got dizzy and fell down on the sidewalk.

"Are you talking about Ralphie? I did not kick her down the stairs," I sniffed. "She was on the stairs barking and barking at the front door. I went out there to get her to stop. I yelled and clapped my hands but she's deaf! What was I supposed to do?"

"And?" Daniella said, licking the bottom of her cannoli.

"And I just touched her back with my foot to get her attention, but she got startled and down she went. I mean really, what was I supposed to do? She's deaf!"

George looked appalled. "Oh my god."

Daniella was nodding. "I heard this thump out in the hall and when I went out to see what it was, Deb was looking down the stairs and Ralphie was at the bottom. The poor old girl didn't stop until she slammed into the front door." Nan shook her head.

"Oh for god's sake, she didn't "slam" into the door. She just sort of rolled into it, and she's fine, by the way. You forgot to tell him that part. And the stairs are carpeted." I was trying my best to defend myself, but the truth was that the sight of Ralphie falling down the stairs, yipping every third step or so, had been pretty horrifying. I hadn't pushed her. I had only touched her, but that had been enough.

George wadded up the paper that held his cannoli and wiped his hands, a contemplative look on his face. "You sent a deaf and almost blind dog down a flight of stairs...I fear there's a nice little table for one waiting for you in hell." He sucked his teeth and threw the wrapper into a nearby garbage can.

I rolled my eyes. "Fine, fine. I tried to kill a blind dog. I trip children and I make old ladies cry. All right? Now can we drop it, please?" Daniella smiled and turned to negotiate the oncoming traffic. I made eye contact with a kid of roughly six years of age hanging out the passenger window of an oncoming late model Pontiac. I smiled at him. He lifted his upper lip and shot me the finger as the car slid past me.

George and Daniella started across the street. A six year old had just flipped me off. I hated my job. I was cold and miserable. What was I doing in this city? My friends were nearly a half a block away, and as I ran to catch up, I was almost clipped by a speeding cab. He banged on his car door and screamed something obscene as he screeched by. I screamed back at him.

This city was changing me. Lately, I didn't recognize myself, and my whining and foul moods were driving Daniella crazy. One day, we were exiting the Mass Turnpike and I stopped at a red light, signaling for a left turn. The guy behind me laid on his horn, wanting me to run the light, which is customary within the city proper. But merging was tricky and traffic was thick. In my rearview mirror, I saw the man get out of his car and saunter over to my window. He was a big guy, with muscles stretching his Guinness t-shirt. His neck was thick and his sandy hair was chiseled into a bristled crew cut. "Why don't you learn how to fuckin' drive?" he asked casually when he reached my car door.

"Why don't I learn to fuckin' drive? Why don't I learn to fuckin' drive? Why don't you learn some manners? Who do you think you are, you no neck, jarhead asshole? Huh? Who raised you, a pack of wolves? Huh?!" I was shaking and spitting as I hung out my window. He shook his head and walked back to his car.

"Are you crazy?" Daniella said, when I was back in my seat. "You could have gotten us killed. You don't know that guy. He could've had a gun."

"I'm sick of everyone yelling at me," I said. "I'm just so sick of the yelling." I put the car in gear and merged into traffic.

The smell and the noise and the wind. Christ, this city." I was mixing up a pot of blue paint. A blank canvas was stretched out on the kitchen table. Daniella was trying to read a magazine. "I was riding the train in from work, right? Dead tired. Just wanting a little peace. And this guy whips it out and just starts peeing. Right there on the 6:15. I watched the stream travel down the length of the train. Nobody did a damn thing. Everyone ignored him. Then he just put it back and zipped up like nothing happened." I washed out a brush and wiped my hands on my paint stained t-shirt. "I couldn't believe it. I could not believe it. People are nuts. They are." Daniella dropped her magazine and got up to leave.

"Nan, did you hear me?"

"Yes, I heard you. I've been hearing you. Why don't you just go back to Texas then? For God's sake, stop griping!" I replaced the lid on the paint and slowly screwed it tight. "Oh. Wow. I'm sorry. Look, I know you're unhappy. I know that. But...I can't change the city. I can't change the people and, believe it or not, I like it here. I don't know what you want me to do. What do you want?"

"I just want to feel like myself again. I want to be able to recognize myself when I talk. I'm afraid I'm disappearing, Nan."

The phone rang and Daniella answered it in the front room.

"Deb..." I gave my hands a final wipe and took the phone from her.

"It's your sister," she said.

Mother!" I left my bag in the hall and wrapped my arms around her where she stood in her bedroom. A black tuxedo was laid out on her bed.

"Oh Deborah, my little girl." As she held me tight, it seemed to me that she had shrunk an inch or two.

"Hi, Sis." Isabelle stepped around Mom and bussed me on the cheek. "Thanks for coming."

"Thanks for paying." I looked down at the suit of clothes and whistled. "Wow, slick."

"Can you believe it? Can you believe what she wants me to wear? Honestly." Mother carefully hung the suit on a hook inside the open closet door, missing the peg twice before bringing the hanger in for a landing. The tux hung like a giant ventriloquist dummy.

Isabelle was president of a small neighborhood bank in one of the suburban communities that migrated around the city of Houston like clustered stars around a black hole. She was active in various charities and supported several youth organizations. She was attractive, well spoken, charming, and she was a public relations dream come true. Therefore, the Chamber of Commerce had overwhelmingly voted her Woman of the Year. She was insisting on formal tuxedoes for everyone in her party at the awards dinner. I was looking forward to the looks of distaste from some of the more traditional Chamber members.

Isabelle put an arm around Ma. "Are you kidding? It's going to be a scream. You pretend you're Greta Garbo and I'll be Clark Gable." She winked at me. "I'm wearing white tails with a red bow tie, cummerbund, and matching pumps. I had them dyed fire engine red."

"Nice," I said. "I too brought for the occasion. Very tasteful. Promise not to embarrass you."

"Perish the thought." She gathered her purse and her keys. "Okay, little sister, I'll see you later. I gotta get back to work. Goodbye, Mother. Love."

Isabelle's speech was a big hit. She was resplendent in that white tux and everyone was riveted, nodding and laughing in all the right places. The audience looked a little dowdy by comparison. Our table certainly stood out in a room full of brown suits and flower prints.

Mother disappeared during one of the many long lectures on the importance of community involvement and I ducked out to look for her. She was pacing in the outer corridor, her hands working at the end of the stiff, black sleeves.

"Hiya, Ma. Everything okay?"

"Oh, sure. I just had to walk," she replied. Her black tails were identical to Isabelle's, save for the accents being in teal. When she stood next to my sister, looking like an uncomfortable penguin, they were the very picture of yin and yang.

"I'll walk with you," I said.

"How is Daniella?"

"She's good. Still going out on those fishing boats, ya know."

"Isn't that something? You couldn't even imagine such a thing in my day," she mused. "For a time, my dad cut down trees for a living, and I always wondered what that would be like. It was great fun climbing all over those mountains. There weren't any women lumberjacks, of course. I wonder if that's still true. Do you know? And how is my Q.T.? How do you like the East Coast?"

"Well, I fear your youngest child has turned into something of a whiner, Ma."

"What? That doesn't sound like you. I've never known you to complain. Are you getting enough to eat? Are you keeping warm? I sure worry about you."

"I'm fine. I'm just...I feel like I'm drowning out there. Drowning in people. There are just so many people. People everywhere. And no place to hide."

"You always did like being off by yourself. You were different than the others in that way." She nodded her head in the direction of the banquet room. "That's the artist, I guess. Or maybe because you were alone so much growing up."

"Do you ever dream about flying, Ma? You know, just soaring above the rooftops and freedom and the lovely air up there?" Sadness washed over me and I blinked tears away.

"Dreams about flying? No, I don't think so. I've always preferred to walk."

"I've never dreamed like that either. Friends tell me about these fantastic experiences where they just take off, feeling the wind and seeing the world far below, but I've never been able to do that. If I'm up high, I fall. I fall, and you know, people say that if you die in your dreams, you die in life, but that's not true because I die. I die in my dreams."

She stopped and pulled me close. The coarse fabric on her shoulder smelled vaguely of plastic. "Oh, Deborah. Honey, if you're unhappy, come home," she said. "You can always come home. I'm always here."

I squeezed her and took her elbow. "I have to work some things out, Ma. Maybe." We continued to walk in the quiet corridor. Her pumps echoed over the muffled laughter from the crowd inside.

"Are you meeting any nice men out there?" she asked, squeezing my hand.

"Well ah...no. I don't really like men like that, Ma."

"That's good," she said. "They're nothing but trouble."

The banquet had been held in a big hotel out near the airport. After the event, Isabelle worked the room, shaking hands and posing for pictures. I was in the middle of a yawn when she grabbed me from behind.

"Uh-uh. None of that. The night is young," she said. "We're going dancing in the club downstairs."

"What? In this monkey suit? I don't think so."

"Oh come on, don't be a dud. When did you become such an old lady?"

"Birth," I answered. She rolled her eyes and pulled me out of my chair.

The club was loud. Music thumped up through my rib cage. The dance floor was populated with suburban looking folks jabbing and swaying just this side of the actual tempo.

I sat at a table with a group of Isabelle's friends and colleagues while she went to the bar to fetch drinks. One of them leaned over, attempting to make chitchat. Thankfully, she gave up after a bit, screaming that it was good to see me and leaning back into her chair to sip her umbrellaed cocktail. Isabelle carried the drinks to the beat of the music, bobbing and sloshing watered down spirits onto the table.

"Whoops," she giggled, handing me a drink. "Here, I got you a Tom Collins."

"Uh, thanks." I took the drink and dabbed up some of the drabs with a paper napkin. "Where's Mother?" I yelled into her ear.

"Jack took her home. She was tired. Ooo, I love this song. C'mon, let's dance." She grabbed me and hustled me out to the dance floor, positively glowing under the spotlights, an incandescent beauty in a man's suit and red silk high heels.

"God, Isabelle, I feel ridiculous," I said.

"No parking on the dance floor." She grabbed my hands and began to pull me around, occasionally twirling me under her arm. Her hands were small and delicate in mine, and she was an inch or two shorter, but she led with authority. I laughed in spite of myself as we danced and shimmied in a kaleidoscope of color and noise.

By the time she pulled into Mother's apartment complex, my tie and cummerbund were in my pocket and my head was spinning from the gin.

"Congratulations, Isabelle," I murmured, as we sat idling by the front gate. "I'm glad I got to see this. Thank you."

She sat, hands on the wheel, still pristine and buttoned up. "It wouldn't have been the same without you, little sister. We miss you."

"I miss you too," I said. I eased back into the seat and closed my eyes. "It's good just to...thaw."

Seventeen

YOU CAN'T GO HOME

I was wondering when you were going to show up. You said you'd be here at six." Isabelle greeted me on the walk outside Ma's apartment. "How's the new place?"

"Yeah, sorry. I got hung up. I bought a couch today. It folds out, so now I have a bed too. I feel so grown up. Too bad my bank account's still adolescent." I survived nearly two years before leaving Daniella and George in Boston. There had been hurt feelings and the pain of something ending, and Nan and I were still unsure and tongue-tied through phone calls, but it was getting easier. Now I was broke and back at square one.

A moving truck was parked just off the curb, the lift stacked with packing boxes. "What's all this?" I asked.

"Mother's coming to live with me and I'm recruiting you as an official mover," she said, grabbing my hand and leading me inside.

"Oh wow." Open boxes were stacked throughout the living room and kitchen. The walls were bare, and even the bird cage was gone from its customary spot in the corner. "I can't believe it. Where's Mom? How's she doing with...with all of this?" Jack tottered past, his arms full.

"She's great. She doesn't know." Isabelle laughed and looked around the room, itemizing everything that had to be thrown away or packed.

"What? What do you mean she doesn't know?"

"She doesn't know. She's watching the kids at home. I'll tell her this evening." She walked to the kitchen and surveyed the damage. "You can start packing up dishes. These boxes here have the compartments for the various pieces, and you can use this stuff between the plates. Okay, Sis, have at it." She smiled brightly and started for the bedroom. "Jack, have you loaded the drawers yet?"

"Isabelle—" I followed, close on her heels.

"Isabelle, about Mom."

"Oh, I know, poor thing," she said. "She just shouldn't be living on her own anymore. Do you know she fell twice last month? And she's been so depressed and listless. It's hard to even get her out of bed. The boys will keep her engaged. Keep her present." She was pulling clothes off of the rod in Ma's closet and stuffing them into large garbage bags.

"But don't you think we should tell her all of this before we just pack up everything she owns and give the keys away?" She stopped and fingered her bangs out of her eyes.

"Why? Do you think it would be easier for her? Do you think she'd agree to it? No, of course she wouldn't. I can't even move the couch from there to there without a fight. Now, we have her room all ready for her, and we're going to move her furniture and all her things in so she can feel at home and be comfortable. She'll be fine. She'll make a fuss at first, but at least she won't waste away in bed." Isabelle tied a knot in a bulging plastic bag. "Now do me a favor and take these out to the truck, would you?" She picked up the bundle and passed it off to me. I struggled outside with the shifting load and plopped it up on the lift.

I followed the walk around the complex to the pool. The evening was warm, the sky washing a brilliant orange as the day seeped away. I pulled a chair to the edge of the water and stared at my lapping reflection. It hadn't occurred to me that Mom would ever leave here. This was my home, too. The front walk where I'd kissed dates goodbye and kicked off sandy beach shoes. The cat snoozing on the patio, the birdcage. All gone. It was the most normal place we'd ever had together, and it was the last place we'd ever share. I heard my mother's voice ring in my ears. "You can always come home."

226

I took a brooding walk back to say goodbye and help with the move. Isabelle was on her knees, searching through bulging sacks that spilled out onto the carpet.

"There you are. I need your help. I can't find Mother's medication. It's in a white pharmacy bag and she's due for a shot this weekend. If I can't find it, she'll have to wait until Monday, and you know how she gets if she goes past the scheduled injection." I started digging in the bag next to her.

"Where's the last place you saw it?" I asked.

"It was in her closet, so it might have been packed in one of these bags. It also might have been put in one of the garbage bags that got tossed into the dumpster." We searched all the bags in the bedroom and retrieved several from the moving truck, wrestling with the knots and dumping contents.

"Well, that's it. It's not here. Dammit!" Isabelle sat back on the couch.

"I'm going to look in the dumpster," I said.

The walls of the commercial dumpster towered over my head. I squinted at it with foreboding. "Give me a boost, will ya?" Isabelle laced her fingers and I stepped into them. I grabbed the top and dropped down into the darkness onto springy mounds of aromatic refuse. I held my breath and began tearing open bags. As my eyes adjusted to the dark, I dug through all the collections Ma had squirreled away over the years. Mesh bags filled with small slivers of bar soap, cracked and petrified. Dozens of empty shampoo bottles, packets and packets of fast food salt and ketchup, and of course, actual garbage. Rotten vegetables, old jars of condiments, molding leftovers.

"Yech!" I said as my hand sunk into a fuzzy tomato.

"Deb, just forget it. We don't even know if it's in there. I'll get her prescription filled on Monday. Just get out of there." Isabelle's voice floated over the steel walls of the dumpster.

"Just a few more bags."

"Well, I'm going back in."

"Okay, I'll be out in a minute."

I stepped sideways and nearly fell into the putrid pile. I righted myself and ripped open the next bag, and the next one, and the next. Too far to the right and the bags yielded baby food jars and frozen food cartons. Too far to the left and I dug up beer cans and TV dinner containers. I mentally mapped out the search perimeters and got to work.

"Some kid you turned out to be," I muttered, tossing aside a tomato soup can. "Never there when she needed you. Never there, period. All the work she put in. The sacrifices. What'd you ever do for her? Huh? What?" I went to my knees and dug furiously, tears stinging my eyes. "Please. Please, just let me save her this small pain. Just...just let me do this one thing for her..."

And suddenly, there it was. Halfway down, through a pile of wadded up tissues, I pulled out a white paper sack with a little blue crest. It smelled of my mother's perfume. There, amidst the refuse and the waste, I clutched it to my chest and breathed her in.

"Can I get you something, Mother?"
"No." She sat on the chintz sectional sofa, staring at nothing. I brought her a cold drink and set it in front of her. She ignored it. My nephew ran into the room in his stocking feet. He hurled himself onto the sofa cushions and lay panting.

"What's up there, sonny? You better get your shoes on, you're gonna be late for school." He just grinned and shook his head, pushing his cheek further into the pillows. Magda, the family housekeeper, carried his sneakers to the couch and got down on one knee. He pulled his feet up and tucked them under him. She laughed and said something to him in Spanish. He shook his head. She dropped the shoes and lunged at him, pulling at his feet and finally tickling him into a fit of shrieks and giggles.

"Stop it, stop it, would you stop that!" my mother barked. Magda flushed and busied herself opening laces and pulling the tongues from the shoes. My nephew allowed them to be slipped on and tied.

"He's just a little boy, Ma," I said. She looked at me and went upstairs to her room.

The days passed and my mother became resigned to her new surroundings. She was sitting under an enormous umbrella on the back patio. Palms and banana trees grew green and lush, providing the illusion of a private oasis. I took a seat across from her at the patio table. "Hi, Mom," I said. "It's nice out here, huh? Not too humid today."

"I suppose. How's work?" she asked.

I shrugged. "Same ol'. Ma, a friend of mine is moving to Seattle, and I think I'm going to go with her."

She looked out over the yard and nodded.

"Houston is just not the place for me, Ma. I've never loved it, not like Isabelle. You understand?"

"Of course. You have to find your own way. You're a grown woman now. It rains a lot there, doesn't it?"

"That's what they say. It seems nice, though. Hey, remember when we'd watch the rain out at Mrs. Shussler's place? Everything washed clean and the dust settling out of the air? I just loved that smell. We'd stand in the doorway together and just watch it come down."

"Oh, Mrs. Shussler. What I remember is that ugly dog of hers."

"Mom! Jimi was sweet," I chided. "I wonder what ever happened to him."

"He died, I imagine."

"Well, yes."

"Are you okay, Mom? You want to talk about anything?"

"No, I'm fine."

"I'm gonna miss you, Ma."

"Well, you know where I'll be."

Eighteen

THEY

Ipopped the last of my sandwich into my mouth and rinsed the plate, leaving it to dry near the sink. My sparse living room was littered with poster board, magic markers, and cans of paint. The airy Seattle apartment was really more than I could afford on my own, but I was in love with the place. The only furniture I had was a mattress on the floor and a drawing table tucked into the corner. Partially completed stacks of paintings leaned here and there, and raw pieces of painted canvas splashed across the walls. I was living the life of the bohemian artist, and I loved the funky cafes and coffee houses that were a Seattle staple. Tonight, this room would be wall-to-wall with loud chatter and happy party goers. My friend Carry and I were throwing a shindig, complete with barbecued chicken and a rented snow cone machine.

To offer people somewhere to sit, I'd constructed a quick bench from a hunk of two-by-eight lumber and some steel pipe. Canary yellow, with my own red handprints stamped down the length of it, and the thing looked precariously top-heavy standing near the wall. I touched a finger to the surface and it came away smudged with paint. "Come on, dry." I opened all the windows, hoping to cure the paint before guests arrived in a few hours. I was tapping the lid back on paint cans when the phone rang.

"Mmyellow."

I heard scuffling and close breathing. "Hello? Who is this?" I said.

"Hey little sister."

"Judith? Wow, sorry. That was weird."

"What's that supposed to mean?" Her speech was thick and slow.

"Nothing. What's going on?"

"Something has to be going on? I can't call my sister?"

"Of course, of course. How are you?"

"I threw Matt out." I could hear her children playing in the background.

"What? Oh my god."

"Yeah, he didn't come home from work and I went to the bar and there he was, sitting with his brother, having a fucking beer. I said, "Are you kidding? I wash your clothes and cook your dinner and you're sitting in a fucking bar? Don't bother coming home."

"Uh, wow. I'm sorry."

"Sorry? Don't be sorry for me. Be sorry for his sorry ass. It's no big deal, I've done it before. I get tired of his shit."

"How are the kids with all of this?"

"Fine," she said brightly. "We went to McDonald's."

"Uh-huh. I was kind of..."

"What about you? How come you're always Pollyanna? Huh? Don't you have any fucking problems?"

"Of course. Course I do. Everybody has problems."

"Like what?"

"What? I don't know. Money, job sucks. Life. What is this? What's going on? Are you okay? You sound...funny." With that, the phone went dead. My mouth dropped open and I sighed. I picked up the phone and dialed Isabelle.

After the general niceties, I told her what had happened. "Oh yeah, she's drunk. She hangs up on me all the time. She's an alcoholic," Isabelle said, matter-of-factly.

"What? Since when?"

She laughed. "Since forever. High school, maybe? How could you not know?"

"I don't know. I mean, she's always been erratic, but she's never hung up on me before or called me sounding like that."

"You're lucky. She likes to call me in the middle of the night crying. Then the next day, she acts like nothing happened. I used to get really upset and worked up about it, pleading with her to come live with me. Anything to get her to stop drinking, but she's got to want it."

"How could I not have known this? All those years, she always had something. Beer, Yukon Jack."

"Oh, yes. She loves her Yukon."

I transferred the phone to my other hand and cleared my throat.

"How's Mother?"

"Speaking of messes, huh?" she laughed. "Oh, she's fine. I think she's sleeping now. I'll get her."

"No. Don't do that. I'll call tomorrow. Tell her I'll call tomorrow."

"Okay, sis. Don't let Judith bother you. She'll be fine the next time you talk to her. Half the time, she doesn't even remember what she said. Or she acts like she doesn't." She clicked her tongue.

"Thanks. Talk to you tomorrow." I hung up and eyed the sunny, yellow bench. Suddenly, I didn't feel much like a party.

I love your work." I was putting out more chicken when a blonde guy in a tight t-shirt sauntered over. He stood staring at the painting on the wall, arms partially crossed, clutching a cherry-red ball of ice in a mangled paper cone.

"Thanks," I said.

"There's so much depth and color. It's wonderful."

"Glad you like it. Everything's for sale, by the way."

My friend Andrew sidled up to me and slipped his arm in mine. "I need to borrow her for a minute," he said, steering me away.

I pulled my arm free. "What the hell? The guy was interested in the painting."

"I don't think you should be talking to him." Andrew was licking at an orange stream trickling down the side of his paper cone as he glanced around the room at the milling crowd.

"Why not?"

"He's a vegetarian."

"So?"

"I don't trust vegetarians. Or non-drinkers."

"Ah."

"You can't trust 'em. Anyone who's never cut into a thick, juicy steak or uttered at least one "I love you man" in a drunken stupor does not know what it is to live."

"I see."

"And therefore cannot be trusted to feel passionate about art."

"Uh-huh."

"Trust me, I did you a favor. The guy has no pulse. You don't want someone like that walking past your painting every day."

"All I care about is the passion in his bank account."

Andrew looked horrified. "You don't mean that."

As the crowd parted, one of the guests walked past with a yellow and red print in the shape of my hand stamped to the seat of her pants.

As the evening waned, the barbecued chicken disappeared and dancing ensued. A mirrored ball threw tacky, beautiful stars around the darkened room while my boss poured straight vodka over shaved ice and knocked it back in one shot. Her husband thanked me for a lovely evening and steered her to the door. The cops came, complaining about the noise. All in all, a great success.

Late the next morning, Carry cleaned out the snow cone machine while I made my way around the room, a large garbage bag trailing behind. Sticky paper cones were everywhere. Carry's dog, Jake, was in the corner, licking himself with great ferocity.

"What was going on in the bedroom, anyway?" I said, as I wiped lime syrup from my fingers onto my pant leg.

"I believe that was spin the bottle. Or truth or dare. Or both."

"Oh man, I missed it." The telephone rang and I dropped the garbage bag, reaching for the phone before it could ring again.

Isabelle's cheerful voice chimed a hello in my ear. "Oh, hi Isabelle, I was going to give you a call in a bit. You beat me to it."

"Yeah, I've been thinking and I have a favor to ask. I wonder if you could come stay for a few days and watch over Mother? She's been a handful lately and I'd like to take the boys skiing."

"A handful?"

"Yes, she's stopped eating. She says they are closing her throat and choking her so she can't swallow."

They. How I hated They. I could hear my mother's voice. "Are They making you say that?" "That's what They want you to do." "Are They hurting you?" I had gotten used to not having They around. I sat down heavily on the unmade bed. "I thought you said she was fine."

"Oh, she is, she is. There's nothing really wrong with her, medically speaking. She's lost a lot of weight though, and she's weak. She fell again and she needs help going to the bathroom. And she shakes, of course, poor thing. She's hallucinating again, too. Her doctor's trying to get her on another medication that, you know, doesn't have the side effects too bad. All she does is sip Pepsi from a straw up in her room. I think she's single-handedly keeping them in business."

I had the urge to slam the phone down and run screaming from the room. I cleared my throat. "When do you want me there?"

When the conversation was done and the line between that world and this one had been severed, I sat with my knees up around my ears, hunched on the rumpled mattress.

"You okay, bud?" Carry came and sat next to me.

"I have to go take care of my mom. She's stopped eating."

Carry put her arm around me. "I'll come with you."

"No. Thank you. I should go alone. She's not well. It would be awkward. Thank you, though. Really." I sighed. "It'll be all right. I knew I couldn't stay away forever."

Hiya, Shayba." I leaned over the bed and enfolded her frail figure. She held me close with bony arms and uttered a mushy, "Oh, Deborah."

Her eyes were glassy and her cheeks sunken, making her a distortion of her former vigorous self.

"Oh Deborah, I can't hardly swallow. My throat is all closed up." She floated a swaying hand above her neck.

The furniture here was the same stuff that had been in our home together. Here was the same bed where she'd read her magazines and Sunday paper, giving me an interesting bit of gossip or news now and then. Here, the same good dresser and mirror stood, waiting for her smile as she admired a new blouse, tugging and smoothing and asking what I thought. How could this sturdy, reliable wood and glass and glue have stood by and watched this steady decline? It was a cruel joke to see the same bedding, bright and cheerful as ever, with my mother wasting away beneath.

"I'm sorry, Mother," was all I could say, and I sat and held her hand.

Her gaze wandered past the walls and she slowly adjusted the shoulder strap of her blue silk nighty with a stiff hand. I watched it work. Her nails were perfectly manicured and painted, her hands smooth and youthful. Isabelle did her nails regularly, tenderly massaging in lotion along with wry humor and conversation.

"You sure have nice hands, Ma," I told her.

"Oh yeah? You think so?" She looked at her nails and then her eyes got all soft as she drifted off again. I sat with her like that the rest of the afternoon. We watched the game shows and bad sitcoms in her clean, white room. Past the gauzy film of the curtains, the sun disappeared below rows of neat suburban rooftops.

You should look before you back up!" my sister shouted at the man in the dark green minivan. He nodded, smiling. She returned a tense smile and smoothly raised her driver side window with the push of a button. "Stupid," she said, under her breath. We were cruising the parking lot of one of Houston's many chain restaurants, searching for a spot. I felt sorry for the man. He was a gray-haired Asian guy with glasses, and he looked like he was the type of grandpa that would slip a kid a ten spot with a wink and a sly smile.

My sister shouted over the pandemonium in the back seat. "Boys, I shouldn't have called that man stupid. It's not polite." Her three sons were playing video games on the built-in console, punching and slapping each other between points. The youngest whined and complained that something wasn't fair. They all ignored my sister completely.

When we got inside the restaurant, Isabelle put her name on the list and gave the boys each a twenty for yet more video games. She and I made for the bar.

"I make sure they know their manners," she was saying as we perched on the heavy bar stools. "Like that Chink back there? I made sure I let them know it wasn't right to call him stupid, even though he was." She laughed and put her hand lightly on my knee. "We don't say "stupid" in our house."

"What?"

"Can I get a glass of white? Sis?" She had motioned the bartender with a little wave.

"Gin and tonic please. Double. Uh, Isabelle—"

"It sure means a lot to Mother to see you. She seems better, don't you think? I think it's really lifted her spirits."

"Well, thanks. I mean, I hope so, but—"

"I tell her we're going to Mexico when she's better, to lie on the beach. We always have a good time there and it's been awhile."

I nodded and had a sip of my drink. I knew my frail mother was not likely to see the white, powdery sands of Cozumel ever again.

Isabelle talked about her sons' grades and achievements, her work. Finally, she pulled me into a bear hug, rocking me unsteadily on my bar stool. "My little sister. I wish you didn't live so far away."

Everyone was up bright and early the next morning to catch their flight. Jack and I made the usual mutterings at each other, never having much to say. Soon my sister glided in and wrangled her three boys out the door, kissing me on the cheek as she passed.

After seeing them off in the driveway, I turned and headed back for the gate. The house was still, except for the muffled television in my mother's room. I sighed and started for the stairs. Taki, my sister's green parrot, wolf-whistled at me loudly from a large brass cage in the corner. "I bet you say that to all the girls," I said.

I climbed up the stairs and peeked in through my mother's door. "Hi, Mom. How's it going?"

"Uhhhh," she replied in a high-pitched, dismissive grunt.

"Do you need something?"

"I need to go to the bathroom," she croaked.

"Oh. Uh, okay, no problem. What do we do?"

"Help me up." She propped herself up on one elbow and turned down her covers. I winced at the sight of her gaunt figure, feeling clumsy and strange with her. I freed her feet of the bedding and held her elbow as she stood. Slowly, we made our way down the hall. She walked, hunched over and with deliberate purpose. Step, feet together, step, feet together, an agonizing wedding march. I helped her with her undergarments and eased her down to relieve herself, and then I waited outside to give her some privacy. When she was done, we reassembled everything and made our way out the door.

An enormous sense of accomplishment filled me. I had been so afraid to see her. So afraid I wouldn't recognize her. That her vulnerability would translate into a foreign thing that would render her lost and nonexistent to me. She was the only home I had ever really had. She was a place to me, strong foundation and too many memories, and I had been terrified that the brick and mortar that was herself would have been laid to waste, leaving me homeless. But here she was. Oh yes, still here, all ninety-some odd pounds of her.

"I'd like to go downstairs," she said.

"Excellent idea," I chirped a little too loudly. We turned for the stairs.

"I feel like we're getting married," I said, as we shuffled along. She chuckled. "Yeah."

We negotiated the stairs with little incident and she settled into a nest on the sofa. The remote was found. The giant television ignited.

"How about something to eat?" I offered.

"I'd like a Pepsi," she whispered.

"You're not hungry?"

"Pepsi." Her right eye was squinted shut.

I went to the kitchen and plucked a can from the mountain of sodas in the refrigerator. I plopped down on the sofa next to her, popped the top, and put a bendy straw in it for her. She took a pull on the straw, coughing and sputtering. I brought a box of tissues. She pulled one from the box, held it to her mouth, and spit into it. She wiped the sides of her mouth and her tongue with the tissue and wadded it up in her fist. After a bit, she took another shaky sip, swallowing more easily this time.

As we watched the nearly life sized figures on the television, it dawned on me that I was catching bits of my sister's voice through the din. Then I heard her laugh. I got up and took a few steps from the noise of the TV. I listened. There it was again. It was coming from the kitchen. As I got closer, it got louder. It was unmistakably Isabelle's voice. "Oh, I know. Uh-huh, yeah. Umm." My sister's laugh twinkled throughout the room. "Uh-huh, yes." I rounded the corner and it stopped. I sat at the table and listened. Nothing but Judge Judy. Then—

"Uh-huh, oh yes." More laughter.

It was the parrot. His cage was near the phone. He'd heard my sister talk here so many times that he'd learned her voice perfectly. Her phrasing, inflection, even her laugh was perfect. It was both wondrous and disturbing. I chuckled and went back over to the couch to sit with my mother.

"Wow, that was weird. I thought Isabelle was in the kitchen. That bird sounds just like her," I said.

Ma rolled her eyes. "Oh, that bird. Don't get me started."

I studied the side of her face and smiled widely. "It's good to see you, Mom."

She turned, looking vaguely surprised. "Well, it's good to see you too."

Nineteen

RENTED SHOES

I've got bad news." That was how she'd put it. Isabelle had asked me how I was, muttered pleasantries, and then she'd said that she had bad news.

"Your cousin Paul is dead. He shot himself."

Shockwaves rocked me. I'd never really thought of Paul as being mortal. I suppose I thought he'd just create another version of himself when the old one wore out. This time, maybe a bird of some sort, with glossy feathers and sharp claws, still making his own special brand of reality, high above the rooftops.

Nearly two months after that phone call, I was listening to Judith as we sat in her back yard under a blanket of stars. "I was really nervous about going to the funeral, seeing all those people again. I hadn't seen them since I was a kid." She pulled a cigarette from a rumpled pack and held a flame to the end until it glowed red in the cool night. "I was shaking. I was. I'm glad I went, though. Everyone was so nice to me. Poor Charlene. She was a mess. We get together sometimes now. You know, Isabelle doesn't think he killed himself."

"Yes, she told me that."

"What do you think?"

"I think that if I was a drug dealer and I was pissed that someone narced on me, I wouldn't go to the trouble of making it look like a suicide. I'd want everyone to know. "This is what happens to you if you screw me." I think Paul finally ran out of tricks."

"Yeah, that's what I think too. Maybe he was high. It'll make you do some fucked up things. Talking about all this stuff in AA, it made me realize how sick I was. I either had to stop drinking or I was going to die. You know, I used to think that I couldn't be happy. I couldn't just be happy or I'd have to pay for it. Now I'm trying to just be. Trying to believe that happiness isn't something that comes with a price tag." She took a sip of her tea and a deep drag on her cigarette. "I'll tell you something, though. I hope that when you die and go to heaven that you can drink as much as you want. As much as you want, with nothing bad coming with it, because I love it. I fucking love it so much."

That evening, the sofa was prepared with goodnight kisses and wishes for pleasant dreams. I lay stretched out, reading under a yellow tent of light shed from the bedside table lamp. A shuffling made its way from the shadows and I looked up to find my sister's six year old son, Marcus, standing just beyond the light. He clutched a blanket and a book. He spread the blanket on the floor behind my makeshift bed, disappearing as he reclined. Occasionally, I'd hear a page turn. An hour of silent reading passed and he stood, dragging the blanket up by a corner.

"Whatcha reading?" I asked.

"Book about a mouse."

"Mmm. Is it good?"

"Pretty good."

"I'm reading a detective mystery. I think your book sounds better."

He nodded solemnly. "Goodnight," he said.

"Goodnight, Marcus," I said.

Judith had found a tentative serenity hiding in each day. She doled out patience and tenderness with her children and she practiced a deliberate nature in her movements. She devoured tea and cigarettes with voracity and lit scented candles throughout the house. She did seem genuinely happy, though she trembled visibly and her eyes would shift to empty places. It was as if she worried that the bottle hid behind every piece of furniture, waiting to jump out and inflict itself upon her. And indeed, I suppose it did.

"Good morning," she said, as I stretched sleep from tight muscles.

"Morning." I rubbed my eyes and sat up. She was in her robe, holding a can of cat food and a spoon. She opened the back door a few inches and a petite gray cat stepped in. Judith rubbed the carpet in front of the cat with a slippered foot and the cat took a few steps forward. My sister backed up and repeated the process across the room to the door that led to the garage.

"She's blind," Judith explained, after she'd fed the unfortunate cat. "I gotta lead her to her food. We feed her in the garage because it would attract coyotes out back. She gets around pretty good, though. She bumps into the other cat, Blackie, sometimes and Blackie'll slap at her. Cats can be so mean, can't they?" She took a sip of tea. "What do you want to do today?"

"I thought I'd go see Ben. You wanna come?"

"Oh, no. I don't get out very much anymore. Besides, I have so much laundry to do."

"Can I take the kids with me?"

"Emma is at a friend's all day, but Marcus might want to go. Marcus!" The boy emerged from the recesses of the house, already dressed, his hair neatly combed.

"You want to go with your Auntie Debbie to your Uncle Ben's house today?" He looked at her with wide brown eyes. He turned to me, looking thoughtful, and then nodded once.

* * *

He hadn't said a word during the drive through the city and out into the wide open spaces. He sat small and sweet, buckled to the enormous seat, staring out the window.

"Are you hungry?" He shrugged without looking at me.

"You can have anything you want. Anything. Pizza, hamburgers. What do you want?" He rested his elbow on the door and put his chin in his palm. After a bit he turned to me.

"Vegetable soup."

"Vegetable soup? You want vegetable soup?" He nodded, his jaw set.

"You sure you wouldn't rather have a hot dog or fries or something like that?" He shook his head.

"Okay, we'll try finding vegetable soup in Belen, New Mexico, population six thousand and some."

I drove the short length of the town, searching for a sign touting the best vegetable soup in the state, but could find none. We settled into a little family-run place near the end of Main Street.

"What'll it be?" the waitress said, after water and clean silverware had been set on the checkered oilskin table cloth. Her name tag said Imelda.

"Do you have anything like vegetable soup?" She sat back on her hip and put her pencil to her lips.

"Vegetable soup... We have posole. Corn is a vegetable," she said.

"It's not spicy, is it?"

"Naw, green chili comes on the side."

"You want that?"

"What is it?" Marcus sat with fingers entwined on the table in front of him.

"It's a soup with large, white corn and pork in it. It's pretty good."

"Okay," he agreed, though he didn't look too sure about it.

"We'll take two," I said. "And bring some tortillas. Please."

When the meal was over, I paid the check and held the door for him. "So what'd you think of posole?"

"Good," he said. When the waitress had slipped the check under my plate, he'd insisted on paying for his meal, producing from his back pocket a tiny stitched wallet with a hand-tooled bucking bronc.

"Are you sure you're a kid?" I said, taking the bill from him. He smiled at me, showing off his dimples.

"Of course."

We took a left onto River Road and drove over the Rio Grande. The river sat in fat brown puddles, too lazy to move in the heat. We passed Golf Course Road and the Del Rio Apartments, with their strange stuccoed walls jutting from the center of the parking lot.

"I used to live there," I said. He looked out the window and nodded.

We pulled into the familiar gravel yard, the fence long since repaired since I'd knocked it down trying to get the Vega out of neutral. Ben emerged from the house, slamming the screen door behind him.

"Debbie..." He pulled me into a bear hug. His hair had retreated up his scalp and a small goatee was rooted to his double chin. I noticed flecks of gray. "And there's Marcus. Man, you've gotten so big. He was a baby just yesterday, wasn't he?" Marcus pretended not to hear him.

We went inside and planted ourselves on his overstuffed sofa. The place was a time capsule, looking exactly as it had when I was in high school, a little more wear and tear perhaps. My brother brought out cold drinks. Marcus sat beside me quietly, sipping ginger ale.

"You heard about Paul, huh?" he said.

"Yes, I heard. I couldn't make the funeral because of work. Did you go?"

"Yeah. I think the whole family was there. Poor Charlene, I can't even imagine. But you know he was involved in the drugs so badly. Something was bound to happen."

I took a sip from my perspiring can. "I can't remember the last thing I said to him," I said. "Probably wasn't very nice. He sure knew how to push my buttons."

"Really? I thought you two were close. You were always playing in the dirt together."

"Yeah, he loved playing in the dirt. He liked that red Chevy you used to drive. He shoved me off the roof one time."

"Oh, the Chevy. That was a good car. Real roomy. You know who had a nice car? Your dad, uh, James Clark. It was a Jaguar XKE. Leather interior. Cherry." He whistled.

I nodded and knocked back a swig of orange soda. "What's that now?"

"A Jaguar. Perfect condition."

"Who's James Clark?"

"Oh, come on. You know this. James Clark? Your dad?" I shrugged. "Nobody ever told you this? Huh. Yeah, he had a British accent and red hair. He had a daughter a little older than you. Man, that was a great car." He had a wistful look. "Come on out and see the addition I'm putting on the back of the house."

I stepped from the frigid air-conditioned driver's seat and leaned against the car. The wide-open mouth of the valley yawned in the morning sun. I wrenched the miles from my bones and took a sip from a two dollar bottle of water. The silence was absolute, the sun relentless. I hadn't seen another car for hours.

I was on my way to Roswell. I'd always wanted to see it. So many myths about the place. As far as my family was concerned, I was with Julie. I'd had lunch with her, marveled at her growing daughters, and then I'd hit the road. A small fib. I had envisioned the look on my sister's face at the disclosure of my solitary trip to a place that had no apparent portent. No family there, no friends, no real attraction, only the tackiest of histories. "You're going by yourself?" I could hear her say. "Why?"

I had the rental for three more days and the freedom of my anonymous journey filled me with a strange giddiness. A bit of debris in the breeze, free to float and shift direction on a whim.

A dust devil materialized and danced over sagebrush. It courted the wind and disappeared as quickly as it had come.

"Lil Debbie," I whispered, squinting at the place where the devil had been. Paul. Paul was gone and I was a bastard child. I sighed and walked down the road a piece, kneeling to snap a photo of a yucca in bloom. Focusing on the milky petals, I conjured Paul's face. Ten years old, grinning maniacally, his hand on my wrist as he pulled me along. Click.

Out in the world somewhere was a sister I didn't know, as much a sibling in blood as those closest to me. And a father, too. The word meant Ward Cleaver and Ozzie Nelson, so foreign was it to me. It had crossed my mind that I might search. Hire someone to comb through records, dig up the family tree, pick at old bones. But why? I searched my heart and could find no restless need. Nothing in me cried out for the comfort of strangers. Besides, the family I had was quite enough, thank you.

Roswell's your typical Small Town, U.S.A. Folks are friendly, time moves slowly. And alien faces with oversized liquid stares are everywhere. Even the streetlights have the teardrop black eyes on them.

In 1947, something plunged into the remote desert just north of the little sleepy town and since then, the local merchants have elevated merchandising of the event to a bona fide art form. The corner diner depicts the little almond eyed green guys scarfing down a hearty breakfast on the sandwich board out front. "Our waffles are out of this world!" A gleaming flying saucer hangs in front of the consignment store. "Deals that are UFOkay!" Even the seal on the police cruisers have a saucer integrated into the artwork. Extraterrestrial activity is seamlessly woven into the fabric of life in Roswell, as casually accepted as death and taxes. This plain and simple fact makes the town folk here a bit different.

I checked into my hotel late in the afternoon. The girl at the desk advised me of parking restrictions and ice machine access.

"Has anyone around here seen a UFO since 1947?" I asked, signing the slip on the counter.

"Oh, sure, just about every summer someone sees something out there. It's usually written up in the paper. You can see some of the photos taken in the museum on Main Street.

But if you talk to people in town, you're bound to find someone who's seen one." She smiled and me and wrote something on the paper I pushed at her. "Enjoy your stay," she said.

My room was cool and quiet, smelling of mass-produced cleaning products and hotel chain soaps. I dropped my bags and wandered Main Street, ducking into a homey looking cafe. I ordered a hamburger and a milk shake with my mother in mind. The waitress set down a large plate overflowing with a burger and home cut fries. She wore a pair of beaded moccasins and a t-shirt with a faded Coca-Cola emblem on it. She had the hurried, efficient manner of a woman that had waited on the same customers most of her life.

"Anything else I can get you?" she asked.

"Uh...Do you know of anyone who's actually seen a UFO?"

"Are you a reporter?"

"No."

"A kook writer?"

"No."

She sized me up. "Yeah, I know a few people who've seen 'em. You go out in the desert the right time of year and they show up. Lights in the sky. UFO don't mean little green men, just means we don't know what the heck it is. Enjoy your meal." With that, she hurried off to refill the coffee cup of a grizzled man in a stained felt hat.

That night, I dreamed of wolves running in fresh snow under a full moon. They moved like sheets flapping in a breeze, billowing across the white, intangible and ghostlike. My breath came in great clouds and I ran to keep up, wiping tears from my eyes, straining to see them whole and solid. A stitch cut my side and one of them stopped to stare at me. Yellow eyes glinted and his grin was terrible. A light streaking through the sky caught my gaze and when I looked back where he had been, there was only snow.

My mother and I were cuddled up on her bed watching a tense game of *Wheel of Fortune*. I had landed in Houston that morning, having completed the first leg of my family visitation obligation.

"What's new, Ma?" I said, watching a large woman from Nebraska spin the wheel.

"Not much. My leg's been hurting."

"Mmm, that's too bad. Listen, Ma, Ben mentioned something about someone named James Clark?"

"Ooo, James Clark. He was so handsome. He had hair like a new penny."

"Really? Where did you meet him?"

"Oh, all that was so long ago. Crazy like a fox," she said, to the television.

"Crazy like a fox," the woman from Nebraska said, solving the puzzle. The audience burst into applause and Vanna revealed the letters on the big board.

"But why did you have another baby so late, Mom? The other kids were growing up, you could have been free."

"Free to what? The other kids were growing up. I needed you to keep me company." She patted my hand. "Aw, did you see that? She should have bought a vowel."

"Hey, Shayba girls." Isabelle plopped down on the foot of the bed. "How's my mother?" she said, resting a hand on Ma's foot.

"My leg hurts."

"That's because you never use it. I thought we'd take Debbie and the boys bowling tonight."

"Oh no, not bowling."

"Yes, bowling. It'll be fun. But I'm warning you, I'm not renting shoes for all of your friends." Isabelle tapped a finger against her temple.

My mother rolled her eyes. "Oh, Isabelle."

Twenty

LOST AND FOUND

I sat cross-legged in the middle of the living room floor, sur-rounded by the stuff of happy holiday preparations and surprise. Bits of brightly colored paper and ribbon advanced across the rug in every direction. I held my finger across an unruly flap of reindeer paper, pinning it to itself as I stretched for the tape, which was just out of reach. Ribbons were curled, boxes were assembled, and bit by bit, the packages piled up beneath the tree.

Outside, a dusting of snow still glazed the grass. Tomorrow it would be gone, leaving our backyard greenery looking awkward and out of place under the raw winter sky, like a guest that has remained long after the party has ended.

"One down, five hundred to go," I said, stuffing yet another misshapen gift under a low-hanging branch.

"It's not quite that bad. Wow! Which ones are for me?" Kate began picking through my careful pile, shaking packages like a dog with a rag doll.

"That could be fragile, you know." She looked at me skeptically. After all our years together, she knew me well enough to see through my feeble attempt to throw her off the scent.

"What is it?" she asked.

"A lump of coal."

"Aw, you always say that."

"Do you want me to tell you? I will."

She replaced the package with a terse look. "No."

"Come here," I said.

She pouted but allowed my arms around her and a buss on her hot cheek. "Remember when we met?" I coaxed.

"Yeah, I thought you were a stalker."

"Yes, and I felt as if I'd known you my whole life."

And it was true. From the first time I'd laid eyes on her, she'd been as familiar to me as a song that I had dearly loved but hadn't heard in years, the words nearly forgotten but the melody precious and deep-rooted. Up to that moment, we'd only spoken on the phone through the thick, dreary veil of the workday. And so when I saw her small mouth and her round shoulders, I was so pleasantly surprised at the feeling of familiarity that I threw my arms around her and held her tight. For her part, she'd laughed a nervous little laugh and clung to the drink in her hand.

All the rest of the afternoon, I jealously stole glances at her when she was unaware. Over covert shoulders I studied her, absorbed in conversation across a bright room. She would raise her eyebrows and smile crooked smiles and speak in tones I couldn't hear. Her presence caused a raising of the hairs on my arms and a buzzing in my ears.

"You found me irresistible, admit it," I said.

"It's true, you were weirdly charming. Oh, uh-uh. No ma'am, you will not look so pleased with yourself."

Christmas morning, I rose early and picked through the frosty garden in my pajamas. Our black and white cat followed closely and placed ginger paws on the chill ground. The air stung my cheeks and nose and it smelled of snow, though I knew it was too cold.

Inside, there was hot tea and toast with jam. We clinked mugs and lingered with kisses and wished each other Merry Christmas as we settled in front of a fire for the disgorging of swollen Christmas stockings, an appetizer to the treasure under the tree.

I upended my sock and a small cellophane bag rolled out at my feet. I picked up the bag and in my palm, a handful of cat eye marbles clicked and glittered in bright colors.

"I uh, I know how much you loved those as a kid. And, you know, I can't replace all of them, but at least this is a start."

I swallowed hard. "This is the best thing I've ever gotten."

"Really? Oh, good. I didn't know what kind to buy. I don't know very much about marbles. The guy at the store said everyone should have some of these."

"Yes," I said. "Yes, everyone should. He's absolutely right." I leaned in and held her tight. "Thank you. Oh, thank you so much."

There was a soft knock on the door. "Honey, are you all right?" Kate said.

I wiped my eyes and sniffed. I was crying in the bathtub again. "Yeah, I'm fine. I'll be out in a minute."

My bags were packed and ready to go. It was always the same when I had to go back anymore. The dread. The knot of a fist clenched in my gut.

"Oh honey, it'll be over before you know it. And you know, it's never as bad as you think it's going to be." Kate held my hand as I eased back on my pillow.

I sighed. "My mother was never in one of those places before. I'm scared. I'm scared to see her like that."

"Maybe it won't be forever. Maybe she'll recover."

"My sister says she won't get out of bed. Since she fell and broke her leg, she won't go to physical therapy, she won't walk, she won't even try to stand. The hospital couldn't keep her any longer, they had to put her in an assisted living facility. A home, my mother is in a home."

"I'm sure they're taking good care of her. You know, I can still come with you if you want."

"No, I think I need to go alone. Thank you, though."

"Deb, it'll be fine. She's still your mother."

I had been sitting in the parking lot of the Baywind Village Assisted Living Facility for almost half an hour. It wasn't a bad wait. A pleasant breeze blew in through the car windows, as it will at that time of year in that particular part in the world. The place itself might easily have been a neighborhood recreational center or a preschool. It sat solidly on its plot of land, a single story with well-tended grass and shade trees crowding the winding sidewalk. A bent man sat in a wheel-chair on the walk out front. He was wearing pale blue shorts and a white t-shirt, and he had only stumps where one hand and foot should have been. Finally, I sighed and made my way toward the entrance.

"Buon giorno, mancanza. Giorno bello, non è?" he called, and he waved his one good hand at me.

"Hi, how ya doing?" I said, as I passed. He smiled and nodded, rolling his chair back and forth.

The lobby was a cavernous room, with verdant thick carpet and an enormous bird cage, where parakeets and love birds hopped about on contrived branches. Music played softly and dejected souls sat or shuffled along walls and in corners. I smiled at the nurse behind the reception island and turned left onto the shiny white linoleum. Isabelle had given detailed instructions to Mother's room, and I checked the name plates carefully outside each door.

Childish stickers of Tweety Bird or Strawberry Shortcake dotted nearly every gray, clinical placard. Stuffed animals and balloons littered the plain furniture in each open door, a dis-turbing contrast to the withered and vacant occupants.

I recognized the name long before I could actually read it. The length of the words, the shape and substance of them. Mary McCarroll. It was scrawled in marker, temporary, recyclable. The image of her popped into my head, pacing in her yellow shorts, mid-fifties, vibrant, and eating a bowl of ice cream for some reason.

"Oh, isn't she beautiful?" she sang out as soon as she saw me.

"Hello, Mother," I said, as I bent low to embrace her in her caged bed frame. The television was impossibly loud.

"Turn that down, will you?" she asked, making a stiff effort to locate the remote. I pulled it from her rumpled bed clothes and the room filled with the sounds of the mundane. The rustling of fabric, the squeak of shifting metal springs.

"Oh Q.T., how are you? You look fantastic. This is my youngest," she said, to the wispy bird-like woman in the next bed.

"Hello." The bird woman nodded. I smiled.

"How you doin, Ma?"

"Oh Deborah, there's something wrong with my blood. I keep telling them to give me a blood transfusion. If I could get my blood working all right again, I could get out of this bed. I could go back to work. I'm still a young woman, I'm only sixty two." Her hands were taut and flat as paddles as she waved them in front of her. Her eye was closed and she had a sunken look about her, as if her flesh and bones had begun to pancake and turn in. She had been sixty two since I had been in college. Like a needle skipping on a record, the years continued to turn, but to her, time never advanced.

I took her hand and it relaxed, closing around mine. I looked at it, so known to me and still vital and smooth. Her nails were neatly filed and painted. "Your blood looks okay to me, Ma. Your hands look better than mine. Look." I lifted the hand I was holding. "Besides, you see your doctor regularly, don't you? Don't you think they'd know if there was something wrong with your blood? They take good care of you here, don't they?"

"Oh yeah, they do. They're all so nice, they really are. But look at my feet. Just look." She moved the sheet aside and ugly bedsores showed themselves on her toes and ankles.

I suppressed a flinch. "Those poor feet don't get used, Ma. They need to move. You walked across the state of New Mexico, for God's sake. You telling me you can't get out of this bed? There's nothing you can't do, Ma. Not if you really want to do it."

"Yeah, that's true, isn't it? That's right." Her eyes got soft and she looked away. "Your uncle Bill wants you to call him."

Uncle Bill was years in the ground, but I agreed. "Okay, Mom." Alarm must have touched my face, because she watched me for a time and then she said, "I better not say anymore. I get myself into trouble."

I smiled. "You can say anything you want, Ma. You never have to worry about saying anything to me."

"There are thugs in the hallway," she whispered.

The thing I remembered most about my Aunt Charlene was her hair. It was always a work of art, whether it was high and round on the top or swept off to the side in a magnificent, sculpted wave. Sometimes, she'd wear a colorful sash that tied in some unseen place underneath it all so that the back rose above the beautiful silk like a towering wall of blonde, Aqua-Netted brilliance. She wore big jewelry, painted nails, and layered eyelashes that sometimes left tiny claw marks of black on her cheeks when she blinked. My sister told stories of cruelty, of my aunt's drinking and volatile temper, and I certainly did see some of that. But my Aunt Charlene was always kind to me when I was a little girl, winking in my direction as she stood in our tiny kitchen, a smoldering Salem 100 clutched between two long fingers. She'd occasionally bring a box of groceries, and she once gave my brother a hair cut that looked more like he'd been scalped. My mother actually cried when she saw his bald head.

"Aunt Charlene visited Mother." There was an edge to Isabelle's voice. This was the first call from my sister in weeks, and I was happy to hear from her, since I relied on Isabelle for any contact with Ma, as her eyesight and her Parkinson's made writing impossible, and the phone by her bed had been efficiently unplugged and carted away due to her frequent calls to the local police.

"You're kidding! Mom must have been so happy."

"Oh, yes. Very happy. But then Charlene cried and carried on afterward, going on about how frail Mother is. Then she calls me saying she wants to take her back to New Mexico, where she'd be Mom's legal guardian. She made it sound like she'd be doing me a favor. A favor! I told her over my dead body. Years go by and where is she? Then she drops out of the sky with that boyfriend of hers, thinking she can cash in and collect Mother's disability benefits. Can you imagine letting Charlene take Mother? She can barely take care of herself. Like I would ever let anyone take Mother anywhere, much less out of the state. What a loon."

"Do you think that's what it is? The money? They used to be so close, I'd hate to think that."

"Whatever. She's nuts to think I'd let Mother go. I mean, I feel for Charlene, I really do. She fell apart after Paul, but good God!"

"Still, Mom must have been so glad to see her. I remember them all getting ready to go out dancing. All the sisters laughing and bumping to the radio through caked mascara and clouds of hair spray. I'll never forget that image. Mom was just hardly ever like that, you know? She always seemed a little less, I don't know, less nervous around Aunt Charlene."

"You were little. You don't remember the bad stuff."

"Yes, I suppose that's right."

Isabelle sighed. I could tell her hands were busy. She constantly needed to be in motion, and I could picture her picking up the boys' abandoned video games and soft drink cans or folding a sheet back on one of the beds. "Well, now Aunt Helen is threatening to fly in. Pretty soon, we'll have the whole familia waiting in line at Baywind Village."

"If only. Mother would really love that."

Twenty One

A WALK OF HER OWN

A rose was in bloom. A crazy, perfect yellow rose displaying its delicate petals in the harsh January rains. I laughed when I saw it. "Aren't you cold?" I marveled. I reached out to touch the milky softness and listened to the pit, pit of the rain on my hat. The rose remained defiantly cheerful against the gray. From inside the house a telephone rang, pulling me from the little flower that could, and I thought about cutting the bloom and taking it with me. "No. You've come this far. I suppose you deserve to see it through, hm?" The phone continued its insistence. "Come on, cat. We're gonna drown out here." The cat tip toed across the wet, happy to be heading for the warmth and comfort of his favorite perch, which was near the window, and perhaps a little cream.

"Hello?" I negotiated the phone as I slouched out of my wet coat.

"Someone here would like to say hello." The background wind noise was so terrific I could hardly hear Isabelle. There was some additional rustling and then a series of grunts and my mother produced a sound akin to branches scraping against a window.

"Hi, Mom. Out for a drive?" She was silent. The Parkinson's had progressed to the point where her speech was severely impeded and her frustration was palpable. Again, she mouthed words that I couldn't translate through the clamor.

"I saw the weather last night. Looks like you've got some good sunshine, huh? We're all cold rain and we're expecting snow." I kept my voice light and casual, but my hand was shaking.

Isabelle was laughing when she came back to the phone. "We're having a drive. It was such a beautiful day. We had a nice lunch and now we're cruising along the water. Mother wanted to call and see how you were doing."

"Well, that sounds great. Uh, are you actually driving? Maybe you pulled over."

Breezy giggling bubbled out of her. "Oh we're enjoying ourselves, aren't we, Mother? She's been feeling pretty good and I asked if she'd like to get out and she was all for it." The cacophony decreased as I assumed she'd slowed for a red light. "We miss you, though. When are we going to see you again?"

"I have some time in March. I'll look at fares." I chewed my fingernail and looked down the garden at that brave yellow rose.

"Great! Mother wants to say goodbye." The wind noise escalated and my mother grunted into the phone.

"Enjoy the sun for me, Ma. I'll see you real soon. I love you."

I had lunch in my car. As I ate my sandwich, I watched the rain sweep in across the Puget Sound in great billowy gray sobs. Sea gulls swooped and balanced wings on the wind, calling now and again. Some insane jogger struggled past in shorts and rain gear. I kept her in my rear view mirror until she disappeared around the bend. This part of the country was a different world from the place I came from. It was wet and lush and it ticked at a faster pace, but there were still quiet places to sit and think and let the day wash over you. I finished my lunch and headed back to work where the world, as I knew it, ended forever.

It continued to be one of those slippery days, with chores to do and phone calls to make, and seconds melting off the clock at a glacial pace. All afternoon I passed the studio door, stealing glimpses at the work in progress propped on the easel. A large raft of muslin and lumber, big enough to paddle, were it seaworthy. A sail, billowy and pure, waiting patiently for the picture inside to fully appear. Now and then, I would pause to tilt my chin and narrow my eyes, mentally finishing the picture. Finally, I left the dull and necessary things and snuck off to better work, full of color and light.

It was a lonely, airy picture of an old woman, hips full and settled as risen dough. Her hair was blizzard white and she buried her hands in sagging sweater pockets and trudged in slippered feet away from me down to the sea. Kate had asked if it was my mother and I had laughed, thinking that the woman was far too old, though in truth she looked to be years younger than my Ma was now.

The phone rang in the other room and I muttered at the sound. "Hello?" I said.

"Bad news sis, I'm on my way to Baywind Village right now." Traffic shrieked behind Isabelle's voice. "The nurse called and told me to come down."

"What's happening? Is she all right?"

"They wouldn't tell me anything. They just said that I should come. I asked if she was in pain and they said no. I asked if they had called her doctor..." Her voice caught. "They said no."

"Oh, no."

"I know." She choked and gulped and began to sob, letting the levies break. "Maybe she's just unconscious. Maybe she's okay. I'll call you when I get there."

"Okay," I said and I hung up, knowing Mother was gone.

It was as if a stone were thrown from thousands of miles away. When Isabelle had let me know, through her pain and tears that really, the unthinkable was true, it was as if an unseen hand had tensed muscle and bone and sent that cruel projectile hurtling across the ether to splash the placid waters where I stood.

It was her hands that I saw clearly. Her hands in the air, next to my own small things, with dirt under the fingernails from mud pies and bike rides. Such beautiful, graceful affairs, strong and supple, but in the end rendered stiff as dry twigs in winter.

I ran cold water in the basin and washed my face. Tears ran down the drain, rivers of them it seemed, and I wondered idly if I might throw up. I sat staring at the phone. Finally, I picked it up and dialed, seeing it all as if I were watching a silent film.

Judith picked up and answered brightly when she heard my voice.

"I'm sorry," I said. "I have some bad news..."

"No, no, NO, NO, NO!!" she screamed.

"I'm so sorry. Mom passed away. I'm so sorry." I heard the dull thud of the phone dropping to the floor and her mournful wailing, sharp and primitive.

A man's voice answered. A stranger. Someone to drink with and flirt with and fill up the empty places in my sister's house. "Hello," he said.

"Would you please tell her that she died peacefully, and that she was not in pain? Tell her that I'll call her again in awhile. Please."

The stranger answered softly that he would tell her and I heard him hang up.

I had a layover in Dallas. As I walked in a daze to my gate, I was surprised to find water leaking from my eyes. Weeping, I had reckoned, that came from a conscious thought. A sadness conjured that reddened the eyes and caused the lip to tremble. But this was its own thing, independent and wholly separate from my right mind. And so I shuffled, head down and closed, so as to hide my unruly grief from the bored and irritated commuters.

The moving walkway gave me a chance to rest, and I dropped my bag to rub my chafed shoulder. Out of the corner of my eye I would see her, just out of my sight. When I turned my head, these visions of my mother would disappear and wickedly transform themselves into strange faces and unfamiliar limbs and gestures.

I arrived at the gate and dropped into a seat. Here were the same unyielding black chairs and relentless lights. It was the air that took me right back there, still too cold for any comfort and smelling stale and slightly acrid. I looked down to find a sad little girl sitting next to me, her shoes scuffed, her hair in need of combing. She turned to me. "Now what?"

W elcome, Ma'am, how can I help you?" The man at the hotel desk was a groomed gentleman, skin the color of cinnamon and smelling of clean citrus.

"I will be needing a room for a few nights," I said.

"Ah, very good, Ma'am." He turned his attention to a screen hidden in the granite counter top. He asked me smoking or non, name, address, and all the other things that made it possible to hunt me down in the event that I skipped on the bill. Then he asked me if I was visiting for business or pleasure.

"My mother passed away and I'm here for the arrangements," I said. He stopped his typing and looked at me closely.

"Oh Ma'am, I'm so sorry. Please accept my condolences."

"Thank you," I replied.

"I am going to give you the bereavement rate and I have a room for you with a view of the garden." He smiled sweetly and turned back to the screen. I was very grateful to him for his discreet kindness. He wasn't embarrassed or awkward, neither did he pry or cajole. His genuine grace allowed me to be wounded and sad and human without shame.

He handed me my key and said, "Please let me know if we can do anything for you, Ma'am, and again, I am very sorry for your loss."

I thanked him and picked up my bag.

D eath is an embarrassing inconvenience these days. In some cultures, death is revered as a crucial cog in the fragile mechanism of being. The ancient Egyptians dedicated lifetimes to the preparations and celebrations of death. It was golden and gaudy and commonplace. But in the modern world, death is feared and whispered over when children are lurking. For us, to be thrown out of those reliable clockwork priorities of picking up dry cleaning and preparing meals and going to work, unravels the very fabric of what we know of life. Colleagues and friends blush and mutter condolences, unsure of how to stand or where to put their hands. This I knew, and this I was sure would be particularly painful for my eldest sister. For her, the reliable clockwork of the day-to-day was a compass that guided her and allowed her the confidence of her worth and her life's purpose. And so when she greeted me with a smile in her gleaming kitchen, perfectly pressed, not a hair out of place, I wondered for an instant if it had all been a terrible dream.

We chatted about unimportant things. Work, my flight. Clockwork. Then we sat in the kitchen, with our cold drinks to give us somewhere to look and something to hold, and we got around to the elephant in the room.

"They said she just breathed deeply and then...went. It's strange, she was doing better. Remember that drive we took? We called you? That wasn't that long ago. Course, she couldn't really speak by then, but she enjoyed hearing your voice. Do you know I got up this morning wondering what I was going to bring her for lunch?" She shook her head and took a sip from a can leaving rings on the counter. "Angels appeared to her sometimes, you know. The Virgin Mother would come to her. Did you know that? I saw her once, Mother Mary. We were just kids and Mom was working nights, like she used to. We were in the kitchen and suddenly, there was a figure wearing long robes and bathed in light. Ben picked up a knife and she disappeared."

I contemplated the sight of the Virgin Mary manifesting in our humble kitchen, my brother and sisters bickering and bored as children will be, interrupted by a transcendent figure, glowing and tranquil. I wondered if my brother, even now, regretted brandishing a weapon against the mother of Jesus.

"Ben and Judith arrive tomorrow afternoon. His daughter gets in tomorrow morning," she said.

"Victoria is coming? Lord, I haven't seen her since she was a kid. She must be, what, in her twenties now, right? And Judith. I can't believe she got on a plane. I would have bet money she wouldn't make it."

Isabelle laughed. "Well, she's not here yet, you could still place that bet. Ben said she was coming with him if he had to drag her. He said she would regret it the rest of her life if she didn't say goodbye to Mother."

"How do you think she's going to be?"

"Who knows? I mean, you never know. She's been through so much this past year, with the divorce and all. I offered to have her come live with me. She said no, of course." Isabelle sighed. "Mother's service will be held at a place in Dickinson. They're a client of Jack's. I wish I could afford better arrangements, but it's right after Christmas and all. We weren't prepared for this."

"Please, let me know what you need. I'm happy to take care of it."

"The place is, uh, it's unusual," she said.

"I'm sure it's fine."

She laughed. "We'll see what you say after you've seen it."

She set her soda can down on the counter. "Wait here, I'll be right back."

She was gone a moment or two and when she returned, she was holding a stack of photo albums. I turned the pages, scanning the curled and yellowing faces. Some I knew and some were strange to me. A black and white picture with scalloped edges caught my eye. My own face, small and pale, before lines had creased the cheeks and built a web around the eyes. The only photo I had ever seen of myself that was dated before the steady parade of crooked bangs and shy school picture smiles. In the gray photo, I stood in front of our little house, staring into the camera. Streamers decorated my arms and neck and I held them with tight fists. Paul stood next to me, an inch or two shorter, his face open and sunny as always. I picked up the photo.

"I remember that day," she said. "It was the parade, remember? I took the picture from the cheerleading float. You looked so happy with your little streamers flapping in the breeze. Let's see, you were..."

"Seven," I said, staring at the photo.

"Yes, that's right. I was just about to graduate. I guess that must have been right before you and Mom took off."

That afternoon, armed with large hefty bags and cardboard boxes, my sister and I cleaned out Mother's room. The nurses and caretakers of the place gathered around my sister and hugged her and held her hands, saying how much they loved my mother. When I was introduced, they would smile politely and nod, as if I were a late arrival to someone else's family reunion. There was a different woman in the bed next to the one that had been Ma's. She was a good deal more substantial than the last occupant. The last roommate had died in her sleep. It had shaken Ma, sending her into a depression that hung onto her for weeks.

"Oh, honey, I'm so sorry about Mary. She was a good egg. We would talk and we would watch TV. You know, I'm gonna miss her." The woman's voice was husky and a bit louder than was necessary.

"Thank you, Helen. This is my sister, Debbie."

"Hiya, hon. Your mom was a peach."

"Thank you."

I wondered if Helen had been in this room when my mother had breathed her last breath. If they had been watching television. If she had been chatting at my mother as the synapses and sighs and the very things that made my ma laugh and cough and cry were disappearing and if, like the curl of smoke when a flame is extinguished, there had been a sign of its leaving.

When I had last seen Ma, she had gripped my hand and said, "You have to help me or I'm going to die in here." I had hugged her and stroked her cheek and talked about the people she loved and the places we'd been, trying to smooth the corners and round the edges of her fear until she could laugh again.

I snapped a garbage bag open, sending it billowing wide. "Keep anything that's half full or more–here's a box–and throw away everything else." Isabelle had begun efficiently pulling clothes off of hangers in the tiny closet near the window. Sighing, I looked around the place. A whole lifetime fit into half of this small room. I opened a drawer and began pawing through the contents, conscious of the invasion of privacy. I worked through lotion bottles, bobby pins, old birthday cards, lipsticks, letters from her sisters, silk flowers, and of course, jars of Pond's cold cream. I removed the crowded photos, drawings, and bits of ribbon from the small bulletin board by her bed. I pulled a pin from my own smiling photo, the image stupid and callous. I dropped it in the box. I pocketed a rosary I had sent her one Christmas.

When the last box and garbage bag had been loaded into the car, Isabelle gave a final embrace to Mother's friend, and to the nurses, and we left that place.

In the car Isabelle began to cry, her voice strange and smothered, unaccustomed to tears. She talked about regret and wishes that would never come to pass, apologizing repeatedly, saying that she did not like to show emotion in front of others.

I pulled into her driveway and she got out of the car, opening the garage door before slipping inside the house. Twenty minutes later, after I had stacked boxes and stowed garbage bags, she reappeared, nose reddened, makeup reapplied, lipstick freshened.

O
h my god, is that Judith? She's so thin." My niece sat in the passenger seat of my sister's cavernous vehicle as we

pulled up to the entrance of the small Ellington Field airport. She had transformed from a gangly little girl, teeth too big for her mouth, into a beautiful young woman. She sat staring out the window, her knees prim, her hands clasped in her lap.

Judith and my brother Ben waited outside the glass doors, luggage at their feet. Judith brought a cigarette to her lips and it trembled noticeably. When we embraced, the whole of her shook against me, making her seem positively breakable. "They took my lighters," she said. "I had six lighters and they took five of them. I need to buy some more. I need my lighters." She held up the cheap blue plastic lighter and clutched a carton of cigarettes to her chest.

M y niece sat patiently, listening to stories of people and events that happened long before she was born. I too was only a spectator in most of the tales, which were told with wide gestures and wistful glances. Stories about poverty and grit and my mother's unwavering perseverance and kindness. "We were down to our last five dollars and she put it in the collection plate. The next day, I found a twenty on the street," someone said. "I remember being on that train, carrying a lamp in my lap. Judith was just a baby," someone else added. "But how about Debbie walking across the desert?"

They all turned and looked at me.

"Yeah, one day she just didn't come home from school, and she and Mom were gooone," Judith added and took another sip of her beer.

"Can you imagine?" Isabelle said.

"How long were you out there?" my brother asked.

"Mmm, I don't know. A few days, I guess." There was a silence and a shaking of heads and then they were on to other things. I turned to my niece.

"How about you? Any stories?"

She smiled and shrugged. "I was so little when Gramma babysat me. I do remember one thing, though. I always heard people say that Gramma was sick, but she didn't look sick to me. I didn't know what that meant, so one day I said, "Gramma, why do they say that you're sick?" and she looked at me and she said, "You see over there?" and I looked where she was pointing, and she said "I see someone standing there, but they're not really there. And that's why I'm sick."

To me, my mother had been something akin to peering into dark water on a moonlit night. Ultimately, all I ever really saw was myself staring back. She never spoke to me with such candor. Now, here was a relic dredged up from the bottom, something tangible and rust-covered and rare. Something real and belonging to someone else. Sometimes, I wonder if I only really know my mother through Isabelle's eyes. My sister spent so many years with her, carefully painting images and stories, so that I might assemble the pieces into the picture that I now have of her. In spite of all those isolated days she and I shared when I was a child, living in a single room, hair entwined, I know her as everyone does. A kind, courageous person that persevered and sacrificed, but I cannot say that I know the woman that she really was. Any dreams or regrets she may have had, any passions or desires were her own, and she guarded them zealously.

Tow's it going?" Kate asked. The air conditioning hummed behind smooth papered walls and warm light bathed the hotel bed where I lay, safe and exhausted.

"Horrible," I said. "I always feel like I should be doing something else. If I'm laughing, I shouldn't be laughing. If I'm crying, I shouldn't be crying. It's exhausting. My sister Judith is a wreck. At dinner, she confessed she didn't want to go to the funeral and my other siblings were hurt and angry, so they lashed out at her. She ended up leaving the table in tears. Oh, and the usual racial stuff, of course."

"What about you? How do you feel about going to the service?"

I looked across the room at my black suit. "Scared. I have to go, though. If I don't, I don't know. Closure? Something like that. I'm just so sad."

"I'm so sorry, honey. I wish there was something I could do."

"You're doing it. Believe me."

The next morning, all dressed up in my new black suit, I let myself in through the kitchen door. My brother was sitting on the couch, reading the paper.

"Wow, you slept late, huh?"

"Not really, it's only ten," I said, glancing at my watch. "I got up and had a muffin. Took my time getting dressed. I didn't sleep that well, actually."

"I didn't hear you get up," he said.

I stared at him. "Uh, you know I'm not staying here, right?"

"You're not staying here?" He put the paper down. "Where are you staying then?"

"I have a hotel room."

"What? I thought you were here last night." He laughed and scratched his beard.

"Let's get some photos." Isabelle smiled and touched me on the shoulder. "You all look so nice." She corralled us out to the patio by the pool.

"What's going on?" Judith was having a smoke as we passed.

"Pictures," I said.

"You're kidding."

Isabelle posed us at various locations, plucking at lapels and gesturing for us to move a little more this way or that. We all smiled for the camera. I never wanted to see any of those photos. Never.

"Boys, time to go!" Isabelle yelled up the stairs as purses were gathered and last minute lipstick applied.

They thundered down the stairs in basketball shorts and t-shirts, jostling and shoving. "Okay, come on, let's go." She put an arm around the youngest and kissed his temple. They moved with a loose-jointed self-consciousness and careless innocence, shoes too big for their lanky bodies, safe under the sheltering wing of their mother. I watched them with envy and scorn, feeling utterly orphaned. They would never know hunger or want. They would not be boats set upon the sea without rudder or oar. I wrung my hands and bit my lip and listened to the words that no one spoke as we left the house.

I followed Isabelle closely, not wanting to lose her but wanting to all the same. The air in the car was thick and warm. I turned up the radio.

"Where's the service?" Victoria asked from the back seat.

"I have no idea," I said, and we settled in for the ride in silence.

I drove for twenty minutes or so, unable to see anything beyond the hind end of Isabelle's towering SUV. Her turn signal flashed red and I followed her into a Kentucky Fried Chicken.

She must be lost, I thought. Instead, she pulled into the drive through and she began yelling at the large, cheerful order board.

"You have got to be kidding me," I muttered.

"Well, maybe it's better to have the kids fed, you know? Maybe they'll be calmer," my niece offered.

"Can I get a Coke?" Judith said, wringing her knuckles white.

"I am feeling a little funny. Maybe I should eat something," Victoria added.

I dug my fingers into my eyes and sighed. "Oh, all right."

I ordered and pulled up to the window, handing my money to a shy girl in a crooked red visor and a shirt three sizes too big.

"Uh, that lady already paid for it," she said.

"What?"

She jabbed a finger at the Suburban idling at the curb in front of us. "The lady in the last car already paid for it." I could see Isabelle watching us in her rearview mirror.

I felt us very conspicuous as we sat lined up on a pew against the wall in the entryway. Not just because we were the only white faces in the place, but because there was such a collection of us. People in twos and threes milled about the room. Occasionally, someone glanced at us.

The strip mall funeral home had been a used furniture showroom until recently, and the scuffs and wear still showed. The pew had been added, I'd imagined, to lend an air of reverence, but it only succeeded in looking decidedly out of place.

A man rushed through a pair of ornate gold trimmed doors and hurried over to my sister. He was wearing a blue jogging suit in a parachute material that made a shushy sound as he passed.

"Hello, Darius," Isabelle said.

"Hello, Mrs. Fairbault," he replied, taking her hand. "Please excuse my appearance, I am terribly behind today. I can't seem to find a moment to change. We'll be ready in a minute here." She nodded and he hurried away.

A woman sat at a computer screen behind a railing near the door. A man in a light colored suit and chestnut snake skin shoes reached behind the railing and picked up a well-worn Bible.

"Can't do much without this," he said, to the woman. She swung around to face him and leaned her chin on her fist.

"Mmm-hmm," she murmured.

"This Bible has seen ten years of weddings and funerals and too many babies getting blessed to count." His fresh skin shone like warm dark chocolate. "I don't need it for the words, but I gotta have it to hold."

Darius and another man emerged, pushing a pearly-finished white casket on a telescoping gurney. We all watched it wheel by and the white doors close behind it.

More people filed in. A woman in a black dress and a wide brimmed hat crossed to the two at the railing. "She looks so good," she said. "She'd be real happy, they did her makeup real nice." She opened her purse and started digging around in it. "I ain't afraid of dying. The Lord takes care of us, ain't nothing to be afraid of." The others nodded, saying, "Ain't that the truth," and, "Amen."

A moment later, Darius propped the doors open and we filed into an enormous room. The walls were painted in a bright magenta that showed its age. The floor was covered with a worn, gray Berber carpet laid in long pieces, fraying and curling in places. Fluorescent light rained down from above. At the far end of the room was the open casket, a single flower arrangement on the floor in front of it. Two rows of gray folding chairs waited like soldiers standing at attention. We filed in and took our seats.

I could just see my mother's face over the edge of the box. Judith sat next to me, weeping softly. The man with the Bible stepped in front of us and cleared his throat.

"My friends, as you come together today to remember your loved one, I remind you that as you keep her in your hearts, then she is never really gone. Hang on to those moments spent together that are precious and uniquely your own. Find comfort in those you love and hold them near to soothe like cool rain on parched tongues, knowing that when we pass from the bonds of this Earth, we will know no more pain or sorrow, and we will rest comfortably in God's love. This life is but a journey that leads us to the perfect home that God prepares for each of us. May the Lord bless you and ease your pain in your time of grief. You are welcome to stay as long as you like." With that, he nodded his head and retreated.

I stood behind the chairs and watched my family file past the casket. My brother came over and stood next to me. "Don't you want to go up?" he said. I smiled and shook my head. He touched my arm and moved away.

As I watched, I thought how Mother would think this was so much nonsense, all the fuss and staring, without her able to offer so much as coffee or a bite to eat. I wondered if she had been surprised by her death. If her eyes had grown wide and her mouth slack as she stared down at herself, and if now she stood on her toes, searching crowds for familiar faces. If my grandmother was there to smooth her hair and kiss her cheek and speak to her in trickling Spanish, asking after children and grandchildren.

My grandmother had been a stern woman, but she had a rattling cackle of a laugh and an appetite for embraces and a full, happy kitchen. She was a commanding sort of woman and for the most part she frightened me, causing me to keep to the corners and say nothing at all. Usually she was preoccupied with cleaning or cooking or watching her soap operas, but one day she asked me to help her make up the bed in the whitewashed guest room of her cool adobe house. As we worked over linens and hand-worked quilts, she told me that it was my mother that had taught her to make up a bed properly. To tuck the ends and fold the corners with careful hands, coaxing the fabric and feathers into a tranquil lake, swollen pontooned pillows moored at its head.

I said goodbye to my mother then. I told her I was sorry that I couldn't have done more for her. Sorry that I wasn't with her when she needed me. I told her how grateful I was to her, and I told her that I loved her.

I can't take you any further, I'm sorry. I'd never make it down that hill." It was the worst blizzard Seattle had seen in years. They closed the airport just after my plane landed. I'd waited an hour and a half in a freezing cold line of desperate commuters to climb inside a warm cab. My fearless driver had slid through drifts two feet high and taken the flattest surface streets he knew to be passable, until skidding to a halt four blocks from my house.

"It's okay, I cannot thank you enough for getting me this far. You are my hero." He pulled my suitcase from the trunk and set it on the snowy road.

"That'll be forty six fifty, please." I handed him seventy five dollars and considered hugging him before picking up my case. "Be safe," I said.

His brake lights threw a rosy glow on the blanket of white until he was out of sight. The silence was absolute, as it is in heavy snow, quiet of sound and quiet of sight. The storm is not yet corralled and made polite by plows and salting. It roams free, leaping and whirling in lamplight, tickling lashes and tucking the city under a thick quilt with a wink and a soft kiss.

I breathed in the cold air, feeling at home and at peace. My clothes hung on my frame like melting icicles and my hands were red and pruned with the raw weather. I dragged my heavy bag up onto the sidewalk, pulling mounds of snow with it. Every twenty feet or so, the snow would build to such a height that I had to stop and lift the case over the drift. My breath came in great plumes and I laughed at the sight of my driveway.

The door flew open as I trudged the final steps up the walkway. Kate wrapped around me with ferocity, kissing my face and pulling me along. "Come in, come in," she said. "Oh, I'm so glad you're home. Please don't ever go away again."

The power went out at 6:22 the following morning. Somewhere, a line had snapped under the weight of the wet freeze, or perhaps a pole had tumbled along the shore, leaving most of the west side in darkness. In a light sleep, I was vaguely aware of a sudden absence of the hum of appliances and furnace sounds before succumbing once again to the relentless tide of dreaming.

My mother was setting places for a banquet in an enormous hall under an elaborate chandelier. She was young, her nails neatly painted red, and she was barefoot and wearing her yellow shorts. As she handled china plates and made sterling salad forks and butter knives orderly, she was telling me that she had been helping my friends plan my fortieth birthday party when she'd died. I was forty now. The same age she'd been when she'd had me.

"One of them, I don't remember her name, the pretty one with the long hair, said that someone was an "ass." Well, I don't know what got into me, but I made such a fuss and I gave that poor girl such a hard time." She shook her head and rolled her eyes.

I laughed and went to her. "Mom, I miss you so much." I said, and I started to cry.

She put down the plate she was holding and put her arms around me. "I know it, Q.T.," she said as she held me tight.

Later that morning, I wished Kate luck getting a bus and lit a match to kindling in the fireplace. I boiled water for tea on the open flames and thought of other fires that burned out years ago. Fires of survival and hardship and need. As I sipped at my cup, I watched the blaze paint pictures inside a glass marble and remembered the gifts that were given so freely. Strength, compassion, humility.

Not a day goes by that I don't think about my ma, and every day I am reminded to truly live in each moment with eyes wide open. I whisper thank you's and remembrances, and I hope that wherever she is, the sun shines warmly upon her, the grass where she steps grows lush, and the walk is peaceful and sweet.